T0355758

THE EARLIEST ROMANS

THE
EARLIEST ROMANS

A Character Sketch

Ramsay MacMullen

The University of Michigan Press • *Ann Arbor*

First paperback edition 2013
Copyright © by Ramsay MacMullen 2011
All rights reserved

Published in the United States of America by
The University of Michigan Press
Printed and bound by CPI Group (UK) Ltd, Croydon, CR0 4YY

2016   2015   2014   2013   5   4   3   2

A CIP catalog record for this book is available from the British Library.

Library of Congress Cataloging-in-Publication Data

MacMullen, Ramsay, 1928–
    The earliest Romans : a character sketch / Ramsay MacMullen.
      p.   cm.
    Includes bibliographical references and index.
    ISBN 978-0-472-11798-7 (cloth : alk. paper) — ISBN 978-0-472-02779-8
(e-book)
      1. National characteristics, Roman. 2. Rome—History—Republic, 510–
265 B.C. 3. Rome—Civilization. I. Title.
DG78.M329 2011
937'.03—dc23   2011020871

ISBN 978-0-472-03570-0 (pbk. : alk. paper)

CONTENTS

PREFACE

How should we tell the story of the earliest Romans—scattered first over their seven hills and then in time spreading across the whole center of the Italian peninsula, until their state was grown great enough, and their destiny sufficiently grim, to engage them in their endless wars with Carthage?

There is no easy answer. Now, after some centuries, archaeology still shines its light only on a handful of sites among those hills, and illuminates the later processes of Roman growth not one bit better. Certainly there is a written record of this period, and a very ample one it is. The work of one author alone, Livy, was once in the West more read and familiar than that of any other of Antiquity's historians. The relevant part of his text survives in some hundreds of pages. But he is rightly seen as "a romantic novelist" (chap. 5)—which is a problem, is it not? We might turn also to Dionysius of Halicarnassus. His account of those early times survives in equal bulk but is equally to be challenged because he, like Livy, wrote many hundreds of years after the events and developments he describes. It is by no means clear how or how much he or Livy can ever have known about their subject. The same difficulty infects various other sources of information that we might try to learn from.

Where there is so little information that we have good reason to trust, what we do have we must arrange in some form that will satisfy our skepticism and yet allow our time-travel, our curiosity, to take us among those most ancient toga-clad fellow human beings. The method I propose requires us to think of that entire people as one personality, who, like any real individual, makes choices at crossroads, and so traces a path through life at the dictates of personality; so to know the one is to know the other.

To explain: thanks to scholarly books I have written in U.S. history I am acquainted with one certain period: the second generation of the young republic, say around 1830. The human types of that time are recognizable today. There, once, and still today, we see the man of business focused all on the risks and chances of the market, bent on winning; or women young or perhaps not young but unafraid, cutting loose from the old to try a brand-new life on their own.[1] At the time, these were not worldwide human types at all; they were as they remain *American;* and the first real genius in what we would now call sociopolitical studies, Alexis de Tocqueville, marked them out as such, distinct in the new nation that he observed in his travels around the country, comparing what he saw with what he knew in the Old World and doing so in the hope of discovering what sort of society it was that he then saw in its adolescence.[2] What sort of person did it produce? He believed that, at such a point in its history, a society's characteristic individual, or individual character, would be already shaped. Here was where we should look "if we would understand the prejudices, the habits, and the passions which will rule his life. . . . The entire man, is so to speak, to be seen in the cradle of the child".[3] And he goes on to unfold his thought:

> The growth of nations presents something analogous to this: they all bear some marks of their origin; and the circumstances which accompanied their birth and contributed to their rise, affect the whole term of their being.
>
> If we were able to go back to the elements of states, and to examine the oldest monuments of their history, I doubt not that we should discover the primary cause of the prejudices, the habits, the ruling passions, and in short of all that constitutes what is called national character. . . . This might explain the destinies of certain nations.

The ideas expressed may not be scientific but, perhaps better yet, they are close to common sense. This much I infer from the pages of the *New York Times* where, on average every year over the half century and more that I've known that useful publication, you can find at least some reference to Tocqueville's *Democracy in America* or some review of a new book on that oracle. The traits of Americans' nature that the visitor once observed, and those of today, are seen to correspond; to a striking degree, those of today recall those of 1830. As Tocqueville himself might have said, *Plus ça change, plus c'est la même chose.*

And if that is so, can we not apply his reasoning to a period much more remote, as I intend to do in this essay, asking, What were the ancient Romans really like? Can we not make some estimate, with some probability? Making that estimate, is it not then easier to grasp a very large body of reported acts, constituting their history, which is at the same time too full of gaps and deficiencies for any close, exact analysis?

An estimate of national character may be ethnocentric, picking out for emphasis those traits that seem salient because they seem different. So Tocqueville compared the New World with his own Old Europe, selectively. Alternatively, estimate may be wrapped up as anthropology or sociology or psychology. Or perhaps, less pretentiously, it may be sought in what seems to be the actual record of behavior. The four traits on which I choose to focus can, I believe, be discerned in well-attested actions on the Romans' part, considering the Romans collectively, and both explain and are explained by results of obvious historical significance.

If we had better data, perhaps other traits would look more useful to the historian. Who can say? We could aspire to such wonderful depths of understanding as Geert Hofstede laid out before his readers in many hundred pages of small print, with reference to many hundreds of other scholarly studies and a hundred graphs and tables, telling us all about modern national character.[4] But a Roman historian must stay inside the boundaries of his evidence.

It would be best, as Tocqueville would advise, to look at the Romans' childhood for the formation of their nature, perhaps at the very moment when they were wondering about their own birth, asking the question likely to occur to children: Where had they come from? Andrea Carandini knows the Romans well enough to tell us,

> Romans would have thought historically, not like storytellers; in terms of the nation, not the universe; in practical terms, not logically; politically, not in a moralizing way; like lawyers, not mystics.[5]

It is thus that Roman nature should be understood; thus Romans should be imagined in the explaining of their origins. From a lifetime of reading and thinking about them, Carandini could claim the right to say how they would have expressed the answer to their questions, "not in myths but in rituals".

In exactly the same way another veteran scholar, Alan Watson, considered a text in Rome's earliest law code. He wondered if the lawmakers took some certain detail into account. No, he concludes, "the practical Romans are unlikely to have wasted much thought on the matter". He can settle the question because he knows the society's proclivities—its nature.[6]

And other illustrations of this approach could be supplied easily enough. I tried, myself, long ago.[7]

Anyone like myself, interested in Roman history, might well want to consider the matter of national character. Paradoxically, the reason lies in the very inadequacies of our knowledge, as I indicated above. Their extent must occupy my pages again and again, perhaps to the impatience or puzzlement of readers; yet this book would never have been written without my taking the huge gaps and sloppy parts in early Roman history so seriously. At this point, let it be enough only to repeat that our traditional sources for the formative period, despite their seeming richness, in fact allow us to see *and to trust in the true report of* only a thin scattering of disconnected dots and bare names. Such is the fact, as I judge; and there are many other much better judges than I to say the same, without quite confronting the logic of their own conclusions. We lack believable accounts of the human individuals involved in action, their motives, the wherewithal of any causal analysis. We can't say *why* anyone did *what* he did. More simply, we can't connect the dots. What we might use instead, in the absence of reliable knowledge about individual motives, are not scattered dots but *the whole society's general proclivities* directing the broad flow of development and events. The Romans can be seen all together as an entirety acting in characteristic ways because such was their collective nature; and out of this view, a story line of some sort can be attempted, having regard to historical consequences and analysis.

This is my hope, that such an attempt may serve readers wishing to form a first impression of the Romans. I carry it down to around 264 (that is, B.C., like all the dates in this book). At this point, on the brink of the Punic Wars, somewhat better sources might be supposed in the memory and official records of the generations that fought against Carthage, and thereafter. But there is no need to count every king or consul in all the preceding centuries, or every conflict against some neighboring people. They can only be, "as some historians have said, one damned thing after another".[8] I see it as a virtue of this approach of mine that it waives arguments about detail over that long period on which (I would say) far too much learning has been expended out of far too much belief in the truthfulness of the ancient annals.

For specialists in the period (among whom I certainly don't count myself) I include in notes whatever may better explain my reasoning (and some of those specialists have been most generous with their help, whom I now have the opportunity to thank sincerely: Nicholas Horsfall, Stephen Oakley, Seth Bernard, Carol Mattusch, Bruce Frier, Larissa Bonfante, Christina Kraus, Gabriele Cifani, R. Ross Holloway, Fred Kleiner, Jerzy Linderski, Lynne Lancaster, and William Metcalf).

Part 1

TO 509 BC

I

CONSERVATIVE

The Romans were a people distrustful of novelties, slow to adopt a change, grudging in their surrender to it. They liked the old ways. This trait appears, for example, in the fact of their being only twenty miles from the sea and yet never for a half-millennium bothering with it: building no fishing fleet that's ever mentioned, no port, no navy, or even a watchtower.[1] For their own countrified purposes they had a cattle and a produce market but no interest in market tolls. Their riverine location invited them to look beyond their immediate horizons, but there is no sign of their attempting this, themselves; at most they allowed others from elsewhere to conduct business among them in an assigned, convenient spot: notably the traders in salt from the flats at the mouth of the Tiber, coming upriver on the right bank, who found at Rome the first fording place and could so continue up the so-called Salt Road on the left bank to their inland markets. They passed through leaving no trace. To judge from the problems of interest to the Romans' earliest laws, down to the mid-fifth century, it was lands and family property that they were concerned with, not commerce or banking.[2]

We have in view, here, not just two or three generations but several hundred years of opportunities neglected. Another people would have behaved differently, with different historical consequences. Surely there would have been some such effect as Plato imagined, had the Romans chosen to engage themselves in the scenes beyond their own home at the invitation of the nearby waterways. We would have, or it would have produced, a different people; for "the sea", as Plato said, "is pleasant enough as a daily companion, but has indeed also a bitter and brackish quality, filling the streets with merchants and shopkeepers, and begetting in the souls of men uncertain and unfaithful ways" (*Laws* 705, trans. Jowett). The philosopher had in mind and detested the very Athenians whom Pericles described in his funeral oration, loving them: always ready for something new, always the active agents of it at the cost of everything fixed and trustworthy. Indeed the early Romans would have suited Plato much better than Pericles.

Something can thus be inferred about the earliest Romans from what they chose to do or not do on a grand scale. Nature unfolds in behavior; "actions are proof of character" (Aristotle, *Rhet.* 1367b). If inferences are indeed fair, then we should be able to identify and similarly learn from further illustrations drawing on our familiar sources. We don't lack for a good base of information. On the shelf, inviting our inquiry, the ancient writers seem ample enough. Their appearance, however, is itself a problem that I need to explain before I go any further.

Among those that tell us about early Rome, one of the best known was Marcus Terentius Varro (born in 116). Though his work survives only in bits and pieces, he counts as first in a long line of scholars called antiquarians. He served as a prime source for most historians who came after him. For this authority and for his successors, whatever was very old and very odd was of interest. He collected absolutely everything, generally in lists, in volume after volume, some devoted to religious rites, others to city monuments and their origins, and so forth across a variety of subjects. A gigantically learned if often ridiculous hobbyist, he and his writings earned immense respect. In proof, it is enough to quote Cicero: "You unlocked for us the secrets of our country's age, the divisions of time, sacral and priestly law, the learning of war and peace", etc.[3]

Antiquarian method may be illustrated through the use made of etymologies: for example, in the tale of the Sabine chief Curtius. Though Rome's enemy, he was generously remembered and his gallantry confirmed in the so-called Curtian Lake, a swampy section of the city. Varro indicates no less than three explanations for the name. One is as good as the other, all involve the invention of history. Or, for a second illustration, we have a certain Olus inserted into the historical record, a little-known king of Rome, whose remains were dug up by chance atop the city's citadel with the inscription in Etruscan writing, "Head of Olus", *Caput Oli,* to be interpreted as one *Aulus* in Latin spelling. Thus he explained what Romans called the citadel itself: the *Capitolium.* Since our sources had no reason to place this figure in any particular period, half of them put him in the 740s, the other half, two hundred years later.[4]

A second tradition or category of historical literature, and by far the more familiar, was the narrative of action. As its representative I name Livy (Titus Livius, born in 59, the year of Caesar's consulship). He was equally comprehensive with Varro but in quite other ways, and equally laborious in research. His account *From the Founding* gives us as rich a resource as we could ask. We exclaim, rightly, at how readable his work is; for here are dramatic episodes, passions at their most heated, outsized personalities, beauty and bravery. We exclaim at the work's prodigious bulk, too; for, were it all in our hands along with *Anna Karenina,* both in an English translation, the two would weigh in at about the same 350,000 words. True, we have a little less than a quarter of the whole in our hands today; yet this portion is not only a wonderfully generous gift of words, by the standards of surviving Classical literature, but it happens also to contain a long run of his opening chapters devoted to just the centuries in which to look for the origin and development of the Romans' adolescence—my subject.

With such a resource ready to hand, it might seem easy enough to learn about early Rome, and in some detail; but we are deceived, not in the richness or proportions of Livy's work but in its quality. Like other ancient authors, he no doubt deserves a special veneration for his very antiquity, at least from a philological viewpoint, as literature; but Livy as a historian . . . His level of analytical sophistication—his sense of all that needs to be looked at and indeed that sense among other ancient historical authors earlier and later, with the rarest exceptions—could be matched today by any clever fifteen-year-old, surely. It can hardly satisfy readers older or further along in their education. No need to flinch from the fact: for, after all, we are glad to point to mankind's progress in other disciplines, let us say psychology or linguistics. The world has changed, as we think, for the better.

The casual reader might conclude after a first glance into Livy that nothing at all could be better. The flow of action he offers is not only satisfactory as literature but secured by specific names and dates. It's even called *historia.* Livian "history", however, isn't what one might think of under that term today. For a test, put Livy with Dionysius of Halicarnassus, the two together providing us with a good 95 percent of the surviving written data for the seven kings (down to 509). Scattered here and there in the total will be found a hundred pages and more of word-for-word conversation among the principal actors as well as countless insights into their innermost feelings. "Fine speech is found where the facts are all unclear" (Livy 3.56.3). We have really to confront the conclusion that the art of these two writers is not what we thought it to be but a sort of fiction. It is fiction not improved by the writers' criticisms of their predecessors for untrustworthy method, and by occasional displays of a preferable accuracy, for example, through exact numbers. Some of these latter are patently ridiculous, like those for the population as a whole and for its wealth-divisions in a quite imaginary money economy; and, alas, broader areas of agreement among the ancient writers in which modern scholars can find anchorage are too few to yield a clear picture.[5]

Writers like Livy in the first century might, however, be excused for any failures in their treatment of the most remote past because of a simple lack of factual material. To fill their page they had to invent or elaborate on somewhat earlier inventions that they found in their libraries. Indeed that was their difficulty; for, in their search among predecessors to draw on, they could get no further back than 200. It was around this date that Fabius Pictor, a senator, put together the first Roman history of Rome, choosing to write in Greek. He was "the oldest of writers", *scriptorum antiquissimus*.[6] For this if for no other reason his Latin successors evidently felt the greatest respect for his work and are generally believed to have built on it and thus to show some degree of agreement among them.

But as regards the period of the kings, just where we would expect the thinnest sketch of events or where we would expect nothing at all, hidden as they were behind so many intervening centuries, Fabius and others after him provide a surprisingly full story. So great was the value set on the most hallowed ancestors—on the most ancient times and their nearness to the very gods, to Romulus and to others of beloved legend—Roman writers felt not only the freedom but a patriotic obligation to amplify, to fabricate, to dramatize, and to draw lessons for their own times. The result, of course, could only be bad history as we understand that discipline today. Modern scholars in fact generally agree on such a judgment. The ancients (to repeat) were not historians at all, on our terms, but storytellers; and we all know what telling stories amounts to.

"A liar in one thing, a liar in all"—such is courtroom wisdom.[7] In other fields than Antiquity, historians generally have so many witnesses to choose from, they don't have to depend on the doubtful. The doubtful can be omitted or ignored, they needn't be laboriously confronted. But in ancient history there is no such large supply. It is tempting, then, to make do with the dubious and to shape or accept such testimony as probable. "Probabilities" can then be made to serve not only as the mortar but as the very brick of historical reconstruction. Indeed they absolutely must serve in this fashion; for how could one deny all reality to such figures as the pious old Numa Pompilius? Or events like the Rape of the Sabines or institutions like the Luperci, known down to Caesar's day and Shakespeare's? These all are too precious a heritage to discard; nor could they be satisfactorily replaced by the yield of excavation, if that bleak proposition were to be actually considered.[8] Relief is thus to be sought in an effort of salvage— salvage to connect the dots, the few things known beyond question; to fill in the gaps by resorting to conjecture and by so doing save the past in its familiar literary form, that is, in Livy and Varro and the rest. Where ingenuity and learning in the attempt are tolerated or even rewarded for themselves, interpretation need never end.

In illustration, a problem and an answer offered by a prominent specialist, T. J. Cornell, who has given a good forty years to the study of the centuries in question and who is, for any English speaker interested in the period, an obvious point of repair.

To determine the site among the seven hills that became the city center (not the very first settlement anywhere on the seven hills), Cornell looks to the ritual running of a certain group of priests, those Luperci just mentioned, who cleansed and sanctified what their course marked out. He cites Varro to argue that they ran round the Palatine, and did so from some most ancient time; therefore it was here that the city's historic beginnings lay. But the idea would involve a two-kilometer circuit, and the only encircling that Varro describes is done not by the priests' course but by "flocks of people"; and this too is physically impossible. So the interpretation of all other ancient sources except Varro must be right, as A. K. Michels (1953) argued. With their help she places the course up and down the Holy Road, the Via Sacra off the Forum, a quite natural site which Varro actually indicates.

How then can Michels be rejected? In answer: by appeal to Cornell's admired mentor, Arnaldo Momigliano (1966), who cited Kurt Latte (1960); and Latte agreed with Michels but only as applying to Varro's own times, without Latte's explaining his disagreement further. Nevertheless, "the tradition" (Cornell indicates Varro, meaning not all the other writers) "is perfectly sound. . . . The archaeological evidence is therefore consistent with tradition, but not adequate on its own to confirm it. Once again it is tradition that helps us to interpret the archaeological evidence, rather than the other way round".[9] The same scholar goes on to say elsewhere, "the archaeological evidence cannot tell an independent story of its own; only by interpreting it in the light of written sources can it be made to speak at all".[10]

Though Cornell's aim is to show the superiority of antiquarianism and philology over archaeology, the matter of the Luperci seems actually to prove the opposite. Written evidence, so exiguous, so long tortured, settles nothing. In contrast, the results of excavation, showing the Palatine settlement as the center of the later city, are perfectly well known and happily established—thus, no need of Varro at all! Nor is it the case that archaeology can afford no narratives without written sources, whether of events in the style called "political" or narratives of trends, *de longue durée*. Many of both sorts are in fact quite familiar.[11] For my own interest, then, in the picking out and describing of trends rather than events, the data recovered from the earth certainly seem to likely to help the most, and it is to these that I now return.

To throw light on the Romans' conservative nature, after what was said at the outset of this chapter regarding their disregard of trade and exploration, I instance religion, next. It is an area where particularly useful evidence can be found, under both headings: private and public.[12]

Private and domestic worship was of course dominant, little as that fact would appear in modern accounts. To bring to mind an image and belief in some superhuman being, and to address and if possible conciliate that being with associated feelings, thoughts, words, gestures, or rites—all this that constitutes religion was a daily matter with the Romans as with other peoples. So much is clear from Cato the Censor in his personal handbook, turned into a published form *On Agriculture,* where he prescribes how a good estate-owner should begin his rounds of supervision: "The head of the household, the *paterfamilias*", he says—meaning the oldest male in charge of the core family, of the extended family, and of slaves and dependents—"when he comes to the manager's home, and has paid his respects to the household deity, its Lar", should then get into the business of his visit. He should remind the manager to observe holy days and remind the man's wife to be equally observant in rites thrice monthly at the hearth and such other days as she prays to the household's Lar; and in estate work, "according to Roman rites, offer a pig in sacrifice" to the spirits of a grove, using the following form of prayer: "whether thou be a god or goddess to whom this is sacred, as it is right to be offered a sacrifice of a pig for the thinning of this holy space", may this pig be acceptable. *On Agriculture* passes on, then, to other similar rules of estate management, specifying what observances are right for the working of the animals, every day or on holy days, and for the overall purification of the lands and the *familia* collectively assigned to the keeping of the Manes, the deceased. Manes are to be conciliated by a larger offering (pig, lamb, and calf), with specified prayers also to Janus, Jupiter, and Mars for the good fortune of the land, its crops, and its flocks and shepherds.[13]

Cato is writing up his management notes for the benefit of other big farm owners like himself, looking beyond their homes to the duties of their workforce. It is no part of his purpose to talk about religion in his own home. His contemporary, however, the playwright Plautus, presents the Lar of a family as an actor in one of his comedies, telling the audience how the daughter of the house prays to him constantly every day with incense, wine, or some other offering.[14] Such routines of worship find mention in later literature, at least in poetry, and appear in archeological evidence, too, from as early as Plautus' day.[15] Earlier still, the Romans may perhaps have had all the beliefs and rites that Cato and Plautus tell us about—the guardian spirits, the Lares, to protect each family's food stores, while the particularly chosen deities, Venus or Mars or other, were invoked collectively as the Penates.

Perhaps that is so. But for domestic or private religion demonstrable among the most ancient Romans and still to be found in well-documented centuries, thus illustrating the Romans' conservatism—for this purpose Cato and Plautus reporting only on the earlier second century of course cannot be of any use. What is needed lies far back in time, beyond them. Fortunately for the argument, in that remote period we do in fact have thousands of burials well excavated in Rome and the territories of its nearer neighbors, Etruscan and Latin; and most of these contain articles along with the body or the ashes of the deceased to indicate a belief that life continued into the Beyond. "The gods, the Manes" as the dead are called in many hundreds of epitaphs of Livy's date and afterward, enjoyed a cult at the graveside in the form of family meals, with toasts or at least the sprinkling of wine on the tomb—witness among the most common articles in and atop the grave, everything needed for the preparing and enjoying of a memorial picnic. This one act of cult, addressed to the deceased, was evidently universal, or nearly so. The celebration took place not only at the moment of cremation or inhumation but at set intervals in the weeks thereafter, and on the date of death of the deceased, not only the most recent such but, apparently, other persons to be remembered at the choice of the survivors. Lest any dead be neglected, the people as a whole celebrated a period of remembrance, "The Giving" (*Parentatio*) in February, which was a three-day fixture in the calendar by the mid-fifth century and, as everyone supposes, much earlier, too.[16]

The cult more broadly may count as ancestor worship if it can be shown that successive meals or memorial feasts were held by families well after the day of inhumation itself. We would hardly expect perishables to survive above ground: uneaten bits of piglets, goats, kids, calves, fish, and various kinds of vegetables such as are identified inside covered tombs from the day of burial. Telltale evidence of this sort survives only from the best-documented times, much later. However, the preparation of a Roman tomb half below ground level—this on the Esquiline hill in Rome—and the presence of votive material within a cemetery on the Quirinal from the eighth down to the fourth century—suggest a wish by families to maintain contact with the spirits of the dead long after the funeral.[17] The publicly inscribed Twelve Tables then carry the story down into Roman law of the mid-fifth century (chap. 5), with mention of rounds of toasts at the grave-side in the "Ninth-day Rites". Such picnic times on set days were still cel-ebrated in Cicero's day and later. To sum up, then: family cult that fits the usual description of ancestor worship appears from at least mythic times, those of Numa in later tradition or even those of Romulus in archaeologi-cal evidence; and it can be seen essentially unchanged a thousand years later.[18] The surrounding society may certainly be called conservative, in at least this quite significant respect.

Ancestor worship which was essentially private could be expressed also by the community. This was the case in the cult of Romulus, and from an early date. Among the Greeks at home and familiar also in their Italian and Sicilian settlements, a city's people might honor the man or the name in which they saw their founder, their common father, and call him more than human, and set up an altar to him for thanksgiving: from the eighth century on at Eretria in Euboea or at Athens near the Agora from some un-known early date; and so still in much later times at, for example, Philippi. It was "an older form" and "more conservative than the usual cult of the dead".[19]

Such a cult center at Rome, a *heroon*, grew up on the southwest slopes of the Palatine, indicating the spot where Romulus' house was much later said to have stood; and here in subsequent generations layer upon layer of reverent myth and memorial accumulated. Within an area of not much more than thirty meters on a side, an extraordinary concentration of holy sites and structures took shape (fig. 1.1). Among these the emperor Augus-tus chose to build his own new house, overlooking the Circus Maximus and as close as possible to the legendary house of Romulus. This latter had been no more than a wicker-and-clay-walled, thatch-roofed hut of a type that archaeologists have traced on the virgin soil or rock at several other lo-cations in the city, and more still in other Latin sites as well as Rome, dat-ing to the tenth, ninth, and eighth centuries. It is known also in terra-cotta

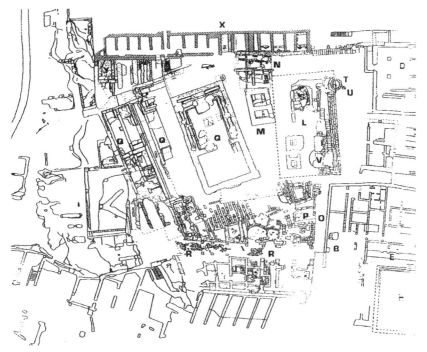

Fig. 1.1. The "Romulus area" on the Palatine
R (ancient hut foundations); M (?augural station); P (Romulus shrine of ca. 300
atop a much earlier burial); H (Augustus' house) and J (well); T and V (cisterns);
A (Apollo temple); L (Victoria temple of 294); Q (Magna Mater sanctuary, with
temple of ca. 200). From Pensabene (1998).

miniatures, buried like dollhouses in cremation burials as a lodging for the
ashes of the deceased.[20] I suppose such things were occasionally found by
chance by later Romans, or could be seen full-scale still in the countryside,
and so provided a model for replication as Romulus' own. An immigrant
Greek already mentioned, Dionysius of Halicarnassus, an enthusiast for
"Roman Antiquities", gave his huge book exactly that title, where he describes such primitive dwellings. He tells his readers, "there was one of
them on the Palatine even in my own times called Romulus' house, . . .
which is kept holy by the people in charge, and they count nothing more
sacred, and if it suffers at all from storms or age, they fix it up as closely as
possible to the way it had been before".[21]

The habit of preservation obliges the archaeologist. Here or wherever
else something had to be taken down or taken away that had once been
dedicated to a god—whether it was construction rubbish or old votive ma-

terials—the Romans piously saved it in the earth in a special pit, as for instance on the southwest part of the Palatine in the area of Romulus and Augustus. Still better-known examples of this conserving custom help us to understand the Forum and the very first chapters in its history, known through excavation.[22] So conservative were the Roman people.

Religion distinguished as "private" in my account, above, which I stretched to include a founding "father", may as well include other gods that evidently began in individual households but at some point rose to honor in service to the community as a whole. Vesta is one instance. Her worship is known, not only very well in later times as the goddess of the hearth and the heart of the home, but in her sanctuary also in the city's principal gathering point, the Forum, by the turn of the seventh century.[23] A fire was lit to her on everybody's account with a dozen priestesses to tend it. They tended it still a thousand years later. A common cult was paid to the Manes and the Penates, too, these being household gods that grew to a larger scale.

Lastly, there was private religion practiced only in common cult centers. Aesculapius' shrine on the Tiber island is an example. Here people came with their personal problems of health and disabilities, which constituted by far the most commonly attested reason for religious acts in antiquity. The Aesculapius shrine was, however, established only late in Rome, by official invitation from the senate at a moment of epidemic, in 293.[24] Before that date, resort was had to a great variety of gods, any that were found to work (for it is a modern myth of misplaced rationalizing, that ancient gods presided, each one of them, over only one sphere of activity, and every society had to have a full team).[25] From some point in the first half of the fifth century an illustrative practice appears in the archaeology: terra-cotta models of this or that afflicted body part offered at all sorts of shrines to indicate to the powers resident there just what it was that needed divine help, or had blessedly received such help already in response to prayer.[26] It was an import from Greece. We know about it on an enormous scale, meaning many hundreds of votive articles, at dozens of shrines, conserved for eternity in special pits throughout Latin territories.

By this custom we are drawn in from private religion to public. This latter is the easiest to study. In the generations before Livy as in his own day, it was not well seen among gentlemen writers and their readers to talk about everyday or personal matters—about one's prayers for better digestion or success in begetting, or about terra-cotta body parts offered at some temple; still less about rites at the family hearth let alone in the kitchen. The surviving literary sources choose to disregard all this, even in their treatment of their own times and of course more completely still in their treatment of the early centuries that concern me, in order to focus on the public not the private sphere. With this choice, modern discussion seems oddly content.[27]

In public cults, nothing especially conservative appears in the Romans' choice or placing of their first and most advertised deities. Jupiter on a craggy citadel overlooking the hills was a friend to all Latin-speakers and it is easily believed that offerings there date back to at least the mid-seventh century. His wonderful gigantic temple, however, was not dedicated on the site until at least the late sixth.[28] Since it was then a three-celled building, no doubt the cults of Juno and Minerva were there incorporated and of equal age. On the level areas below, between the Campus Martius and the Flaminian Gate, Apollo in the sixth century had a shrine and, a little to the south, near the Cattle Market, so too did Herakles, "the most popular deity among the south-central peoples". His was for long an open-air altar of the primitive sort but on a grand scale.[29] Nearby was a cult building dedicated most likely to Herakles and Athena, used in the first half of the sixth century and honored with pigs, dogs, turtles, geese, and more usual animals, generally as newborns. There were terra-cotta statues of the two deities on top.[30] Last among those pre-500 sanctuaries known through excavation, a temple of Vertumnus on the edge of the Forum, its founding date uncertain; and an eighth-century shrine of Vulcan in the city center, in the Comitium.[31] With Vulcan, the census of gods publicly honored among the city's pre-Republican days, as attested by the archaeological evidence, tails off into the less obvious ones. Mars, great god of much of Italy, had his priests and rites established by the city's second king, as Varro believed, but he had no temple.[32]

And a wolf-god needs mention, sacred to Mars, to be further discussed elsewhere (chap. 3 at n. 16). She must have had a name. Lupa was an ancient speculation, or perhaps a memory. Her shrine, the Lupercal, was a cave under the southwest part of the Palatine; for some centuries there were no twins in the picture.

The immigration of deities into the city from afar will need mention, too, in the next chapter; but for my purposes otherwise, there seems to be nothing remarkable in the roster of cults just offered—or if there is, we can know nothing about it. In chief, we can neither read the minds of the Romans nor picture them at worship. We have no idea whether places of worship drew much of a crowd, or whether in fact the public religion on which all modern discussions focus had any general meaning at all.

On the other hand, for the directing officials, that is, at first the kings and later the elected consuls, address to the gods was indeed important. They paid careful attention to the schedule of religious duties and to priests who were as closely listened to as they were actively inventive. Such at least was the later picture to be found in the written sources. It is reasoned, and reasonably, too, that the Cults-King of well-attested times, the *rex sacrorum*, had to be invented after real kings were thrown out, for the purpose of fulfilling religious duties inherited from regal times; and for the same purpose the royal house, the *regia*, was maintained in active service. Thus (with the *lapis niger* to be mentioned, below) we can get back to the period of the kings and first consuls, who were also the community's representatives before the gods.

In intervals between reigns continuity was secured through the royal council, whatever may have been its size or form: the senate. "The auspices return to the senate", *pro tem.*—this at least was the later formula, indicating an identity between ultimate authority and the ability to interpret the inclinations of the gods; indicating also the presence of clan-heads as the power behind the throne, each one supported by the precinct (curia) in which the city's *populus* had gradually sorted themselves out (chap. 5). We have what deserves to be called a "state", then, where power by default rested with kings: "a structural demonstration of the most intimate interaction between the ancient senate and the monarchy—this latter being the governmental form not to be renounced by the dominant groups".[33]

The underlying religious sanctions were clearly important. As in all times and places, exactly what some superhuman being intended to communicate might be expressed in a particular, difficult sign language, the translation of which was by no means obvious. It took much learning; it had to be done right; hence the need for priests and for answering communication in the form of ritual. An early illustration is the calendar of holy days reflecting at least some sixth-century practices, with forty-odd days to keep track of.[34] In certain rites, too, a special sort of bishop's crozier, a staff of office, was to be held and directed in exactly the prescribed fashion: a *lituus.* The belief in the antiquity of this instrument was supported in later times by pointing to the very one that Romulus had used, preserved in a special place.[35] Some sacrificial victims had to be slain by a stone knife; for another rite, a spear with only a wooden tip fire-hardened must be used, or a cake made of a flour long out of use (*far*), or an offering without wine since wine was not known among Romans in the earliest times.[36] It makes little difference for my purposes whether such prescriptions were truly remembered and unchanged from archaic days or were invented much later. In either case, they responded to the Romans' preference for ancient practice. Nor does it matter whether they were acting out their fears that prayer would only work if it followed tradition in every tiniest regard, and thus they were made conservative; or whether instead they thought in the way they did because they were conservative in the first place (and perhaps their religion made them so).

Certain priests, the Salii, served Mars by their dancing around the city (or we might better say jumping up and down), holding sacred shields of an hourglass shape disused in attested times. These were portrayed in gems and reliefs. They recall what any Greek artisan in Rome's regal period would have seen and remembered as very ancient and therefore reverend (in fact, Mycenaean).[37] Other items of Salian getup were also ancient, known to us from very early Etruscan art: a wool or felt cap with a knob on its top, a short cloak, a tunic with bright embroidery on its edges and a breastplate worn over it.[38] The durable items have been found in Etruscan tombs going back to the eighth century, even to the ninth; and they appear again in first-century Roman art celebrating the Salii and approximating or duplicating the items of equipment and ceremony that also marked triumphal parades. That the Salii began their tour of dancing or capering from the *regia,* the old kings' palace on the Forum where the shields were kept, supports the idea of their almost immemorial antiquity; so too do the words of their hymns, unintelligible to a later time.

Ancient lore dictated the actions and paraphernalia of worship. It dictated the form of prayers, too. To judge from first-century ways, a priest would have texts in a book, he would intone the needed parts slowly in a singsong way, and the king or magistrate would repeat them after him. Formulas needed for the initiation of legal proceedings were treated with exactly the same "methodical ceremonial and religiosity", as E. A. Meyer puts it.[39] The fact was familiar to Cicero and many others of his generation, since they had had to memorize all (he says) of the Twelve Tables, and the old terms there and in other early documents, and the old ways of spelling, were characteristic and different. As a specimen says, translated, "If one evades or plies one's feet, one shall lay hand thereon"—this, to authorize an act of self-help by a plaintiff.[40]

The style found in the Twelve Tables of around 450 can be traced back a century further. That brings us to the period of an inscribed square pillar set up in the Forum, later preserved under black pavement called *lapis niger.* On the sides of the pillar are the earliest known texts in Latin. They were crabbed beyond the comprehension of even the most learned of Cicero's day, as they are also to our own. Only "king", "herald", "cursed", "yoke-beasts", "dung", and one or two other half-understood traces can be pieced out; and some part of the pillar was chopped off in indifference to the text, so long as the main part was preserved with obvious piety. Still, what can be read makes some sense. It is a set of prescribed rites and prayers and warnings connected with the Vulcan altar in the Comitium, buried in the last quarter of the sixth century although not newly inscribed at that time. Its forms of expression are just such as one finds in the Twelve Tables. It has the king as the person in charge and his herald as his assistant; and whatever he does mustn't be undone in or near the place of ceremony by the chance appearance of a team of oxen dropping their excrement at the wrong moment.[41] Cicero in his capacity as a priest (he was an augur) explains the need to manage a yoke of oxen in proximity to a place of sacrifice, especially Yoke Street (as it was called, the *vicus Iugarius*).[42] In his day, these rules of ritual had been in place a half-millennium.

In this reverence for the past we may claim to have found the trait of character sought in the present chapter; as also in the forms to assure proper passage of ultimate authority from one hand to the next, by a law of the clan-heads in their Precincts-Assembly; as also in that meeting itself, a dusty bit of antiquity still pulled out of the closet from time to time in Cicero's day, for particular purposes; as also in the unchanged form of government which the Precincts had originally represented, that is, an aristocracy of *gentes* who still loomed enormous and shaped Rome's history to the very end of the Republic. Had Romulus been at Cicero's side, then, might he not have exclaimed, "Yes, yes, there it all is that I once knew, myself"?

2

❧

TOLERANT

The significance of the Romans in history derives, as I see it, from their empire; their empire, from their conquests; their conquests, from their total manpower; and the size of their draft-age population, from their ability to absorb and win over the conquered to usefulness.

This picture of the past stated in the plainest of plain words is, I hope, the familiar and generally accepted one—familiar or obvious.[1] But it takes on life when it is challenged.

In regard to that empire, that supremacy, we may first ask: Why Rome? The Romans were one of dozens of peoples in the peninsula. We know of the Sabines, Etruscans, Vestini, Aequi, Volsci, Hirpini, and a half-dozen others within a hundred kilometers of the city. Some of them spoke a language that united them to each other, or might well have served to do so, in larger coalitions than the population of Latin-speakers. In time, a coalition among Oscan speakers lying to the south did in fact emerge, though not in time nor on a scale to withstand the Romans. The Romans somehow had the solution.

If there was nothing peculiar in the Romans' birthrate, which no one imagines, we must explain the growth of their state through incorporation; for, without incorporation, conquest could only have produced a Spartan state where the conquerors spent their lives and strength sitting on the conquered—"riding a tiger" as we say—and collecting tribute in some form or other. A more effective use of strength required rather the ability or willingness of the stronger to absorb a weaker people into the structure of its own force (whether economic or political or, especially, military).

This could be done only on terms mutually acceptable and more or less ungrudgingly agreed to. From the little we know about the Romans' earliest centuries, amounting to no more than the very barest headlines, it does appear that their constituent communities were somehow able to coalesce for mutual benefit without endless bitter feuding, and thereafter to enfold more remote neighbors as well.

A different outcome to the situation is quite easily imagined. An agricultural and pastoral people like the Romans and the others around them, who had their own land to work and their own herds to pasture, might have seen their interest not in good relations with neighbors but rather in resisting thefts of livestock and encroachments on their arable; and these offenses would only become more common as new generations were added to the population, needing in their turn the wherewithal to marry and raise a family. Where jostling and provocation were common between close abutters, then every free season after planting would be wartime and every war, defensive, until one party or the other confessed itself beaten.

But after winning, then what? Then the two must live together in peace, provided there were no deeper levels of difference and provocation.

As to these latter obstacles, we might think first of religion. Where, however, it was not a condition of service to one superhuman being, that every other superhuman being must be aggressively detested, no problem presented itself. Oh happy world without crusades and saints in arms!

Next, we might think of differences in physical appearance to set peoples apart; but none existed. A distinct dialect, still more an alien language, might have been hard to accept just as the absence of any such would more probably allow easy relations, for instance among the Latin-speakers; also among all the Oscan-speakers to their north and east; also to Rome's northwest, among the Etruscans who were clearly distinct in many ways and could sometimes act as one whole. It will appear, however, that language barriers were easily overcome.

Overall way of life—this too could be divisive, at least in theory. It can be known through our study of what was buried with the dead or monumentalized in stone. What best survives for study and most naturally focuses interest comes from the high end, the richer or richest levels, of society; and, seen thus indistinctly, the Romans appear to have been much like other populations elsewhere in the essentials. The implements they needed for their day's work can in modern times be dug up and examined; doll-sized bronzes show how they looked at the plow. Just like other peoples of Italy, they lived as farmers and herders; even their rich were for long the masters only of big herds or broad acres. Like others, they had ancestor worship to honor and protect the family and its dead; the signs are detectible in the grave contents described in the previous chapter. They had common cults, prominent among them the Day-God (Indo-European Dyeus Piter, Jupiter) who ruled the sky and protected the whole people.

They were, then, not unique. Only the most provident of their neighbors would have seen the future implied in the name of that little hill of the very first long-term settlement, taken from the Greek home *Palantion* of the fabulous Evander—he, of a generation even before Romulus.[2] From *Palantion* we derive our word *Palace,* a place to rule from; from here settlement spread to the next-door little hill as well, from which we derive our word *Capitol*—the two place-names together suggesting Rome's prepotent role in times to come.

A dozen heights reached out to the Tiber banks from the uplands on the east (fig. 2.1). They look a little like the knobby tips of fingers. On these, the earliest settlers at first appeared and then disappeared, until, from the tenth century on, others appeared and endured—forever, it may fairly be said. Clusters of families grew to the size of villages on the Palatine, Velia, Esquiline, and Quirinal. Two hills, Palatine and Capitoline, began to stand out among five others. Excavation shows both their huts and, where adjoining land was of no use to them, their cemeteries. In time, cemeteries were shifted to allow for expansion of residential areas. Down to the eighth century, burials indicate minor local differences among the settlements, thereafter melting into a common way of life.[3]

As to the seven hills on which the ruling city rose, there was never agreement as to which of the seven were the ones that counted. One, the Aventine, lay outside the count even ritually, outside the sacrally marked *pomerium,* until the days of the Empire.[4] Little stretches of wall at times defined one settlement from another and suggest that the inhabitants were not always the best of friends.[5] Of the Luperci mentioned in the preceding chapter, there were two troupes named after two clans, the Quinctii and the Fabii; they acted their part together harmoniously, though the fact of there being two of them shows a division that was overcome and lived with. The same may be found in the two troupes of a dozen priests each called "Jumpers" (Salii) from their primitive dance-ritual with sacred shields in figure-eight shape, resident in different precincts. They served Mars and Quirinus in a single united ritual and date. The citizens called *montani* were somehow not the same as the *collini,* though in what way except for their place of residence is not known; similarly the Suburanenses and Sacravienses of the next chapter. And the city as a whole, so tradition asserted, had been from the eighth century divided into four regions and

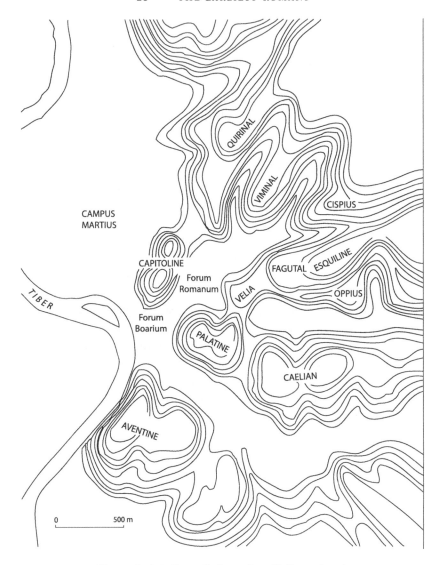

Fig. 2.1. Archaic Rome. Redrawn from Holloway (1994).

into three *tribus,* but without any consequences other than administrative.[6] In spite of all these assertions or at least indications of separate identities—most of them still a reality in Livy's and Varro's day—the many little clusters of huts that are attested archaeologically on the site of the city gradually came together into a neighborly whole. They were able to work out, to learn and demonstrate, just how they might all get along in that tolerating mode that was a part of their nature, or at least pervasive among their leadership classes.

There was of course much interest among the ancient antiquarians, as there is still to this day among their descendants, to determine the exact sequence in which the clusters grew, and how and when two or more became one larger unit; as also, interest appearing in the literary tradition, to show the extent of the largest unit in successive stages of its development toward full-scale urban status. The rites of the chapels termed the Argei are thought to mark out one possible circuit surrounding and defining the whole at some point in its growth; another, those of the Septimontium; still another, the possible extent of the four regions, supposedly proclaimed by a king. It is, however, not easy to see how history of any consequence is better understood through these various questions, as, for example, if the earliest occupied and earliest growing hill had been the Aventine, not the Palatine. The outcome is what matters, unification, and the ultimate cause of success in this regard: absorption without extermination.

Carmine Ampolo has closely studied the various groups among the seven hills, in the end seeing the Romans as "an open society" possessing "a notable facility in integration and social mobility".[7]

Proof may be seen in those many rival pairs and separate precincts mentioned just above. Tolerance, however, was more fully tested by total strangers coming in or passing through. They came for trade, of course, for which the principal site was the Cattle Market on the often-swampy low ground along the river. Here at the landing more than livestock was bought and sold. Indeed location is everything, even location on a river as unimpressive as the Tiber (which I've walked across, no great number of miles upstream in a dry year). It couldn't serve two-way shipping very well before the days of towpaths and barges; but its valley laid out a natural northerly path from the coast to the interior; and further, the first point at which the Tiber could be easily crossed by traffic between Etruria and Latium was at the island. It is thus not surprising that Rome should attract and show the presence of foreigners, Greek or Etruscan, resident or transitory, headed across or up and down the river with their quite alien cultures from at least the seventh century.

Clear proof has been found at the edge of the Market. The site is in the grounds of the modern Sant'Omobono sanctuary where the chief feature recovered by excavation is an archaic temple most often identified as Mater Matuta's, built perhaps in the 580s. From these early years survives the oldest of the site's inscriptions. It is a name in Etruscan. It was scratched on a votive vessel such as was common on gifts to the gods; for, even before the archaic temple, there was an altar here and a cult.[8] Greek pottery was also found, particularly cups that would be expected in a sacrificial meal, along with plenty of animal bones and ashes. A temple would be a likely place to seal an agreement. In any case, a tiny ivory lion among the finds also has some Etruscan on it, the writing not quite so old as in the other inscription. It is interpreted as a friendship token, a *tessera hospitalis*. It too has a name on it, and there is a second tiny lion without writing, perhaps the other half of a bargain struck between traders. In the epigraphic evidence the language experts detect a Latin accent, as also in inscriptions from other Roman sites, that is, a slight deformation of spelling from that of Etruscan spoken to the north; so the writers were long resident among or familiar with Romans. The names of Etruscan merchants can be read on gifts and votive objects found at other sites among the hills.[9] Etruscans in Rome even gave their name to a precinct, the vicus Tuscus with its Etruscan temple. It was situated not far from the Produce Market, the latter matching the market for cattle along the Tiber bank. By the end of the sixth century Etruscan clans had established themselves on a scale to count as aristocratic and, at the start of the next century, to figure among the consuls. The city appears to have accepted them without prejudice.[10]

The plan of the temple at Sant'Omobono cannot be recovered but its molded base and the terra-cotta fragments of its roof decoration are of an Etruscan style with, for instance, repeated lion figures in the decorative frieze.[11] Standing on the roofline were life-size terra-cotta figures of Athena and Herakles, whose battered bits have been pieced together and are often shown in publication. I spell the two gods as I do, not as Hercules and Minerva, to call attention to their Greek origin and the Greek origin also of their art and iconography, even though brought into Rome from Etruria. The temple's terra-cotta frieze figures derive from heraldic felines on Greek models. Greek pottery is found on the site, mentioned just above; it is in fact Greek pottery without Etruscan for company that marks the debris from the still earlier (eighth century) use of the sanctuary. The altar standing in front of the temple and predating it was of a Greek design.[12] Trade at the Market had a correspondingly international character, witness the imported amber, ivory, and alabaster among the finds. Since everyone on business there had to deal with everyone else, including Latin natives, the scene must have been at the least trilingual.

International trade is an obviously important fact of life in the archaeology of the general region from the eighth century on. The literary tradition, for whatever it may be worth, adds a certain Demaratus of Corinth, a merchant of the time belonging to a very prominent clan. He voyaged regularly to Italy and back, eventually emigrating and marrying a rich woman in the Etruscan town of Tarquinii. He had a son Lucumo, who, since the locals wouldn't accept him, moved on to Rome. He had heard that it was more tolerant of foreigners.[13] As to this Lucumo, however, legends loosely festooned about his lifetime in the surviving sources are confused by a quite un-Roman narrative. It is outlined on the walls of a rich tomb at Vulci.[14] Here, some two dozen figures are shown, most of them as pairs in more or less violent action with or against each other and more than half of them with a superscript name to say who they are. One of them is "Caius Tarquinius of Rome". By Livy's account, Rome's first king Lucius Tarquinius had begun life as Lucumo of Tarquinii before changing his name and moving to Rome. Scholars today therefore propose that the king was this very same Gaius of the Vulci paintings and they shuffle about other names and spellings into a great variety of narrative lines and dramatis personae.

The historicity of all this can't be taken very seriously (the Vulci paintings being separated by nearly three hundred years from the period they deal with; the literary tradition, by nearly four hundred years). However, the material does remind us that the Tarquins according to Roman tradition were of Greek descent and were so little affected by the residence of their progenitor in Etruria that they couldn't win acceptance there even in the second generation. Whatever their problem, their Greek origin by itself need not have set them apart in Tarquinii or in any of its neighbor towns, for that matter, given the everywhere-obvious Hellenization of Etruria's religion, painting, iconography, architecture, script, legends (that is, Homer), and social customs. Of this pervasive influence, some acknowledgment in the ancient sources confirms what archaeology shows us.[15]

The Vulci tomb on some of its walls shows Nestor, venerable old man, and Phoenix the teacher of Achilles, and Agamemnon, great leader; Ajax, too, and Cassandra; also Achilles stabbing a naked prisoner. The man who built the tomb for his family saw and had depicted in the Homeric idiom not only the descent of Etruscans like himself from the Greeks but of Romans from the people of Troy. The latter suffering the horrors of defeat were a favorite in figural art among Etruscans at the time of the tomb paintings, witness a full spread of such scenes in a tomb of Tarquinii, roughly contemporary with the Vulci painting. Such popular themes no doubt reflected hostility that had developed in the period of the Roman Republic.

In the sixth century of course the first Tarquin and the Romans could accept each other without prejudice—quite evidently, since he was soon their king. We must imagine him and his family speaking Latin as well as

Etruscan; and they spoke Greek, too, as did some at least of their neighbors
or subjects in Rome. Inscriptions of their time and earlier indicate the current use of that language in private communications.[16] In sum, the immigrants were just like the crowd whose traces are found in the Cattle Market.

It is nevertheless said that Rome became "an Etruscan city" in the period that was believed to extend from Tarquin the Elder to the exile of his
son. There is some support for the claim. Vertumnus worshipped in Rome,
indeed had his roots in Volsinii to the north, as I recalled in the previous
chapter; a temple plan was borrowed; and there were matters of priestly
lore and ceremonial later brought in that belong to another chapter.[17] Still,
the total of influence in religion of the Monarchy amounts to very little.
Literary tradition attributes the temple of Jupiter on the Capitol to one or
the other of the Tarquins, but Jupiter was the most Latin of gods and only
the plan of the building with its three chambers (its *cellae*) was imported.
Its decoration is most naturally aligned with Greek styles, particularly of
Ionia.[18] As to the master hand of the imported artist Vulca, particularized
in written sources, he is said to have come from Veii, of which more, below; or perhaps he is a mere fiction.[19]

In contrast with these meager signs of Etruscan civilization, the contri-
bution of Greece is predictably predominant. In part, it reached Rome in
a more or less Etruscanized translation, indirectly; in part, by direct transmission from cities like Capua or further south and so, ultimately, east to
Corinth, Athens, Euboea, the Cyclades, or Ionia. In religion, its best signs
are the gods transformed from the shapeless forces of the earliest times. An
early such immigrant was Apollo, worshipped at an altar if not yet in a
temple in the so-called Flaminian Fields. These were down by the river, beyond the two Markets. Diana's shrine on the Aventine was likewise early,
likewise beyond the sacral boundary, the *pomerium*. And bronze figurines
of youths à la Grecque (*kouroi*) are the commonest in Roman votive deposits. In architectural ornament, Greece provided the figures atop the archaic temple in the Cattle Market, Athena and Herakles, and the decoration on the Regia.[20]

Most interesting, perhaps, is the place of the Greeks' symposium in
Etruscan and Roman societies, as well as others to the southeast. Its rituals
and equipment are easily found on display for funerals, though by no
means for that occasion alone, as Etruscan paintings make clear: for example, a wine jug with the owner's name (Kleiklos on an *olpe*) in an Esquiline
tomb. All sorts of specialized service vessels, some very elaborate and taste-
ful, show up in deposits, whether burial or votive or domestic, throughout
Etruria, Latium, and Campania. In Etruria the words for wine jug, wine

cup, and so forth, were taken over from Greek, with a local accent and spelling.[21] The first step had been to import wine, in the eighth century, followed by home production which has left its signs in Rome; elsewhere in Latium, viticulture established itself from the mid-seventh century, with olive-growing a century later.[22] Scenes of banqueting show up in Rome's architectural terra-cottas as in ceramic art in Latium, too.[23] To judge from the expenditure on such festive routines and their ubiquity, they were not only popular but important. It is a good guess that they supplied the setting where the wealthy had their best times and told their best stories, of Troy and past wars and great exploits and whatever else might raise them in the general estimation. The rich for a time in the seventh century set themselves apart by their luxurious Greek-heroic style of burial. A most spectacular success of Hellenization among this class was the chariot races in which competitors for the October Horse (chap. 3) met on the Field of Mars, and for which the site of the Circus Maximus was already reserved around the turn of the sixth century. There, if tradition can be trusted, the Elder Tarquinius instituted games of the sort Homer told of. They were by then well established in Etruria.[24]

In Etruria, Rome's nearest neighbor was Veii, no more than a morning's walk away. The area it once occupied has been guessed at and compared with Rome's in the later sixth century: that is, some 242 hectares against 285.[25] The city was rich well before Rome and therefore a natural source of luxury articles from the mid-seventh century, in a relation called "a kind of symbiosis". Romans lived there, leaving their names on gift-articles.[26] Panther-like figures in terra-cotta reliefs as ornaments on temples—figures ultimately of Corinthian inspiration and popular in Veii—were the choice also at Rome for its chief public buildings: the Regia, Curia Hostilia, the temple of Jupiter-the-Striker on the Capitoline, and at the Sant'Omobono site, as was noticed earlier; so also chariot parades with superhuman attendants depicted on various structures spread over half of the seven hills, and at Veii too. The very same molds were used in both centers to make their architectural ornaments; and close similarities show up also in deluxe pottery found in Veii and Rome, the two being equally engaged in its production.[27]

All this evidence of the closest relations extending over many generations is certainly striking, especially set against the literary tradition of one war after another waged by Rome against its neighbor over the same period. What is even more noteworthy is a cultural continuum that takes in not only Veii but most of southern Etruria and Latium clear down to Campania. The proofs of this are the same as those showing the symbiosis of Veii and Rome, that is, archaeological evidence derived from the close study of the most durable materials: fine pottery and terra-cotta decorative plaques with bas reliefs to mask the roof-tile edges along the sides of temples or the frieze beneath pediments; also images of deities, especially Herakles, of course implying their cult as well. Mater Matuta worshipped at the Sant'Omobono site had her match in an important temple of Satricum; Jupiter was everywhere in Latium.[28] And the continuum includes the plan and materials used in domestic construction[29] and the general content and shape of rich burials.[30]

I go into a little of the detail, here, to make clear how thoroughly imitation penetrated into the lives of the aristocracy, and in how wide a region of central Italy. What people wanted for its intrinsic appeal was offered to them in exchange for raw materials, principally metals. Since these were best found in Etruria and its offshore islands, Etruria led the way in the importation of the best of everything; but general demand spread rapidly. To satisfy it, what had been coastal expanded also into a land-borne traffic so as to reach interior sites like Satricum or Rome. Production could keep up through traveling artists and artisans, for example from Capua, reaching out to markets in both southern Etruria and Latium and through what amounted to mass production of some of the most desired articles.[31] Customers turned salesmen through the making of guest offerings in Homeric style, one chieftain or nobleman to another at lavish feasts, with the name of the generous guest as a graffito on a cup or bowl. As is so often the case, the appearance of luxury products of rarity and refined taste had the effect of drawing out the social structure into an upper class of new wealth, new modes of profit-making and conspicuous consumption; and this phenomenon affected the whole region.

It was thus not only in material culture at some given moment that the continuum is so easily discerned; it shows also in the changes across time. A growing demand for exotic eastern objects of art and display, ivory or ostrich eggs, glass, gold, silver, and perfumed oil, took hold of the region as a whole, though not overnight, from roughly 725, initiating a period called Orientalizing. Princely burials might contain entire sets of arms in precious metals, or beautifully wrought chariots.[32] Then, after less than a century, in Etruria nearest to Rome and in Latium (Rome included) the level of expenditure on burials fell off very markedly. It wasn't a question of less dispensable wealth that remained as before, to be displayed in the large homes of the upper classes and in their gifts at sanctuaries. The change in custom, very hard to account for, may be left unexplained, since it doesn't bear on the subject of this chapter.[33] However, it has some indirect relevance through showing action in common—a more or less united or pervasive culture in which, from Veii across the Tiber into the Latin lands, leaders of society seem all to have been watching each other, and taking up the equipment and conduct of life in whatever way would bring them greater fame. They were their own common audience.

Once more, however, it must be said that the window we have upon the cultural history of south-central Italy through archaeology affords hardly a glimpse of the way of life of the overwhelming majority of the population in the archaic period. Their graves and their gifts at shrines do not well reflect change or locality; there is a generic quality to the evidence, as, for Rome, R. R. Holloway has pointed out.[34] Nevertheless, for reasons that will appear more clearly in the next chapter, it seems safe to say that the quality of tolerance in the Romans' nature, which is my concern here, is best considered at the leadership level. It is at this level that it has obvious historical significance. Whether it extended also into the mass of the population, as I would suppose, can't be known. The nearest thing we have to evidence is the acceptance of intermarriage in law, making no distinction among those of families from other cities or even other cultures, Etruscan or Sabine.[35]

There remains a people whose lands and story equally touched the Romans. They were the Sabines, known to everyone from the story translated into English, quite wrongly, as "the Rape". The outrageous impulse of a couple of dozen Roman youths to grab a wife each from their neighbors to the north, having found suitable girls in too-short supply at home, shows the initial closeness between Romans and their neighbors just across the river. The girls, rather than accepting restoration to their people as damaged goods, preferred to stay with their new husbands; and by the flow of the fable, they lived happily ever afterward. There is no mention made of difficulties in acculturation; their homeland indeed had taken on much of the coloring of the Etruscan-Latin world, if all the imported goods are any sign. There was indeed a Sabine *lingua,* so Romans knew; but, like the word *tongue* as it used to be used, this could mean no more than a distinct accent and a scattering of particular words, not necessarily an entire language. By a disputed or secondary legend, a Sabine chief with all his men followed in the wake of the "Rape" and, being welcomed by Romulus, joined him as king. By yet another, much later and more believable story, a certain Sabine chief immigrated, and was welcomed along with all his dependents, so many of them that with their support he could bulk large in his new community and win a consulship in 495.[36] Thus tolerance was shown when it had become quite easily afforded.

Varro was a great enthusiast for Sabine connections, and other antiquarians joined him to give the Romans a Sabine deity, Quirinus (who is
not attested in Sabine lands) and a Sabine king who joined hands with Romulus (Titus Tatius, who appears and disappears in various versions of
those fabulous times). Two other kings were said to be Sabine as well.[37] Acceptance of such legendary connections, however, may indicate only the
attitude of the forever-Romans toward an alien people fully absorbed into
their community as a result of war, finally.

War with Veii had by that date receded into the past, by almost a century (traditionally, in 386); war with the Latin League had come next (338);
then the Sabines (290). So the principal peoples abutting on Roman territory, with whom Romans were once intimately connected, confronted a
neighbor in arms. It had not always been so. Rather it appears that they
managed to get along, whatever exactly that may mean. So far as archaeological excavation helps to understand their mutual relations, they were a
close family, and if (as especially in the case of Veii) hostilities broke out
every twenty or thirty years over a span of centuries, it was still a family
quarrel. All the easier, then, to arrive at a tolerable truce, in the end.
Whether any such success was proof of a tolerant trait fundamental in the
Romans' nature will appear more clearly a little later (chap. 6).

3

AGGRESSIVE

"The cradle of the child" is the place to look for the grown man, so said Alexis de Tocqueville (quoted above in my preface). If his advice was good, to discover Rome's destiny already taking shape we should look to the fairyland of Romulus and the city's foundation.

Tocqueville I quote again: at the end of his visit to America, reflecting on Americans' thoughts about their country's birth, he reported a view prevailing among the more thoughtful of his hosts, that in the previous twenty years "a great change had taken place. The men had grown smaller". The state of Virginia that had supplied the nation's leaders "was only the shadow of its former self; the great men had disappeared". It was natural to wonder, "Why has Washington become a superman since his death?"[1]

At the time of his observation in 1832 Tocqueville was certainly aware of a part of the answer to his own question, in the form of "Parson" Weems' biography of Washington. Weems had invented and propagated a great amount of nonsense of an adulatory sort and his work was by then in its forty-something edition, wildly popular. From start to finish, it presented its subject as a "hero and demigod", "the greatest among men".[2]

Of all such adulation, the sillier bits were in time discarded. Today Americans remember from the book—and find ridiculous, but nevertheless cherish—only the tale of the six-year-old George with his new hatchet, and the cherry tree he chopped into, and his confessing to the act: "I can't tell a lie, Pa; you know I can't tell a lie". Ridiculous, yes; but back then, it was easy for Weems' readers to fasten on one particular figure as their nation's parent; to simplify so as to understand their own origin; to embellish it and make it wonderful, and to believe it all. Anthropologists offer us a hundred examples of a people's urge to explain and, in explaining, to deify their own origins.

In time, Weems' myths were discarded even though they had achieved the dignity of print and universal familiarity. They couldn't survive in the developing mass of better history. But if, for a moment, we were to suppose that no better history were ever written, we could predict, not only their long life, but an active interest in the myths' many variants and details; and interest would eventually lead to antiquarian research and learned arguments, quite beyond proof or disproof and in this way self-perpetuating.

So Romulus' legend emerged, as I imagine, celebrating a hero who grew up to lead a band of outlaws, to define them as a community on the hills above the Tiber, and to go on from fratricide to a life of warfare against one and all around him. It is a story that may tell us something about those who shaped and believed it. I pursue it therefore through its many uncertainties and disputes, focusing first on the Capitoline Wolf so dramatically symbolical of both the legend itself and what once passed for history.

It was indeed believed, once upon a time, that Romulus was a son of Mars, and that he earned divinization also by his own action in founding a city, and so in the end he was taken up into the heavens. Granted, there were conflicting accounts of all this, not entirely to Romulus' credit. Later patriots proposed this or that exculpation, they argued over this or that link to corroborating detail; but they did nothing to weaken the whole mythic structure. It survived. Nobody doubted it in Varro's and Livy's day; the first emperor asserted his special closeness to the city's founder (fig. 1.1). Cult arrangements shown through written sources and excavation confirm the fact.

And belief in the real existence of Romulus reaches even into the twenty-first century, witness the many volumes by Andrea Carandini supported by his team of experts at the grandest of Italy's universities.[3] To place the legend on the stage of real history, as he intends, he relies on writers of the first century, supported at a very few points by those of the second, and by peripheral mentions in Greek sources earlier still. From all these, by selecting what is least offensive to common sense and best fits together, he manages his own reconstruction of realities. However, between his chosen sources, predominantly late Republican, and the period of the legend itself, a gulf opens of five or six hundred years. The resulting trans-

Fig. 3.1. The Capitoline Wolf with the Renaissance twins in place. Musei Capitolini, Rome, Italy. Photo Vanni / Art Resource, NY.

mission and source problems, which were outlined in my first chapter, Carandini's methods do little to solve.

Evidence from excavation does support the idea of Roman worship of some unknown hero, in the Greek sense, possibly established as early as the sixth century (chap. 1 n. 22); but it offers no link to "King Romulus who is probably an entirely mythical figure". An exception should be made for one piece of recovered evidence, so it is claimed by T. J. Cornell. The famous Lupa Capitolina (fig. 3.1), so-called from its place of residence today, presents us with a tangible proof that "the story [of the twins] was current in Rome in the archaic age. The best evidence is the . . . she-wolf . . . which is undoubtedly archaic and probably dates from the sixth century B. C".[4]

The famous work of art on which this argument hangs was in recent decades usually assigned to some Etruscan sculptor and to the earlier fifth century; but in preparation for a full-scale exhibition in Rome's Capitoline Museum, to be focused on this one masterpiece, an expert (A. M. Carruba) was invited to make a prolonged and careful study of it. When in

2000, after three years, she offered her conclusions, the Administration of Rome through the director of the museum declined to publish them. The trouble was, Carruba declared the Wolf a medieval production, not Etruscan. Labaratory tests proved the point because they indicated that its "lost-wax" bronze casting was, in Antiquity, attested only for smaller works. But "Not definitive"—that was the judgment of the authorities which had commissioned and then suppressed Carruba's study.[5]

A research community is not well served by suppressing opinions, whether those of a well-trained professional of many years' experience, or not. If every study were refused publication because someone judged it not definitive, no doubt the world would be a good deal poorer. Yet on the other hand, it was possible to show that the core left inside the Wolf in the course of manufacture indeed showed the profile of clays of the Tiber valley, which did not conflict with generally accepted views; so also, the origin of its metals in Sardinia; and if the lost-wax process was rarely used by Greek or Etruscan artists, and then only for smaller works, at least one could hypothesize—there was no way actually to disprove—some larger experiment in Etruria at a time not long after 500.[6] Defying her censors, anyway, Carruba went ahead and published, with much support.

Judgment from two points of view thus produced two opinions: one, of science, meaning measurement of technique and constituent elements of production; the other, of trained taste. As to the latter, a New Yorker will recall another piece of Etruscan sculpture bought for that city's principal museum at a most horrendous price because the article was vouched for on stylistic grounds, by Gisela Richter. She was a formidable person to meet, and at the height of her fame then as a scholar; further, she invited separate opinions from a number of other experts; so the sculpture, being so authoritatively accredited, was installed and exhibited with triumph and before long shown up as a fake.[7]

Stylistic evaluation can't be foolproof, and "the shocking allegation that the Lupa was not Etruscan" could be seen as a judgment by only one of the two competing methods. The matter may never be settled in a "definitive" way, as the Capitoline Museum would have it.[8] However, the weight of evidence seems to lie with Carruba and those who support her, ruling out the piece as a means of dating the legend of the twins. We lack any means of verifying the myth from the early centuries.

In the excitement of debate, incidentally, it was forgotten that the Lupa cannot have had anything to do with the familiar legend of Romulus and Remus since the animal as we see it is not depicted in a nursing posture, but instead ready to attack, and she is, of course, without the suckling pair.

The problem was pointed out long ago, in connection with Livy's account of a wolf statue worshipped in the Lupercal, minus twins. His account reports how the two infants in bronze were added in 296.[9] Thus we learn that there was indeed a she-wolf by herself, and that she was an object of cult to which legend had not yet attached the twins, or at least not firmly. To Livy himself and indeed to some generations before him, the attachment to the twins was well known, as may be seen in a catalog of all surviving depictions; but whether in metal or stone, gems or coins or votive terra-cottas from the mid-third century on, without exception, these show the she-wolf with her head turned sharply back so as to watch the nursing babies.[10] There is no match at all for the Lupa Capitolina.

For an early record of the legend, we must look instead at the reverse side of a bronze mirror produced in the late 300s for a philo-Roman lady of Praeneste, twenty miles or so to the east of Rome. For those with doubts about the Lupa, it "is the earliest representation of the myth", showing a nursing wolf and twins in a rocky, woodland setting.[11] The wolf's posture is the traditional, suckling one (fig. 3.2) and they are posed in what might be a grotto, sketchily shown. Very good! But who are the four people around her? Above, to judge from his hat and cape, is Mercury, who is nevertheless not associated with the canonical legend in any way; nor is the owl shown on the tree behind him; next to "Mercury" is perhaps Romulus' mother Rhea Silvia or simply a decorative element like the lion recumbent at the bottom of picture. To the left, standing, is a shepherd like Pan with a leafy crown and holding a stick with a curved end; to the right a humbly clad man with a spear who could be Faustulus pointing to the twins with a gesture of discovery; but so many are the ancient versions of the myths surrounding the twins, there is no proposing, or rather, there is in recent times endless proposing, of some "definitive" identification of all these figures. Plutarch's *Life* of Romulus (§§2–3) gives a good idea of the welter of competing accounts.

Nevertheless, the central figures had become fixed by a date only one long generation after the mirror. A Roman coin issue of perhaps 269 shows the wolf in the usual posture with the twins and, beneath in Greek, "Of the Romans". The story here illustrated and its identification with, or of, the Roman state as a whole, cannot have been just recently invented, nor was it the creation of any one single year; hence, most scholars ascribe that story loosely to the fourth century.[12] And for that reason it belongs to a later chapter.

Essential elements in the Bolsena mirror, however, have a special relevance to the present chapter: "they cannot be detached from a fundamen-

Fig. 3.2. The "Bolsena" mirror. From Wiseman (1995).

tally pastoral origin natural in the earliest Roman community". Their focus is on wolf and herder; and between these two figures, a connection lies in the dangers to be faced by anyone tending herds and flocks. It explains the weapon held by the male on the left, in the mirror scene. Greeks called it "a *lagobolon,* the shepherd's throwing stick". The other figure, a swineherd if it is Faustulus, holds a spear.[13] Away from any city, in the mythic day of the hero, or of the later mirror, or of Plutarch in the second century of our own era, the hills and forested uplands presented nothing resembling a Vergilian idyll, all peace and pipes. It was rather a place for Romulus as Plutarch pictured him: a young man who liked to talk of the chase and the mountains with his neighbors—who "favored exercise, the hunt, running, keeping brigands at bay, driving off thieves, and protecting the weak from violence". To know this life, let anyone even today observe the year-round work of those who guard their sheep in what was once Epirus. Theirs is a job, still, as it once was in ancient Italy, only for the strong and combative; and such persons are valued by their community for the very same qualities that make a tough, ready fighter.[14]

Mirror, Wolf, and herders thus remind us of the harsh world of earliest Rome, fostering aggression. The settlement (though it can't be claimed, among this people alone in Italy) had need and room for those ready and willing to fight; and as such they were honored by the community in a particular public cult. The fact is clear in a connection with the city's very birthday, on April 21, set aside as a feast day particularly for shepherds.[15] Further, the Lupercalia of February 15 certainly had some connection with a wolf, as the name for the day indicates. A goat was then sacrificed to Faunus who was also Pan (Ovid is our source, but the Bolsena mirror recalls the deity in question at a much earlier time).

On both these festival dates, it could only be defense and propitiation that were the object of prayer, against the worst of dangers on the hills; and the cult needs would be very well served by that statue of the standing female in her shrine, the Lupercal. She was sacred to Mars; she was a war wolf, still in the fourth century when animal cults can only have been a wondrous relic from pre-Hellenized times. There in the Lupercal she received a complement of twins in 296, as was said. Though the Lupercal itself, the cave or grotto, has yet to be discovered, it once existed; and its existence suggests both a site and a purpose for such a statue as the Lupa Capitolina. It was apotropaic. So it has been called by Cristofani.[16] Cult always amounted to prayer; prayer, always for help; and help, always against some actual, real-life threat or difficulty to be averted.

The mirror helps us to imagine, then, a primitive Rome not only of farmers plodding peacefully along behind their plows. We need shepherds in the picture, too; and they incidentally explain the very abundant evidence for the spinning of wool by the women of even the richest families; for, from the tenth century on, spindle whorls are indeed found in burials (of course not only Roman) as signs of the chief production of antiquity. The textile industry was basic to every household. Indirectly it pointed to the very word for riches in Latin, *pecunia,* meaning livestock.

Matching the sex-specific wool-working signs are weapons in male burials from the tenth century on, and from the eighth to the seventh with a fashion or display of oversize, Homeric-style shields, war chariots, and weapons with touches of precious metal on them—a fashion growing upon society among its richer classes (chap. 2). Among the middling and poorer, swords appear to identify and to honor foot soldiers, while light spears served just anybody willing to join the fight. Differentiation in wealth which separated the latter two classes and is apparent in the contents of their graves becomes clearer as the seventh century runs into the sixth. The prominence of arms in male burials and the claim made by the better-equipped warriors for prominence and applause thus reminds us of the harsh realities of these early times and the values they imposed.[17]

Further, too, there is the evidence of built defenses. In the same period, these begin to appear as ditches with the spoil thrown up to serve as a berm or earth barrier protecting cities in regions around Rome, and in Rome itself, in the eighth and seventh centuries.[18] On the seven hills, because of the encumbered state of the site, results of excavation have been very limited; only stretches of walls too flimsy to serve except in the gathering of sheep for shearing, or to mark out some pasture owners' claims, or possibly as a religious boundary (a *pomerium*), can be seen on the north side of the Palatine. Construction was thrice renewed over the eighth to sixth centuries.[19] As to any circuit around all those hills together, that is, a "Servian" wall so-named in Livy's and Varro's day and which still haunts the imagination of modern accounts, no clear trace predates the fourth century.[20] Comparison with neighboring cities that made the effort to surround themselves with a full circuit of at least earthworks suggests that Rome by the seventh century was already several times bigger than any of them at least in area and that its inhabitants might feel confident of outmanning any attack.[21] It was to be the Gauls who taught them better.

April 21, it was explained above, marked both the city's birthday and the shepherds' festival, when the dried blood of the October horse was sprinkled on the bonfires of the celebration. In the previous autumn, on the fifteenth of the month, that horse had been on the right hand of a pair that won the annual chariot race in the Field of Mars. The competitors represented the youth (no doubt the richer youth) of two precincts in the city which were the Subura and the Holy Way, the Sacra Via, each with its association, its curia; and the winners earned the right to kill their horse, save its blood, and cut off its head; after which, the young men had a free-for-all to win that grisly object and, if the Suburanenses succeeded, then to nail it on the King Priest's house, the Regia, while, if the Sacravienses won, it was hung on the so-called Manilian Tower. In either case, the tail went to the hearth at the Mars chapel in the Regia. It was all a springtime and Martian showing-off of the skills and strength of young warriors; but more, it was till historic times a proof of the rivalry between quite distinct settlements from earliest Rome. Rivalry was overcome; it melted into make-believe. Yet still the ferocity of the tussle over the horse's head gave youth a chance to prove itself, perhaps also to be purified after the season of fighting.[22]

Language itself hints at that Roman ferocity or belligerence, through the word *populus* in earliest times meaning "infantry" and connected with the verb "to pillage", and this latter right and joy defined the entire community. As to early *hostis,* it meant a *peregrinus,* a non-Roman, a foreigner, *an enemy,* and in the latter sense it came to be standardized. A line called the *pomerium* ritually drawn around the city set apart two zones of life, as the Romans thought of it: "home" and everything on the far side, "military service".[23] They saw themselves as perpetually an army perpetually at war with absolutely everybody.

As the rival precincts of the October rites had somehow coalesced, so also did other little settlements scattered over the seven hills, so as to make a single community. Which they were and how they came together has been sketched in an earlier page. At a very early date some or all of those settlements met to talk over their joint affairs, and did so in a site called "the Assembly", the Comitium, adjoining the Forum and overlooked by a small shrine to Vulcan. Now Vulcan was not only the smith who forged arms as Hephaestus, but a war god, too; and in the lowest levels of his shrine, excavation has in fact turned up bits of lance heads as votive offerings. He was just the right god to have looking over your shoulder when you were voting about your next campaign; and in the Comitium in the month of Mars, when most fighting began, the Salii danced with their shields before the high priests and the noble leaders of the cavalry; so, at least, the Roman calendar declares.[24]

It is a much larger, more consequential question, how the Romans when they were eventually united turned their union against their neighbors; for, ultimately, the resulting conquests underlie whatever is of interest in Roman history. It would be merely circular to say, first, that the process demonstrates aggressiveness as a part of their character, and then to explain it in turn by that urge. An alternative explanation sought in the anecdotes, motives, and details that Livy and other writers provide won't work, either, since classical scholarship has surely shown (chap. 1) how much of this material must be suspected of invention. Hence the other lines of demonstration in the preceding pages, however roundabout they may appear.

There remains only the logic of the thing; but it seems overwhelming. Here was a state grown to a very great size, as no one doubts, at some point in the third century; hence the necessity of explaining it by its actions earlier. Any spurt of sudden growth would have left some sign, of which there is none in Greek sources to the extent they dealt with their own West and its various colonies and interests in Sicily and southern Italy over the course of some centuries. Throughout this long period, construction in towns of the peninsula at no great distance from Rome indicates their independence but their fears of losing it. Without our need of Livy's or Varro's inventions we may thus feel safe in saying that Rome's expansion against its neighbors can only have been gradual and progressive; and we may add that it can only have been driven by the leadership class whose war-won glories were reflected in the tales they told at their banquets and in the splendid arms with which they were buried. We do not confront a pressing, generally felt need for more land. There is no talk of that.

As to the various stages in Rome's expansion, we may turn to tradition. Livy and Dionysius of Halicarnassus show Fidenae, Caenina, Antemnae, and Crustumerium falling to the first of Rome's kings; likewise the Latin towns Cameria and Medullia (their exact location unknown, and they are alternatively said to have been taken over under the first Tarquin). The Sabines, their city Cures, and Veii would be attacked and bested but not occupied. Under Numa's reign peace prevails; but Ancus Martius ("AM" on the map, fig. 3.3, and traditionally dated to 642–617) takes Politorium, Ficana, the obscure Latin town Tellenae; Tullus Hostilius (TH) takes Alba and once more defeats the Sabine armies; Tarquinius Priscus (TP) takes Corniculum, Collatia, Nomentum, and the unidentified Latin Apricolae; Servius Tullius concludes campaigns against the Etruscans by seizing land from Veii, and (off the map) from Tarquinii and Caere. Finally, Tarquinius Superbus (TS) imposes Roman colonial settlers on Signia and Circeii but concludes hostilities with Gabii by incorporating the city under a generous grant of citizenship.[25]

The traditional narrative of conquest, though it fits the map not too badly in its earlier phases with the nearer cities being attacked, and the next nearest, and so forth, nevertheless provokes some challenge. There are archaeological signs of Rome's rule over its immediate vicinity as early as the end of the ninth century and early eighth, thus pre-Romulus. When, later, he was on the throne, he would have had to march his army fifty kilometers through alien lands to gain the Sabine center of Cures, if the written sources have it right—which cannot be imagined. Further, they say the last of the kings imposed Roman settlers on Signia and Terracina, although those two towns were remote from Rome and their prior defeat unmentioned. Archaeological evidence rules out the possibility of it having occurred so early as Tarquinius' reign. At a third site, Ficana, the reported de-

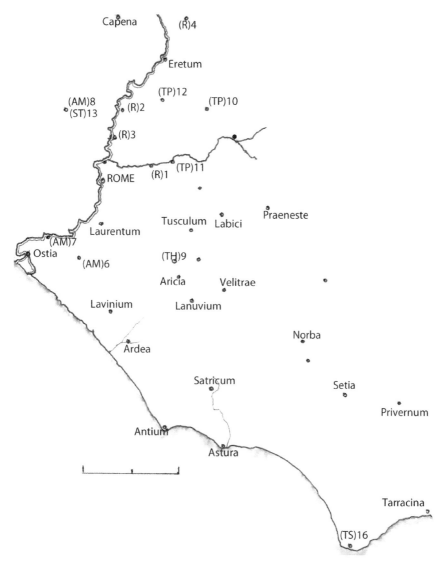

Fig. 3.3. Rome's expansion under the kings

Initial letters indicate the kings credited with conquest ("R" = Romulus, etc.).
Numbers indicate: 1, Caenina (mod. La Rustica); 2, Crustumerium; 3, Fidenae;
4, Cures; 5, Antemnae; 6, Politorium (mod. Castel di Decima); 7, Ficana; 8, Veii;
9, Alba; 10, Corniculum; 11, Collatia; 12, Nomentum; 13, Veii for the second time
robbed of land; 14, Signia; 15, Gabii; and 16, Circeii. Drawing, R. MacMullen.

feat and removal of its people to Rome didn't end the city's life at all. The inhabitants simply allowed their berm and ditch to flatten out so that farming could spread more widely in a lasting peace.[26] At the end, if we wanted to make some use of the events centered in Gabii, we would find the most prominent parts of the tradition lifted out of Herodotus; and who is to say where invention stops?[27] It is a question, unanswerable, though certainly of some interest.

Apart from the evidence of excavation, the written sources include more than the two names just mentioned, Livy and Dionysius of Halicarnassus. Among them all, and even between these two principals, there are obvious contradictions and impossibilities. Julius Beloch in 1926 tried to make sense of them and has been relied on ever since despite his faith in inferences from Vergil and other late writers—some in fact very much later.[28] One witness, however, of whom he makes too little use is Polybius. Here was someone who conducted research for his *Histories* in mid-second-century Rome personally and with the aid not only of his native intelligence but of a real-life knowledge of politics and their patterns. His Greek countrymen had shown their trust in him by electing him to high office. Thereafter, a hostage to Rome, he was not long into his seventeen years of detention before he gained the trust also of the highest nobility among his hosts. When he reports his reading of a text in quite difficult language (that is, very early Latin), placed before the public on a bronze plaque to record a treaty with Carthage in 509/8, he deserves belief. Classical scholars are agreed on that. And what he says is specific and consequential.[29] Agreement with Carthage in that year was struck "with the Romans and the allies of the Romans", that "none are to venture beyond Cape Fair" on the north African coast, where Carthaginian commerce was to prevail without intrusive trading patterns; but the city of Carthage itself and its area of rule in Sicily were to be open to all. Carthage for her part "shall not harm the people of Ardea, Antium, Laurentium, Circeii, and Tarracina nor any other of the Latins who are not subjects" to Rome; yet these latter are, as the treaty says, Rome's allies. If a Carthaginian attack should succeed against one of them, the captured city shall be handed over to Rome, which is thus seen as mistress of the whole region.

With this text as a starting point we can adjust Beloch's findings a little, beginning at the southeast with these coastal towns. They remained free in 508; conquests attributed by the annalists to the last of the kings at Signia and Circeii must therefore be rejected since the two towns lay well beyond the limit of Rome's previous victories. An area far larger than the *ager Romanus* nevertheless had been brought into her alliance. That cannot have been achieved without the use or threat of force of which in fact tradition takes some account. To the northwest, beyond the Tiber, Rome may or may not have had a claim;[30] but on the river's left bank there was no challenger for a considerable distance upstream. From its most northern point, a line of dominion may be imagined stretching to the southeast, down from Collatia perhaps to take in Gabii but not Tusculum, and so to Alba and by a westward curve returning to the Tiber valley. The entire circuit enclosed an irregular area reckoned by Beloch at some 822 square kilometers (317 sq. miles).

His total is perhaps on the low side; but no need to chew at it further. By even a rough comparison with other centers it is possible to appreciate what Rome's aggressive urge had wrought over the course of some centuries: steady enrichment from the spoils of war, of which there is plenty of proof in the archaeology of the city's regal-period remains, and the defeat of neighbors sufficient to produce a state more than twice as large as any of them and five or ten times as large as most.[31] They could have protected themselves by coalescing into larger units. Indeed in Latin-speaking lands, ancient, empty place-names lingered for the recollection of much later antiquarians, where once there had been tiny centers. These had simply leached away into the surrounding towns without making any one of these latter into a great city; nor had the towns relentlessly made war upon each other in a Roman style, so as to confront Rome in the end with some swollen, well-matched champion. Instead, one by one, half of them had submitted to the status of "subjects", as they are called by Carthage in 508. Rome and its people were unique.

Against the estimate of Rome's area, an estimate can be made of the people it could support; for it is the people in whom we are interested. Here it is easy enough to improve on tradition. For example, the numbering of Romulus' troops is set by the annalists at 25,000, implying a city-size at least four times as large, outmatching Athens, with an even larger total rising above 300,000 by the mid-500s. In explanation of such fantasies, it should be remembered that ancient authors generally treated numbers as adjectives, *ten thousand* to mean "a whole lot", and so forth. By today's estimates, a population inferred from the food-production capacity of 822 square kilometers might be around 35,000. The figure is Carmine Ampolo's—a tenth of what the written sources report.[32]

This may be right or it may be too large, the evidence not being good enough to settle the difference. But that too doesn't really matter. What matters instead is the minimum size of the state under the last of the kings, attesting to what was termed (above) a gradual growth, and with results that can only have been attained by growth that was also continual, year by year, war after war, incessant and untiring. The tradition that the doors of the Janus temple, being closed only in time of peace, were closed only twice in the endless centuries stretching from Romulus to Augustus (Livy 1.19.3) seems entirely credible.

The urge to fight and win, all the time or at least whenever labor could be spared from the fields and pastures, invites explanation in its turn. This, for the early period of concern to the present chapter, can hardly be attempted. We would have to know or plausibly conjecture the relations between the classes in control and the masses who made up the armies; we would have to know the community's values and the means of reinforcing them that insured a ready answer to the challenges of war. The annalists don't help on these matters. They simply took for granted the raising of legions. Realities were more interesting than they understood; and the only illumination we have is offered, no more than feebly, by archaeology, in the celebration of arms that characterize aristocratic burials. They were described earlier. The very rich gloried in war; but what aroused a similar feeling in their dependents we can define only by negatives: it was not land hunger or religion, retaliation or grievance. War paid only if you were lucky. I suppose the leadership believed in their luck, they enormously valued fame in arms, and so they could take their people with them.

4

⚜

PRACTICAL

A practical person sees life as an unfolding set of real problems to be solved, not of intriguing possibilities to be explored; and solutions should be the simplest to hand, so as not to present still another set of problems. There is no need to show off, only to get the job done, and the choice of jobs in their sequence should reflect the concerns of the largest number of people possible in matters seen as the most pressing.

The underlying nature that will explain such responses is most often inferred by observing patterns of action. At a great remove, the Romans may be understood in this way, looking at what even the most casually interested person knows about their civilization: their aqueducts and roads and conquests or, in sum, what an army engineer was best at. No more natural culture hero can be imagined than the legionary *faber;* and there is in this humdrum figure a particular quality that the English word catches, "engineering," which underlines the difference between applied and theoretical knowledge. The difference is clear in retrospect, comparing Romans with Greeks (Greeks, by whom we ordinarily mean the Athenians and with whom we so often make our comparisons).

Despite the dependence of the one civilization on the other, in ways already touched on, the Romans were selective in a most revealing way. Not for them, speculation about the origins of the universe and all such idle head-in-the-clouds conjecturing. Philosophy so far as they took it seriously, eventually and characteristically, was of the moral variety and even then, it was to be applied, not theoretical. Ethics might surely be called social engineering in terms of which ordinary lives could actually be lived better; and "better" was to be seen not only in regard to individual contentment but in service also to the larger community.

To illustrate Roman choices, notice also how dependence on Greek storytelling, as it was eventually registered in the Romulus legend from the 300s and in fine literature from roughly 200, was put to use for instruction, not delight. It was applied, as was history likewise, to the purposes of moral improvement. It culminated in the *Aeneid,* celebrating "the pious", no boastful Achilles; and while piety was what Romans liked to draw from the *Iliad,* they preferred to take nothing at all from the *Odyssey,* where the hero was too clever by half, artful deceiver, most un-Roman. By contrast, in the course of a sixth-century siege, the Roman commander "made attempt through the devices of trickery and guile, entirely un-Roman" (so, Livy); or "It was a principle in life for the Roman people", says that Greek Tocqueville, that shrewd foreign observer Polybius, "and it was something on which they prided themselves, to make war in a straightforward, honorable fashion"; or again, as the two consuls of 278 explained to a great king of the time, "we don't like to wage war by offering bribes or rewards or through sly tricks".[1]

As to those endless scandalous doings on Mount Olympus, so dear to Greeks, the educated Roman in the later Republic knew the stories perfectly well, but didn't want to import them into his religion as well as his poetry. He and his class didn't give their collective mind to the invention of their own myths presumably because they didn't feel the need; they shaped their own way of life as much by rejecting as by accepting what was Greek or Greek-through-Etruscan. The resulting selection, the eventual amalgam, the culture of the late Republic, was thus always their own.[2]

From the Etruscans, Romans might have adopted the gloomy gods Vanth and Charuns and all the underworld. Instead, only a few imported cults like Vertumnus took root among them. They did accept the use of the divining staff (the *lituus*) and the science of which it was the instrument, so as to know the intent of superhuman forces around them and thus in effect to know the future. A priest who was especially skilled could stand in a place with a good view all around, and mark what signs, what thunder or what flight of different species of birds, might be vouchsafed in what portions of the sky, exactly distinguished. The *lituus* did the distinguishing. As early as the 390s the story was in circulation that the city's very origins had involved the rite;[3] and, though Rome's ceremonial founding and founder alike cannot count as history, there is evidence that priestly rules were brought to bear on the common interest as far back as the time of the kings; for, at the heart of the city, the Comitium ("Assembly") was cleared and defined by the points of the compass as an augur-authorized site.[4] Thus the gods were known to have approved the site.

The Assembly should be where people naturally came together anyway, that is, in or next to a meeting of streets. Such was the location of the Comitium adjoining the Roman Forum. The latter, lying in a low muddy indefensible area beneath the earliest settlements, was used as their cemetery; but, from very roughly 730, burials there were discontinued so as to claim the whole space for the living; and it was improved with a surface of beaten earth and then in the 600s with paving, and again was paved a short while before the Comitium was more clearly defined.[5] Thus the people on the surrounding hills had a place where they could gather to agree about sales and prices, or to debate matters of mutual interest. Chaffer and chatter will always be good reasons for community.

As to mutual interest: the Forum was not only a muddy place sometimes, but sometimes entirely under water and unusable. Any study of ancient Rome will mention the severity and frequency of flooding at least in the spring.[6] The practical response was to raise the level of the affected parts; and it appears that this was actually done to a new height of as much as six feet in some places with the carrying in of 350,000 to 700,000 cubic feet of fill. "Astounding"!—yes, but there was something on an even larger scale somewhat later to form the terrace under the temple to Mater Matuta in the Forum Boarium; and, earlier, the much smaller city of Ardea in the seventh century also provides support for the conjecture. Ardea mustered the determination, or accepted the dire need, to defend itself with two earthen circuit-walls, one of which would have required a quarter of a million man-hours. Projects on a larger, Roman scale are thus easily imaginable for a workforce of a few thousands in the slack weeks of the agricultural year.[7]

Which should not take us from the size of the flood-control effort, to the imagining of a whole city wall. Ardea of a certain size could build its wall, true; but a circuit enough to go around Rome had to be a gigantic effort requiring the stimulus of some particular threat such as the Gauls delivered in the fourth century, and a degree of community cohesion that is not attested before the Gallic catastrophe, to assemble the labor force. I am not inclined, therefore, to imagine that the great barricade attributed by tradition to Servius Tullius was of his date, simply because it would be "curious" if Rome had nothing of such ambition in the sixth century.[8]

The fill effort of the seventh century on the Forum and Comitium, attested archaeologically, was repeated in the building of the great open drain (*cloaca maxima*), the Palace (Regia) and the Senate Building (Curia Hostilia);[9] also a number of temples, of which the most famous was that of the latter sixth century dedicated to Jupiter on the Capitoline, Jupiter Best and Greatest. Following the so-called Etruscan plan, actually Greek in derivation and first realized earlier in Rome for the temple of Mater Matuta, this was the largest of its style in archaic Italy (62 × 53 m). On the Aventine outside the *pomerium* another ambitious temple went up to Diana.[10] Of aqueducts and roads there were no pre-Republican beginnings—only paved streets inside the area of the hills, the best known being the Sacra Via.[11]

Making possible all these large projects, and no doubt others of which we have no report, was a strong sense of community. This we have before us among the Romans of the seventh century, demonstrating (but also among many of their neighbors of the period at other places in Latium) an ability to decide on something all together, for the good of all. A sense of community may seem a very obvious gain, therefore a thing that every population will arrive at as soon as any common need is felt; but in practice, of course, separateness and the mutual hostility of smaller groups come first. A good half-dozen inhabited parts of the seven hills defined themselves in this latter fashion, as can be later read in their various competitions and duplicative institutions described in the preceding chapter. Somehow neighborhood rivalries could be sublimated in harmless ceremonies; somehow small projects such as boundary walls at this or that weak point of the Seven Hills could be attempted jointly, and then larger ones requiring larger efforts from more people. At some point in this story of reconciliation, the largest portion of the whole population may fairly be called a city.[12] It may also be called a "state" (chap. 1).

It is natural to wonder what were the building blocks from which this whole was made. Together the Romans showed themselves capable of such grand enterprises as the leveling up of their Forum. This was beyond the powers of any one single hill's inhabitants. The possible constituent elements seem to have been three: the clans (*gentes*), the so-called Gatherings (*curiae,* "co-viri"), and all other persons whom I will simply call Residents. Regarding these last, likelihood gives weight to the tradition that Rome's situation always invited not only traders coming and going or passing through, but immigrants as well and, from the very earliest times, conquered Latins by incorporation.[13]

In the development of little communities that might in turn coalesce, where did the process begin? There is no risk in hazarding a first answer: they were families to begin with, and then larger ones by extension as time went on, until at an obviously arbitrary point they attained a size to be called clans. We have no knowledge when the word came into such use.

Gentes were the initial building blocks of "Rome" in a sociopolitical sense. In the Latin lands generally by the end of the ninth century, the clustering of a few dozen up to a hundred tombs is taken to show kin groups. In the following century something better defined can be seen at nearby Gabii: an arrangement of burials of a few score in a circle of poor folk around a pair, man and woman, of whom the man is signalized by special rites of interment (still cremation, not inhumation) and with grave contents suited to a warrior. Mention was made in earlier chapters of the so-called princely tombs which, in Latin towns like Praeneste, contained such glorious beautiful shields, swords, and so forth as declarations of the deceased's prowess.[14] It was prowess that made him princely, a clan chief, sheltering his dependents in a circle under his protection.

D. J. Waarsenburg confronts the obvious fact that, "as it may happen in archeology, Rome abounds in literary documentation on the regal period while archeological (burial) documentation about the elite class is entirely lacking". Considering all that has happened to the site, we could hardly expect to find anything at all. Some connection between arms and kinship, between group identity and war, is in fact attested in the city, but it is better seen elsewhere within the same cultural milieu. At Satricum only thirty miles down the road southeast, excavation has had some play not only in the town's famous shrine but in one of its cemeteries. Two rich burial mounds in particular were opened up long ago, the contents of which told much about social structure. The larger one labeled "C" covered a circle of many burials originally all in the open air dating from around 775/750 to the late 600s. There was no special chronological pattern in their position but there was indeed an order in their wealth or status: the poorer ones lay toward the edges, the rich ones nearer in, though all were "of the corporate clan". Compared with other sites, what could be recognized here was *gens*-organized and not merely for the use of a family. Eventually a mound some eighty feet across and over fifteen feet high was constructed to protect and memorialize them all.[15] The feat was proof of the cohesion and workforce that the clan commanded.

In the second mound, "F", there is a clear ordering of far fewer burials in stone-built chambers in a fashion to respect the male line of succession, and a princely character in the complex overall. Grave contents show all the deceased to have belonged to the gift-giving, show-off exclusive upper stratum of their society, as does the position of the mound itself on the edge of the cemetery. Each male had his own full set of vessels, tripod, and so forth as needed for symposia; also weapons, and more in the later burials than in the first. Structure and contents alike show the command of labor and wealth, implying not only land ownership on a large scale but control of bronze-working for more than the clan's own uses. "F" exemplifies a way of life that enjoyed its glory days in the later eighth and earlier seventh century, flowering in the so-called Orientalizing period for a few decades; but it had come to its end by the date at which both mounds were closed, in circa 620/610. A sign of the cause may be read in "C", where a piece of stamped bronze of the sort beginning to be used as currency was discovered. Such guaranteed metal was the precursor to coinage and appeared at the same period as the coalescing of small towns into larger ones. Other forms of exchange than gifts were establishing themselves in the Latin regions; old ways were discarded.[16]

Throughout Etruria and Latium in the period of the two mounds, for a time, people needed only single names like "Romulus" without anything to show what kinship they belonged to. Only a patronymic might be added, like "son of Pompus" (Numa Pompilius). Then the double-name, gentilitial practice came into gradual use, showing (it is supposed) the acceptance and significance of larger bloodlines. The change appears in the epigraphic evidence from the eighth century on.[17] So nomenclature tells the same story as the mounds, regarding social structures, families, and clans. And to show how clans could assert themselves, we have at Rome the Fabii and Quntilii as self-governing entities of a size and dignity to represent the whole community through their wolf priests, Luperci.[18] Clan chiefs would also explain the row of rich big stone houses that were built on the Palatine in the later sixth century, at a location of great prestige.[19]

No clan of which we have early records was more powerful than the one led by Appius Claudius. Consul in 495, his election validates the story of his immigration from Sabine territory, a few miles away, a decade earlier, along with the entire body of his *gens,* his dependents, and his supporters, of whom tradition said no fewer than five thousand were able to bear arms. He and they were granted a place to settle beyond the Tiber; they and their lands became a Tribe, the Claudian. He was enrolled in the senate; all were granted citizenship, including those outside the clan; and the integration of any and all through marriage with other Romans presented no problem.[20]

Claudius' reception shows the existence of state lands (*ager publicus*) of which he and his people received very handsome shares. We are told by Varro that Romulus once gave out land in two-*iugera* lots (two and a half acres), which would provide a much earlier example of such distributions; but this report was doubted even by our enthusiastic informant himself.[21] We are left, then, knowing very little about state land as a category, and how it was parcelled out in order to be farmed. As to private ownership, however, we have the practice established in the Twelve Tables and surely of sixth-century date if not earlier, whereby clansmen were to inherit jointly if no male in a family survived.[22] Here is the recognition in law of both joint ownership and individual. Existence of individual owners is discovered in excavation around the environs of Rome and in the parts given out to Claudius: in quite modest little holdings, but plainly treated as private property where one could bury one's dead.[23]

We must assume that distribution of *gens*-land was at the will of its senior members whose much greater wealth enabled them to help or hurt their neighbors, and hence really to command them; and they would certainly not neglect their own families; but they would see it in their interests to place others under obligation to them as well. Hence, a body of dependents on the nobles, the latter asserting their rank and means by conspicuous consumption—big feasts, an open house to travelers of any distinction—and by the show of chased splendid arms, a chariot, a company of retainers. All these fine things have left their signs in burials: the rise of an elite from the eighth century on, the princely tombs of the next century, their exotic eastern imports of the sixth, these are features of life common to Etruria and Latium alike.[24] Among the proofs of rank, finally, are the mounds covering the dead at great expense of labor: group projects. Gabii and Satricum, above, supply some of the recoverable signs of these developments.

Group projects were my target from some pages back, to be explained from the known evidence. Some of them required an effort by the whole membership of a clan, of which burial mounds are the demonstration. Very good; the existence of *gentes* can be certainly established; but none of them singly could raise the level of the Roman Forum or dig the Great Drain. All must join together as a practical matter addressing a practical need, not only in Rome but in dozens of other centers in Latium that saw the urgency of an earthen or cut-stone wall of defense around them and managed somehow to build it. In what political institutions did they find this capacity? If the proposed answer is, in monarchy, then kings must be supposed everywhere over the course of centuries; and this is indeed possible. We have little sure knowledge, but kings are what traditions placed in charge of Veii, Clusium, Ardea, Alba Longa, or Caere and what are certainly attested in sixth-century Rome.[25] On the other hand, Rome under an aristocracy post-509 could build a number of temples on a large scale; so monarchy appears to be one key to cooperative efforts, but not the only one or essential in every period.

I turn from clans to "Gatherings", *curiae,* the second social unit attested and perhaps better suited to serve in state-building. Surviving information on these is little and late. They numbered perhaps four at some unknown date under the Monarchy, and then seven and then twenty-seven before rising to thirty in the early fifth century, as the inhabited or incorporated area of Rome grew bigger. Later traditionalists preferred to think the eventual total was the original one, just as they believed Rome itself had been brought forth upon the hills by a single Romulean act. However, unlike the family with its *pater familias* and the *gens,* which may be called natural, the *curiae* were indeed artificial. They united both people who were related and those who simply lived close to each other—for example, in the *curia* Veliensis, where the hill Velia is indicated and where the members cannot all have been of some single kinship. Some were what I have called Residents, belonging to no large known clan at all. Their inclusion is what we might expect if assignments resulted from the carving up of the population for administrative convenience. To exclude Residents many of whom would be dependents of some clan would have served no one's interest. They were, after all, citizens. All *curiae* were expected to meet in the Comitium, there to vote on the legality of an adoption or an inheritance or similar matters. They also voted to authorize electoral outcomes pro forma even in the first century.[26]

In creating *curiae,* it is safe to say that Rome's kings didn't decide just how to split up the city's population by walking around from one district to another, personally; rather, the job was delegated to persons known to them as locally prominent; for it can only have been on such persons and their support that the monarchy depended for its influence, its authority. They were the leaders in their clans, princely, chariot-borne, each speaking in turn for a dozen less ambitious cousins who were nevertheless to be counted among the elite, themselves. Kings and nobles worked together; they had always done so; for, to explain the very beginnings of a monarchy, we can only suppose that some smaller or fewer clans had yielded to the larger in support of some one individual as ruler over all. How else can such a step have been taken? The realities of power were recognized in the king's council, composed of the senior clansmen: it was "The Elderhood" as it may be clumsily translated, the *senatus.* There is no reason to doubt that such an institution existed from the seventh century, by the end of which a special chamber had been built for its meetings, the *curia* Hostilia; so it is known archaeologically.[27]

A monarchy, a nobility, an advisory council, a national assembly, and the capacity to act as one in the achievement of common goals, all together constituted a practical working state. Considering its size and heterogeneity, being so much bigger than any other Latin city before the close of the seventh century and welcoming immigrants as citizens from the start, Rome's was a notable achievement. The incentives to achievement had of course been great as well. The raising of the Forum above flood level or any similar construction project had been very desirable; so too the smoothing out of relations among the smaller settlements, through ceremonies and honors nicely apportioned. But the most urgent necessity by far was the common defense, for which the need is reflected archaeologically in the arms and armor of men who could afford them, buried with them in their graves, and collectively in the circuit walls that protected so many Latin cities of the seventh to fifth centuries. Without any great state as a police-man, piracy was rife along the coast, and cattle theft and organized attacks were rife in the interior. Armed bands like condottieri formed in regions close to Rome and with a strength sufficient to take over the smaller cen-ters—this, in the later sixth century.[28] It was a dangerous world if by no means a barbarous one. To the institutions just named as the elements of a state, we must add, finally, an army.

To offer an organized response to the times required a muster of men at arms. In picturing the necessary scale of this, as it changed with Rome's growth, we have a scattering of exact figures in the literary sources. They are all nonsense. One instance was noted above: the 5,000 ready to fight who followed Appius Claudius. With allowance for women, children, and the elderly, his company would number above 20,000 all told! But then, Livy and others more or less agree on 80,000 Roman males ready for ser-vice in the count conducted by the next-to-last king, implying a total pop-ulation above a quarter of a million.[29] This figure too may be dismissed, but modern attempts have accepted the literary tradition of wars fought and won, lands thereby conquered, the area of rule increased, and citizen numbers increased in proportion. The base of calculation is itself a little doubtful before the end of the sixth century; but at that point Roman lands may be estimated and the population they could carry, as was at-tempted in the preceding chapter: say, 30,000 and an army under 10,000.[30]

On the matter of statistics and their reliability, I may add what seems to me a specially illuminating blunder, where Livy (7.25.10) marvels at so many as 45,000 standing to arms for Rome in the mid-fourth century, though only thanks to a great effort of conscription. "Today", however (as he writes, in about the last decade of the first century), the state with all its size and reach could hardly match the effort, "so strictly has our expansion been limited only to what we work for: wealth and luxury". Yet in the most publicized wars of his own life, armies of hundreds of thousands had been raised in the peninsula.[31] I wonder, had the Roman annalists spent their entire lives looking at nothing but their books?

A modern estimate of army size says nothing of its nature and use. Techniques of war changed over time, affecting the call to arms. Once upon a time it had been enough to announce a levy en masse, in the days when the nobles had their swords and shields and fought from chariots, hero-style, or from horseback, while their retainers had a sword and a spear, and mere *hoi polloi*, a spear alone.[32] By more advanced practices, fighting in formation proved far more effective. It has been supposed that, by the seventh century, the preferred formation had become the phalanx; supposed, even, that there was "a hoplitic revolution" in Rome to drive, or to be driven by, the new way of fighting. This latter we can see in such a representation as survives at Vulci in Etruria (fig. 4.1).[33] Yes, but we should note that the war scene is painted on an ostrich egg! Ostriches favor deserts, they are not at home in Italy; neither are the phalanx depictions painted on pottery, likewise imported (or their decorative conventions imported) from Greece or the Near East. True, in the Vulci tomb was also buried a full bronze panoply: greaves, big shield, corselet, spears, and sword. But just such have been found in many eighth- and seventh-century Etruscan burials and in Rome and Latium, too, long before any phalanx importation is imagined. The arms were deposited in honor of the warrior but not of some particular military formation.[34] They cannot support conclusions about the arrangement or handling of force.

Preparation for war presented practical problems of the first importance. It is not surprising that they should be addressed with interest and that necessary change should be accepted. First, everyone fit to fight should turn out; next, all must have arms; and last, they must be in the best fighting order. How Rome responded, however, is not easy to say. Of the first of the problems, a full muster, we know nothing, though the silent assumption among scholars is that military service was enforced in the period of the kings as it was in better-documented times. Of the second problem and its solution, likewise, we know only that some men fought on foot and others, mounted; and regarding the third—up-to-date battle formation—a great deal more is reported in written sources than makes any sense, and more still is hypothesized in hopes of reconciling the various bits of conflicting information. The whole subject area therefore remains quite uncertain, a kind of quicksand in which the learned who asked too many questions have been sometimes sucked down, and never heard from again.

It was, for example, supposed by writers of Livy's time that a cult

Fig. 4.1. Etruscan phalanx-fighters and chariot. From Ducati (1927).

officiant in charge of the Salii, called the Tribune of the Swift, had once stood high among the military ranks. The Swift were said to be Romulus' own cavalry, numbering 300, or perhaps better, his royal guard.[35] But the latter had a sinister, tyrant-protecting character. Better to believe that the model was taken from the so-admirable Spartans and incorporated by the city's founder into a grand division of his people into three, as *tribus* (the word of course dictating this numerical interpretation), within each of which there were ten *curiae*. There had to be ten because, at the time of the antiquarians and those other writers who followed them, the *curiae* did indeed number thirty; and the impulse was irresistible to refer everything possible to Rome's most remote and semidivine beginnings. Three Tribes there must have been, then; thirty *curiae;* three hundred cavalry; three thousand infantry; everything in threes.

Under a later king commanding a more numerous nation, three hundred more cavalry were added. Somehow all together then totaled 1,200; for when Servius Tullius added another six hundred they made 1,800. He it was who also discontinued the division of all his subjects into three tribes, and reassigned them to four instead, which were partly inside the city walls and partly in the extended suburbs; but there were variant views in antiquity and modern doubts whether any of this is true.

But enough!—"in the present state of our knowledge, further speculation along these lines becomes unprofitable", as T. J. Cornell declares.[36] The confusions in the evidence seem to me beyond repair. Clarity can only be found as the fifth century goes on, and the subject of the army and reform should therefore be deferred to chapter 8. Before the fifth century all that can be said with certainty is what is too obvious: the Roman army consisted of infantry and cavalry, both of which figure in decorative architectural reliefs and whose equipment is sometimes found in tombs.[37] How they were assembled by conscription, how armed, and how massed and directed on the field, where Livy and other annalists have so much to tell us, we unhappily know nothing for certain.

Part 2

❦

FROM 509 TO 264

5
CONSERVATIVE
(continued)

Transition to a republic with elected magistrates was handled by the Romans through their clans. These were prominent and established from the earliest times, as evidence makes clear.[1] All the rest of the Romans' history is to be explained by the role of *gentes* down to the moment when the monarchy was restored in the person of Augustus Caesar, five hundred years later. To cling so long to any institution surely shows not only the conservatism of this people but still more, the strength of the trait in their collective character.

Details, too, in their transition to a republic show the same trait at work. As Livy tells it, the last of the kings was condemned to exile by an aristocratic coup, led by the two highest of his own officials, one of whom, Junius Brutus, Junius "the Bonehead", then became one of the new consuls and promptly filled up the senate with members of the elite whose commander he had been, *tribunus celerum*. Dionysius of Halicarnassus for his part stressed the importance of class, the old nobility, patricians, as distinct from and set above the general populace. Junii, Valerii, Lucretii, Horatii, were the leaders bearing names of clans also prominent in the early years of the new republic; and in the overthrow of monarchy the tradition emphasized the need not to disturb an institution of the first importance through the exiling of all kings absolutely: a *rex sacrorum* was to be created, that is, retained, by a piece of simple humbug that might pass for truth. Let it only fool the gods! Holders of this office were still around five centuries later.[2]

If this outline of what happened is easily accepted, it is almost by accident, so elaborately is the whole traditional account dressed up in much posturing, a glorious suicide, galloping about, rhetoric, high morals, appeals to ancestral values and customs, selfless love of country, and at last treachery avenged by rightful assassination. All these dramatic elements simply sustain the style that gave us the Roman monarchy: it is to history as Vivaldi's *Seasons* is to the weather report, that is, more art than reality. Yet Livy has readers today who will protest, whatever he recounts we should accept so long as we can't actually prove it wrong.[3]

It is Livy of course on whom we most depend. How he went about his work has often been described. I quote T. J. Luce:

> Livy's dependence on his sources is nearly total; he trusts himself to follow only one at a time (rather than produce a conflation), and when he is forced to alternate among several over long stretches, an appalling pastiche could sometimes result: skewed chronology, contradictions, the same story repeated twice, cross-references to stories told not at all . . . [and] no evidence that he was ever a senator or involved in public life; hence his treatment of the workings and traditions of government betrays ignorance and naiveté. . . . Indeed, the general feeling is that he was a romantic novelist who wandered into history by default.[4]

This characterization is offered by someone who very much admires his subject, taking him at least as an artist, and who is himself rightly seen as Livy's champion "against the hypercritical emphasis on the historian's perceived shortcomings".[5]

Let me, however, call attention to the charge latent in a term occurring here: "hypercritical". It waves away any reader of the ancient historians who might seem too ready to doubt them, as for instance Ettore Pais a full century ago.[6] He extended debate by defending his views after their first expression. The term was then taken up for frequent use along with less polite expressions, "bizarre", "absurd", "fantastic", "astonishing", and more, by which antagonists subsequently and to this day seek to dispose of each other's interpretations. Strong feelings are engaged very naturally; for, if the surviving written accounts should be totally discounted, a great library of exegesis must lose all meaning, on the instant, and half of the debaters retire from their business. Instead, like Pais, they defend themselves, provoking a reminder from a veteran of the scene: "The most difficult virtue required by the historian of early Rome is that of being able to renounce the greater part of the information the ancients have handed down to us".[7]

In this nonmeeting of minds no doubt I should declare where I stand, given the natural expectation that in this latter half of my book I address, not the period of ancient huts and legends but the quite different one of the Republic. For the Republic was, after all, a going concern with consular dates and all sorts of governmental continuity. Surely the Romans, after driving out the tyrannous Tarquinius and as a people taking over their own affairs, should emerge a little from the mists of legend; surely there was some improvement in record-keeping. A Classicist, therefore, and one with the authority to speak for all and cautious about the historicity of the literary tradition for the period of the kings (though perhaps not cautious enough)—a Classicist could even conclude, "the end of the monarchy marks a new era in historiographical terms: better chronology and constitutional continuity make tradition more reliable".[8]

The statement, however, does have two terms in the comparative degree; and "better" and "more" need not mean very good.

At first, in fact, a change in the surviving account did not mean anything much fuller; rather, the opposite: a sharp pinching down that characterizes the coverage of several generations of the narrative post-509 before that coverage gradually swells out again to more generous dimensions. An hourglass shape in the historical record down as far as Augustus was noted in my first chapter. That shape on a small scale can be seen in what Fabius Pictor wrote about Roman history; and he was acknowledged as first and father in the annalistic tradition. Although his work survives only in passages that later writers quote, they do suggest the distribution of his coverage; and there is a further hint to be found written up, very unexpectedly, on the walls of the culture center of a Greek town in Sicily. We have a section of a catalog listing the more interesting scrolls in the library in about the year 130. It says of Fabius, "he has given an account of the arrival of Heracles in Italy, and later the homecoming of Latinus and his ally Aeneas and Anchises. Much later were Romulus and Remus and the foundation of Rome by Romulus, who was the first to rule as king"—at which point, the writing fades away. But we are able to estimate how much space must have been given to the rest of the book. The continuation, lost, can't have amounted to very much more than what is preserved; for we know the height of the lines and must imagine that the catalog was meant to be easily legible, extending no lower down than the waist of a person standing before it and no more than a foot higher than eye level. Thus in the rest of the entry there would have been room for little more about the rest of the Monarchy and so forth, down to 225, before entering fully on the events of Fabius' own lifetime and involvement.[9]

The intervening period rather summarily reported in the waist of the hourglass is what I now turn to, looking for evidence that inspires some confidence. What can we trust if not the standard written accounts, "the tradition"? In answer, we have the remains of quite a few public monuments, notably temples, which are archaeologically datable to the year or at least the period in which the written account sets their dedication; and thus the accuracy of the written account in this regard is strengthened. From the Twelve Tables, posted up in the mid-fifth century and still memorized by the sons of the elite as late as the first century, we have many excerpts. We have also a treaty copy of 493 from a bronze column seen and read by two of our reporters from the first century. We have the magistrates list by which the Romans counted the years (the consular *fasti*); and these seem to be pretty reliable once they get past the first decade or two of the Republic. By the end of the third century, or not many decades after the end, a flow of names of high officials was beginning to be pieced together by those interested in family records, and it could be aligned with the Greek dating system and the mythic founding of the Rome, giving us what can be at last turned into the common era. Discrepancies, to be sure, remain a sometimes serious problem.[10]

All these (but they are lamentably few) documentary remains are used today to justify belief in a far larger number of more or less public but barebones items of record to which people like Fabius Pictor must have had access and on which they could draw. Inference from the few to the many seems to me acceptable and, furthermore, adequate to defend at least those large events about which more than one source speaks without much disagreement from others, in increasingly trustworthy fashion as we get down toward 200.

Further: Roman noble families naturally liked to recall their most noble forebears, occasionally in wall-painted scenes that could serve a mnemonic purpose (not always accurately) or in individual portraits surmounting eulogistic *c.v.*'s[11] From later times, in inscriptions that may more or less faithfully copy texts from as early as the turn of the third century, brief outlines of a man's career survive.[12] It was believed that certain speeches from the third century also survived in copies to the time of our surviving annalists; and there were narrative ballads, too, though these had all passed out of memory centuries before Livy. Paintings, published eulogies, speeches, and some memory of ballads should count as historical sources available to the Roman historians and so to ourselves; but all could of course be embellished *ad lib.* with whatever descendants cared to invent. About the oral tradition which supported them—familiar as a form of art and sometimes called "orature"—there is a huge amount known from around the living world, for comparison's sake, as well as much discussion about the Roman variety. Here as well, embellishment and lapses in transmission must be acknowledged, and evidential value correspondingly reduced. Where the lapse of time extends two or three generations further back than written histories, the value of the oral falls almost to zero. It is discouraging to have the foremost of modern authorities on the literary tradition suggesting no better material than this to flesh out the "mere bones" of centuries.[13]

Last, we have reports of events not only in Fabius Pictor but in partially derivative accounts such as Livy's, in which we can notice occasional items of information in a particular wooden, laconic style reflecting an earlier age. Surely these were retrieved from official records since there could be no literary advantage from their invention: a senate vote for a public building or a notice of the actual start of the work, or its final dedication; a banquet for a god (a *lectisternium*); or the reception of ambassadors, the sending out of a colony, names of consuls, consular tribunes, censors, and other elected officials charged with the care of religion; reported plagues and other natural disasters; portents dealt with by due rites; or the bare fact of some military campaign, perhaps rating a triumph. Such written items look very much like the materials we need for "real" history.[14] They include the names of magistrates by which the years were numbered and, with them, the only chronological framework that the Roman historian had to work with; and they supply other bald facts in chronological order.[15] They were thus of importance, undeniably; they fit without difficulty in a context of accustomed if quite limited literacy; and they were supplemented by whatever might be written on trophies, armor, or other objects in temples, or on temple walls, to which later writers refer also.[16]

Unhappily, however, these various items remain, as I called them on an earlier page, disconnected "dots". Cato the Censor, already mentioned, had a dim view of what had been preserved in the official style by a succession of the city's high priest: "I would rather not set down what is in the Tablets kept by the Pontifex Maximus, the occurrences of food shortages or of the obscuring of the moon's or sun's light or whatever blocked it"; "nothing could be more jejune", Cicero says of these same records, impatiently; and "the ancient authors themselves seem to have made little use of them", as a modern scholar points out.[17]

In taking our measure of the facts, so-called, for the period after the kings as far down as 264—this, a date from which witnesses survived to offer living memories to others who wrote them down—we might look beyond the Latin sources to the Greeks. Alas, their works are largely lost to us, so far as they dealt with Republican Rome before its sack by the Gauls in 390; nor did any continuous narrative in Greek pick up thereafter until nearly the end of that century. Those later Greeks convincingly condemned the earlier while, themselves, provoking our distrust.[18]

We are thus reminded of our dependence on the late, surviving annalists, Livy in chief. How much to believe them is too broad a question to be useful. They had one idea of how to go about their job when they had what we would call relatively good evidence in their hands, with details provided by eyewitnesses. This would be their situation as they wrote about, let us say, the lead-up to the endless struggle with Carthage beginning in 263. As they looked further back, however, into what has been rightly called a fog, other ideas of how to fill their pages intruded, and they resorted to invention without fear of their critics, if invention wasn't on too large a scale. It is important to see the whole long flow of Roman historiography and its aims and rules not as one thing, all of a kind, but rather as a living tradition that changed across time.[19]

It was these writers' aim to be believed. They had no wish to amplify beyond plausibility. Paradoxically, however, they were often troubled by too much information, in conflict with itself, and had to choose among irreconcilable versions. Which of these, if any, might be the true? Judgment of probability was the key. Gary Forsythe is the most recent among many scholars to have confronted the matter, wondering how Livy responded to the confusions and contrarieties that he found in the books he depended on.[20] It is hard to know what best illustrates the state of our knowledge, but I offer this long quotation:

> Livy's most interesting use of Fabius Pictor is found in 8.30 concerning the battle of Imbrinium, fought in 324 between the Samnites and Romans under the master of horse Q. Fabius Maximus Rullianus against the orders of the absent dictator L. Papirius Cursor. Livy says that only one battle was recorded in the oldest writers, and this is the version of events which Livy adopts in his narrative. Since he cites Fabius Pictor for the belief that the master of horse had burned the spoils taken from the enemy in order to keep the dictator from robbing him of his glory, it is quite clear that Livy's *apud antiquissimos scriptores* refers to Pictor. Livy, however, also notes that some writers did not mention this battle at all, but ac-

cording to others two battles were fought. Apparently Fabius Pictor knew of this battle and of Imbrinium, a toponym otherwise unattested, from members of of the Fabian family. Thus, Livy has preserved for us an incident reported by Fabius Pictor from oral tradition concerning his kinsman's [Rullianus, his great-uncle's] exploits during the Great Samnite War. Some of Pictor's immediate successors failed to mention the engagement altogether, but the later annalist added a second fictitious battle for the greater glory of Rome and the enhancement of their narrative.[21]

What serves the present chapter is the illustration of the historians' method, quite tolerant of fiction in a good cause. I might add the battle to avenge a long-remembered and disgraceful defeat in this same Samnite war, through a wonderful Roman triumph—made up out of whole cloth—or the fate of Spurius Cassius as it is offered for moral instruction, likewise pure fiction.[22] These two along with the story that Forsythe picks apart are enough, perhaps, to illustrate the freedom with which the Roman historians employed embroidery, bias, and choice among competing versions of events, so often detected by Classical philologists.

We need finally to consider not only the narrative product but its underlying purpose. Did writers conceive themselves to be on oath, speaking only the truth, the whole truth, and nothing but the truth? Their impulse was instead conservative in the most literal sense, to recall and recommend the past in its moral values and institutions; and this can be detected in clan legends, used as a source, as well as in the historical literature that built on these and addressed the general reading public. What must be honored was ancestral ways, *mos maiorum.* Instruction to this end began for every Roman at home, where no father, no grandfather, could do anything but encourage respect for one's elders; and, notoriously, every paterfamilias enjoyed that most enviable right to execute a disobedient child. Romans gloried in historic instances of this actually happening, as they believed.

Even beyond the teaching of such a top-down moral code, or rather, as an extension of it to the realm of the gods, these latter were to be respected in the most minute way, encouraging and shaping the religious traits and practices already noticed in my first chapter. Anxious piety ruled every action of the state. For illustration: in the most vital business, that is, war, the senate had first to vote for it and then direct certain priests (the *fetiales*) to deliver a bill of complaint to the adversary, against whom, if intransigent, an attack could then be made with the certainty of divine approval. Mention of these ceremonies by a playwright around 200, and in later sources with reference to the second and earlier centuries back to the regal period, make credible a hoary age for the whole business, of which also the strange get-up and instruments of the *fetiales* seem a proof.[23] Fetial rites were gradually reduced to little more than a minor nuisance in the course of the third century.

After a declaration of hostilities, Rome's army must next be mustered outside the city's holy boundaries (the *pomerium*) in a space, the Field of Mars, sanctified by priests through the observation of signs in bird flight; and still more priests must purify the army by their rites. The highest officer must be of a rank (consul, dictator, or other) qualified in the name of the whole people to inquire about divine favor through auspices; and before any battle began, as an ancient text describes, "enjoying the highest authority [*imperium*] and the auspices, he must take his seat on the *sella curulis* [a special sort of camp stool] inside his tent in the presence of the armed host to consult bird-flight; and the [sacred] chickens being let free from their hutch and directed into the space around his camp-stool shall indicate"— but here the text becomes fragmentary and all we can see in it is the bobbing heads of the chickens as they eat, described as a dance, and this, to the more lucky side, a fully satisfactory omen. A relief depiction of the sacred chickens takes these rites as far back as the third century, matched by literary mentions for that period but also for more remote times.[24] The procedures have the quality of a truly primeval agricultural society preserving its customs to generations at quite a different stage culturally.

In a second setting familiar to every citizen, litigation, action must begin in the same fashion, religiously, in a sacred space, the *comitium,* presided over by an official (consul or praetor) who "had the auspices" and who conducted business within a time frame fixed by the course of the sun across that space. The Twelve Tables explain. They also indicate the need to observe a religious calendar according to which certain days were determined by high priests to be unholy and therefore closed to court action. Ordinary litigation proceeded in very strict formulas, to be recited word-perfect, resembling spells. Society's supreme sanction was the ritual consignment of the accused to punishment by the gods themselves.[25]

A third setting was familiar: the political. This too, whether in the Field of Mars for major elections or in the *comitium* for minor ones and for legislation, was defined by priests; and they determined also how or if a meeting should begin. Established procedures were reassuring and were observed in these political settings as religiously as they were in the dedication of a temple or the offering of sacrifices at a time of plague. So intimate a similarity in community actions of every sort was, moreover, overseen by the very same people as both priests and secular officials, though not at the same moment in their careers: that is, the leadership class supplied the ranks of both without either one being a caste or a particular calling; and persons in offices secular or holy understood equally that what they did must be "by the book". Though priests, unlike secular officials in the traditional accounts, almost never appear in the sources by name, yet secular action had to await their authorizing; for, if this was disregarded, misfortune was sure to follow.[26] Thus to become a pontiff, augur, or the like was an object of serious ambition, fit for the members of any noble *gens*.

The Romans' beliefs, supporting priestly power in these centuries, we cannot know with any certainty. However, the preservation of primitive features of cult into better-attested times surely indicates a reverence for the officiants themselves. I suppose divine intent to have been very hard to unriddle yet very important to obey in those ancient Roman times as in every other age and society, so that everyone must revere and depend on its interpreters with their arcane but god-given lore, to read the signs granted from above—signs in a language that nobody else could understand. I suppose also *omne ignotum pro magnifico est*, as a Roman once said: what is unknown is seen as a very big thing. Control over religious awe, then, to which Rome's nobility had for so long laid sole claim, surely does much to explain the dominant role of the *gentes* at the moment of transition from monarchy to republic, when "the auspices reverted to the *patres*", that is, the senate; and it explains why they should thereafter cling to their priestly privileges even more tenaciously than to the secular.[27] They were able to do so with some success to the very end of the Republic and beyond.

The conservative trait illustrated in Roman religion returns me to what I set out to describe, at the beginning of this chapter: namely, the state of affairs that brought the monarchy to its end; but I went on to show how uncertain our knowledge about this transition must inevitably be. Caution makes me focus not on details so abundantly surviving and so deceitful in the surviving literary accounts—individuals, motives, speeches, and high drama—but rather on institutions and general situations where uncertainties seem more easily controlled and in which continuity and stability can best be observed.

In the final years of the monarchy, as over some unknown time prior, at least some clansmen were landowners on a scale large enough to give a name to whole areas of farms.[28] Because of their wealth they were sure to be listened to when they expressed a wish. They had influence, that is,

power. Why in the world, then, would they have ever given it up to some
one individual from among them or from some neighboring city, without
assurances that they would continue to be listened to by him also and thus
become a part of his power? In a reconstruction of the Romans' "constitu-
tion", as it may be called, supported from a Roman-law perspective by F.
M. D'Ippolito, a king could well emerge out of and with the help of some
or most of the clan leaders.[29] After a king was chosen they would continue
to gather at his call to be his council, his *senatus;* and at the end of his reign
the consultation of the gods on behalf of the whole community would re-
vert to their hands once more as the state's ultimate authority. They were
thus most naturally the very ones who could bring down a king when it
suited them, in a sort of violent family quarrel exploding among the aristocracy in 509, at least as later writers imagined it—and not implausibly.
When it was over, the clans were still in a position to determine who would
rule. Nothing had changed except the name on top—or names, plural.

The clans' real and not merely fabled existence, and something more
about their structure, was shown above with support from the archaeological evidence. They had their chiefs, the most forceful among the *patres familias,* making a great show of riches and prowess in arms even in the contents of their burials. They were supported by dependents, *clientes,* named
in the Twelve Tables as by then an accepted element in the community.[30]
Corporately they handled land left by some member without an heir,
though how such property was then divided and used, no one knows. Of
this also we learn from the Twelve Tables.[31] And many clans are later
recorded as having their own particular cults that were accepted by the
likes of Livy as belonging to a remote antiquity. Some cannot easily be explained in any other way. They gave a shape and boundary to the *gens.*
Some *gentes* or perhaps all additionally required that a woman being admitted among them by marriage should religiously repudiate the deities
that defined her own clan.[32] Asserting themselves in these various ways,
the *gentes* could stay on top—forever, so it seemed.

It remains only to consider the specific instruments of their control: in
a word, politics. At the start, I assume that landownership in agricultural
communities induced deference. This, since it was as much taken for
granted as the weather, ancient writers had no need to explain; but about
its operation in decision-making by the assembled citizenry we are more
explicitly informed. At some point under the early kings the populated areas of Rome had been divided into precincts (*curiae*) each bearing the
name of a principal clan there resident (chap. 4); and the antiquity of these
is suggested by all sorts of vestigial rites and privileges retained into quite

different times. Most significantly, the vote of their assembly (the *comitia curiata*) bestowed the necessary power to command on any chief magistrate, as has been emphasized above; and by this means the clans held on to their ascendancy. True, in the Twelve Tables "The Greatest Assembly", the *centuriata* in the Field of Mars, had its own competing authority over capital punishment and over the election of its officers; but the choice of a supreme leader had to be confirmed by the *curiata*.[33]

After the expulsion of their last king, Roman tradition had it that the nobles vested supreme authority in a pair of consuls, though the existence of this office from the late 500s is one of many points of obscurity in the early days of the republic.[34] If instead, for some years or even decades, there was a single magistrate with a subordinate, perhaps called praetor, it is not clear that this would require much rewriting of the narrative, no part of which in any case is certain.

What is far more interesting is the consuls' place of business. As a setting for the election of minor magistrates, for trials at law, and for legislation (for which the *comitia centuriata* was hardly ever used) there was a gathering place called the Comitium—often referred to above. Its location adjoining the Forum is known, fitted among structures that have been identified and approximately dated in excavation. That it was square is known, too—a square like the matching space at the center of Roman outsettlements of the fourth century and later (fig. 6.1 in chap. 6). Steps have been found from the Roman Forum to a speaker's platform, the later Rostra, datable to around 500, along with a short stretch of one edge in one of the improved versions of the structure, lower in date than serves the purpose of my book but sufficient to confirm where that edge must always have been. As to the original shape, it was needed for purposes of auspication; internal features are referred to by the Twelve Table fixing the times for court business.[35]

What remains to be determined is the size of the Comitium. This is not much in dispute, either: around 1,600 square meters, encumbered by numerous monuments and statues so that the usable area was diminished by a hundred square meters at the very least. Herein the participants stood for their meetings. If we assign two-thirds of a square meter to each per person, without quite unrealistic crowding, and if we place the speakers out of the way on the raised edge, the later Rostra, then space is left for a total a little above two thousand. If we jammed them in like sardines we could in theory imagine twice that number.[36]

In the area of Rome's territories at the turn of the fifth century, using comparative statistics from adequately known countries and centuries, a population of no more than 35,000 may be conjectured within which a quarter or a little more would be adult male citizens, eligible to vote. Of this number—say, 9,000—in turn a quarter (those who could crowd into the Comitium) evidently made up the fullest expected participation: 20 percent. There would have been much more room for a meeting in the Forum but this was not made use of until the second half of the second century when (in 145 or 123) the speakers on the Rostra turned around and for the first time addressed their audience in the larger space.[37]

Voting was not by head but by unit: by *curiae* numbering thirty at the turn of the fifth century, within which the clans including *clientes* were dominant. *Curiae* were not unwieldy. On the contrary, each had its own dining hall, no one of which earned fame for size or grandeur; none can have held more than a few scores for their common meal; and all members meeting together as the *comitia curiata* may thus have filled but could not have overflowed the Comitium.[38]

The estimate of 20 percent participation among eligible voters in the year 500 is about the same to be found, though with no greater certainty, in Athens before the Peloponnesian war (by the end of that war and in the following century the Athenian population was much reduced and the percentage correspondingly higher). I am surprised that Rome with its less concentrated, less urbanized society could match such a degree of involvement. Perhaps the potential was never achieved in fact; certainly a limited involvement suited everyone, as I explain in a moment.

Livy in his day was familiar only with the Forum as the center of political life. To imagine in its place the far smaller Comitium, he would have had to look back a century and more. This, he and other writers of his time could not do. The Comitium appears in his text as the proper and ordinary place of assembly only once, and other ancient sources such as Plutarch and Cicero know only the late Republican scene, Forum-centered. To their modern readers, too, it is nothing less than "revolutionary" to suggest that the Comitium was "the primary political space, used not just for *contiones* [public debates] but also for electoral and legislative procedures". Could so small an arena as this suffice for the heroics of a great figure like Appius Claudius the Blind? The idea is rejected without need of argument even in the face of the evidence.[39] Yet such was the case both for meetings by *curiae* and, after 493, by tribes.

It was not the case for all elections. To repeat: those for consuls and other top ranks were held in the centuriate assembly in an ample setting and with a different level of attendance; but for lesser magistracies, yes, in the Comitium, which was used also to hear trials or to pass a law (this latter, obviously important but a very rare event in the earlier and middle Republic).[40]

While the area of the Comitium and its assemblies remained the same, the overall population steadily increased. The percentage estimated above, for the year 500, thus changed so that those attending amounted to no more than "a tiny proportion of the Roman citizenry", as Henrik Mouritsen put it.[41] True, his focus was fixed on the political behavior of the later Republic, where, considering all venues for all assemblies of every purpose, he supposes participation ranging between 1 and 3 percent. This figure, however, could well be retrojected to the fourth century. So Robert Develin has suggested; and any estimate of the full citizen population entitled to vote will bear him out. For example, in 290, with something above 150,000 potential voters among close to half a million citizens, the Comitium could hardly have held 2 percent. To anyone dependent on Livy or his contemporaries, this low level of participation seems quite incredible, even shocking.[42] It is easy to see, however, that a small assembly where no one could hide his vote would suit those in charge and at the same time suit the compliant, claiming their reward. A space of forty by forty meters was about right.

Thus far, the *comitia curiata;* but from very early in the Republic an alternative instrument of political action, the tribal assembly, made an appearance.

The cause was the so-called Struggle of the Orders, so famous. "Patricians" effectively defined, or one could say they created politically, the plebeians, their antagonists. Exactly how *patricii* had marked themselves off as an elite at some point in the regal period, so as to keep out everyone else, is not clear. Birth was certainly a part of the answer. Exclusion, however, could not rationally deny a military role to someone able to pay for his armor and even a horse or, with less panache, able to afford at least a stout spear and shield. The state needed everyone's strength. Changes in warfare to be described later (chap. 7) could thus open up a path to honor for anyone with the means to arm himself, even in the ordinary infantry—and in rivalry with the older elite. Warriors of a past time in their chariots or on their mounts had to yield to another style of champion claiming recognition not only within the army but in the affairs of the state generally. According to this justice Have-nots who could afford the necessary equipment and earn their comrades' respect in war could rightly claim the reward of a magistracy. A door opened to prominence and office, and the more prosperous farmer-soldiers who were not of patrician pedigree could force their way in. Or try.

At a certain time, in the 490s, circumstances favored their attempt. The economy was undergoing a serious contraction. The cause is not known but the results are discernible in the public building program, so ambitious in the sixth century, producing several temples in the early fifth and then halting for a long time.[43] In the same period, burials of the dead are honored with less showy, less often imported articles.[44] In the Twelve Tables we find landless sufferers set against a landowner class, harsh punishments for anyone who couldn't pay his debts, and entrenched usury.[45] Short-spoken though the Tables are, they give support to the larger picture we find in the annalists.

The poor, though citizens, remained outside the system of *gentes* and *clientes*. Some were immigrants whom I called "Residents" in an earlier chapter to distinguish them from mere transients, traders, and slaves; some were failed farmers, suggested by a temple to Ceres, Liber, and Libera dedicated in 493 on the Aventine hill as a center for popular protest. The city also had its craftspeople known in the Twelve Tables through mention of their associations.[46] In this class too there would be poor. From all these elements and in this troubled chapter of Rome's economic history arose the famous First Secession of the plebs (494), a walkout in protest against the cruelties of the law and the aristocracy, the law's agents. So began the Struggle.

Its causes and timing are the subject of extensive treatment in the usual sources; but "they have been subjected to severe assault and it is apparently the received opinion today that the Secessions are fictitious and that the tribunate was created in 471 at the earliest"—this, the appraisal of a Classicist worth quoting, in 1965.[47] His discipline, brought to bear on the question what exactly were the working methods of writers in antiquity, could boast of practitioners in the first half of this past century every bit as deeply versed in the ancient languages as those of more recent generations. No one will say otherwise. It is more common now, however, by whatever tilt of argument or fashion, to credit Livy and his company more readily.

And the events as reported do seem to fit naturally within the economy of the times; natural also is the name for the rebellious people's newly chosen representatives (*tribuni plebis*) borrowed from the army, whether these tribunes were at first two in number or four or five or the later-attested ten; and natural was the manner of electing them to speak for and defend the weak. All this seems to me easily accepted in the traditional narrative. Voting was to be by groups in the usual Roman way, but by territorial census units, *tribus,* not by *centuriae* or *curiae.* The *curiae* were too obviously under the control of *gentes* and so as voting units were eventually consigned to venerable desuetude like the *fetiales* and the *rex sacrorum.* They were ob-

solescent long before the end of the Republic, each one of them then contributing no more than a single symbolic representative in the voting assemblies. Still, they were not abolished. In sum, the Struggle in its course
does seem somehow well regulated: one may fairly say, conservative.[48] It is
this trait of national character that I find expressed throughout the internal half of Rome's history to the very end of the Struggle, and which can
be discovered in its other aspects and later chapters.

In contrast to the *curiae* as voting units, tribes had nothing to do with
birth. They registered people in the village or rural district where they held
property, the purpose being taxation and recruitment, as is assumed. There
can have been no other reason to go to the great trouble of dividing up and
counting the people.[49] Voting by tribes, then, the *plebs* in the Struggle
formed and supported resolutions that would be at least binding on themselves if not on the whole state (I think it likely that, before, there had been
no Roman legislation at all—only decrees of kings and consuls). Perhaps
still in the first half of the fifth century this tribal voting was borrowed by
consuls and other high magistrates to supplement and gradually replace
the curiate assemblies.[50]

Given the uncertainties, however, this first chapter in the Struggle of the
Orders must be reduced from the drawn-out drama of tradition to a few
points of better anchorage. To sum them up: the Have-nots had gone on
strike, they had organized themselves, they invented and elected officers to
defend them. Their success was plain, yet only on two fronts: through the
creation of a public office, a tribunate of the *plebs,* amounting to political
power for the ambitious among them, first, and second, through devising
safeguards for the weakest against harsh treatment by the Haves. The outcome never amounted to a state within a state; it was closer to an ombuds-
man system; for nothing had been displaced, nothing was overturned. The
Have-nots remained as before under the authority of priests, consuls, laws,
tax collectors, military service obligations, and military tribunes. In short,
class war was carried no further than this very conservative people could tol-
erate; and it is just this quality or fact that interests me here.

A second chapter in the Struggle begins in midcentury, 452 according
to tradition, and led to the Twelve Tables within a year. The body of law
then published, shaped by custom and "dominated by oral tradition and
symbolic action", could only have been spelt out by the Haves. It had always been held in the mind of the learned among them, just like priestly
lore. Hence the view that it was now "established by the patrician class and
represented the administrative structure that this class imposed and supported".[51] Still, the Tables' scope and publication did serve a proletarian

purpose by reducing the arbitrariness of legal decisions. There was now, so
to speak, a court of appeal against whatever looked like a violation of custom and justice—no matter the magistrate's eminence or arrogance. Just
how these opposing consequences worked out in actual fact, however, to
affect everyday reality, hardly appears in Livy or Dionysius. That wasn't
what historians should write about.[52] We consequently remain very much
in the dark.

Those historians noticed only one section of the Tables: a new law that
forbade the intermarriage of patricians and plebeians. This was seen as important for a reason emerging in the third chapter of the Struggle: it concerned the very essence of the aristocracy, an aristocracy of birth, that is, of
family. It must be held forever separate and superior.[53] No breach of its
boundaries could be allowed through which a plebeian might enter, to
challenge the patricians for public office, whether sacral or secular. The
monopoly was certainly no novelty in 451, no one supposes so; for, if it had
once prevailed in earlier generations, what could be the meaning of names
attaching to some of the kings, to the hills of Rome, to *curiae*, or to consuls of the opening decades of the fifth century, if those were the names of
plebeian clans acknowledged to be such, at least in well-documented later
times? The anomaly or misfit in the evidence is curious. What of apparently plebeian consuls in the fifth and fourth centuries when the sources
say consuls had to be patrician?[54] The shadow of the great Theodor
Mommsen, lawyer turned Classicist, still hangs over these questions, in-
sisting on answers only within the bounds of statutes.[55] But surely explanation is better sought in the compromises and flexibility of politics. The
Haves could claim particular eminence and a long run of it, too, down
through the generations; they could close ranks under a title, "patrician";
but, as their numbers steadily diminished, their ranks gradually opened
lest each, inbred or bred out, should end in only "the tenth transmitter of
a foolish face".[56] Marriage between patricians and plebeians thus resumed
after a few years, accommodating the most eligible among the latter.

As to the monopoly of office, in the Struggle of the Orders from the
mid-fifth century a remarkable story of retreat without capitulation and of
adjustment by increments and invention can be recovered from the tradition; and much of its chief contentions must be believed. In the beginning
there were two consuls for the old nobility alone, so say the annalists, and
then a few tribunes of the plebs were added and the number was soon
raised to the standard of ten; then came two exclusively plebeian aedile-
ships for the oversight of the Ceres temple; and then, barred to plebeians, a
pair of quaestors to assist the consuls (but a plebeian among them first in

421); and military tribunes with consular power from 445, displacing consuls not in every year but quite often down to 367 (the first plebeian among them in 400), when also the consulship was at last opened to the *plebs;* and a pair of censors (443—and one might be plebeian, 351; one *must* be plebeian from 339 on; and the interval of years between pairs might be one, three, five, seven, or nine!). A board of religious consultants was expanded to make a place for plebeians (368); and then a praetorship (from 367) was created which could be held by a plebeian (337); also a pair of curule aediles at first open only to patricians; and the dictatorship was opened to the plebs in 356; finally, the pontificate in 300 was opened to plebeians. It is fair to count this last office among the political, given the role of this and other priesthoods in such secular matters as were recalled above.[57]

With the *pontifex maximus* the story of opening magistracies may conclude. In the course of it, however, notice all the irregularities and inconsistencies in the number of military tribunes with consular power or of tribunes of the people, or in assigning a particular magistrate some particular power or length of term, or in determining how he or they might be appointed or elected, or if a concession once extorted could really be acted on right away; and so forth. Despite modern attempts to make sense of the surviving accounts—meaning, to find some underlying statutory logic—all these signs of disorder seem to me most easily interpreted as simple horse-trading among power brokers or, in more academic language (above), "compromise and flexibility". This in turn I am inclined to read, not as timidity on the part of the Have-nots nor as proof of that sweet temper that will never push an advantage to extremes, but rather as a bred-in respect for past privilege and established claims. "The history of the Roman Republic is characterized not by sharp breaks but by conservatism".[58]

A fourth chapter in the Struggle of the Orders focused on land, something for those outside the circle of patrician clans, of old wealth, *curiae,* and priesthoods. High office was certainly desired by the richer among the excluded—those rising members among the Have-nots who were Have-nots only in the matter of political office. But for the vastly greater number supporting them and in whose name they could claim to be fighting, what counted was something much more modest: a matter of subsistence, an extra acre or two. Whatever they may have deserved as their reward in Rome's wars, the poor got only what little the Haves allowed. Territory won by them in battle became *ager publicus* to be parcelled out both by and to the powerful. Such was the reality as it appears in the traditional accounts a score of times, from the 480s through the next century and beyond; and it is not contradicted by the big estates and villages archaeologically attested at least in the regions closer in to Rome and on the best land.[59]

From these economic inequities the long Struggle at last produced relief wrung from patricians by the consuls Licinius and his colleague Sextius in 367. It set limits on how much public land the powerful would be allowed to retain, by whatever means they might have gotten it in the first place. Excavated sites again make a good fit with the story. They indicate a change in ownership patterns post-367 such as would be expected from the new law.[60] Further, there is something of interest in Livy for for 298:

> In this year a number of court days were given by the aediles to cases of ownership of more land than the law allowed, and almost nobody was acquitted. A huge check was delivered to boundless greed.

What the historian offers here appears to be just what history should be, the real truth: an item of just the sort that Classicists are inclined to believe, serving no obvious artistic purpose, loose-floating, an add-on likely found in some official source. As Stephen Oakley says, "there is no reason whatsoever to reject this notice".[61] Thus from 298 we may look back with more trust in such legislation, earlier, including that of 367.

The Licinio-Sextian limit was, we are told, 500 *iugera* (309 acres; 126 ha). This number like almost any other in our ancient sources provokes doubt; yet it makes fair sense, given what may be conjectured about the extent of Rome's state lands at the time. Close discussion I leave to Oakley; but if 500 can be believed, it gives a numerical definition to class divisions; for, again in the tradition, allotments of state land were a mere two *iugera* in the time of the kings, and in the fourth century still varied from two, to two and three-quarters, to three and a half, and up to seven *iugera* but no more than that. The ratio of the poor to the rich (with 500 *iugera*) was thus in the neighborhood of one to a hundred.

That ratio was inevitably expressed in local influence, so that anyone who challenged the rich and powerful, as an ambitious plebeian might do, would know he did so at his own peril. It must be kept in mind that the Romans neither at this time nor ever in their history assigned law enforcement to the state. Enforcement was left to what we would call civil suits backed up by community opinion; so the cases on trial in 298 (Livy, above), which made some very serious enemies for the plaintiffs, required a good deal of courage or outrage. Small wonder that legislation so regularly lapsed, or wasn't invoked. Thus it must be repeated again and again, into the second and first century, giving an obviously grudging, incremental, never-ending character to the course of the Struggle.

In its final episodes, in 449 (the Valerian law), 339 (the Publilian) and 287 (the Hortensian), the Struggle extended the reach of the plebs in their assemblies to the whole of the Roman state—at first with some restrictions, then with perhaps only pro forma restrictions, and then fully.[62] The pattern is the familiar one, not of revolution but of repeated pressure by the Have-nots to assert their needs and just claims even across centuries of attack and defense. It has not always been understood, however, that what was at stake was not the place (the Comitium) nor the unit of voting (tribal), nor very likely the participants themselves. It was in fact only the question who would preside. A plebeian assembly was one called and run by a plebeian, just as a curiate assembly was called and run by a patrician, while a tribal assembly could be called or run by either. In either case, the presiding magistrate had entire control over the conduct of business, determining who spoke and on what question, and giving a kind of cosy, pro forma, friends-only character to the proceedings. As a consequence, on the eve of the Punic Wars, what fitted inside the Comitium amounted to 1 percent of Rome's citizens, at a guess. And, incidentally, the proportion involved in major elections (consuls and the like) was not very different, though having much less impact on the Struggle of the Orders.[63]

These figures of course define Roman "democracy" about which so much confusion exists for this period and still more noticeably in the most familiar final century of the Republic.[64] In truth, that Republic had begun as a narrow oligarchy with little popular engagement and it ended in the same shape. To changes in the economy and society—changes of a sort affecting a thousand economies and societies across time—the Romans naturally responded as their character dictated, not with sudden and intractable demands, nor with barricades and bloodshed, but conservatively.

6

~~~

TOLERANT

(continued)

There is no reason to think that Romans in a republic were any less open to foreign ways than they had been under their kings. The welcome offered to Tarquin the Elder was also offered to a Sabine immigrant and his dependents on a grand scale in the late 500s: to Attius Clausus remade as citizen Appius Claudius, and still more, as a patrician, and in a decade, a consul. Etruscan neighbors for their part continued to advise the senate, that is, the Roman state itself: it turned to them to provide haruspices, the seers with the only proper credentials still at the turn of the fourth century, if we may trust Livy.[1] In the early *fasti* consuls occur with an ethnic second name, a *cognomen* Etruscan or other ("Tuscus", "Clusinus", "Sabinus", "Camerinus", "Auruncus"), showing the debt or attraction of Rome to other peoples of central Italy.[2]

Most notably, and to a Greek observer a thing of wonder, the Romans freed their slaves liberally and upon freeing them made them citizens straightway, automatically, and this, from the time of the kings. The freed received citizenship and membership in a *gens,* accepted into their master's clan and its cults, in a dependent, duty-laden status. The practice is best explained as a concession to captives taken in wars with Latin cities, who were of an essentially identical language and way of life and therefore easily absorbed; but in time all captives of any sort were treated in the same way. These new Romans, in numbers that rose with every passing generation of wider warfare, best demonstrate the tolerance that characterized the master society. There don't seem to have been any second thoughts about the matter, ever.[3]

Another indication of an open society—although a practice shared across all of central Italy—was mentioned in chapter 1 (at n. 26): people bought terra-cotta or occasionally bronze replicas of a body part to represent whatever was their point of suffering and dedicated them at the shrine of almost any deity (since all deities were healers) along with a prayer for recovery. The rite has left its mark almost everywhere in finds from the opening of the fifth century to the end of the fourth, and touches every stratum of wealth. Over the span of a generation or so, beliefs and articles introduced from outside thus permeated the culture almost from top to bottom.[4] We certainly see in this illustration much movement and openness; we can imagine how, and how well, the market worked.

So much being said, however, it must be conceded that archaeological and literary evidence most often shows us only the elite. Of course, the more money people command, the better the quality they demand for it; the longer trained the artist must be who satisfies them; the more elaborate and carefully worked the idea or product on sale, and therefore the more likely to be mentioned in our written sources or preserved for excavation. All this goes without saying, today; but Tocqueville's reader perhaps needed the reminder that "the aristocratic class naturally derive from their superior and hereditary position a taste for what is extremely well-made and lasting".[5] Thus it was with the Romans. In their response to other cultures, we are able to see a lot of show-off or nonessential things like tomb paintings or eulogies, porticoed temples or parades, while we know almost nothing about how food was cooked or girls got married among the generality of the population. In modern studies of "Roman civilization" this huge fact is generally forgotten, giving rise to the question, whether there was in fact any civilization that was truly Roman, not imported. The answer is, yes, indeed there was; but it lay in those levels of life most often hidden from us and consequently quite forgotten. So far as regards religion, I tried to draw the distinction in the first chapter.[6]

As might be expected, sharing with Latins was easiest. They were closest in every respect. Almost next door was little Gabii from which Romans took a special folding of the toga in the act of worship.[7] Even in conflict, Latin communities were given special treatment by the earliest fetial rites, evidently because the Romans felt themselves to be under the eye of exactly the same gods as the enemy and must therefore behave themselves like good pious folk.[8] No unjust aggression! At least for the city's public cults if not for their supporting beliefs, we have the dates and some of the remains of temples, where our written sources show us Romans adopting the rites and festivals of Aricia's patron Diana and, from Ardea and

Lavinium, Venus; and in Lavinium, Vesta's priestesses were at home as fully as they were in Rome, though there is no saying if this represented some importation by Rome or, if so, at what period. Similarly Mars as well as Jupiter enjoyed worship at many Latin cities besides Rome; so also Minerva; from Tusculum came Juno of the Grove, adopted by a Roman *curia* and with her own special priests; and in 375 a temple was built for her. In 380 the great leader Cincinnatus brought back Jupiter Imperator from Praeneste in the form of the god's statue, to a new site he had prepared on the Capitol.[9]

However much sharing of cults there was among all Latin-speakers, many a city gave its own name and, we must suppose, its own particular customs of worship to gods of common piety. No doubt differences on the human plane might reflect or imply something similar in heaven; but if so, they could be acknowledged in proper prayers. Against the confederated Latins, a Roman hero, Decius "the Mouse" in 340, invoked "Janus, Jupiter, Father Mars, Quirinus, Bellona, Lares, New Gods, Native Gods, deities who have power over us *and our enemies,* and the Manes too", for favor in battle. The names he runs through are easily shown to dominate among the Roman people in the date and size of temples, date of context, frequency of mention, prominence of officiants, and so forth.[10] All but Quirinus were widely shared with Latins.

A Roman once again victorious over Latins, a little later than Decius, concluded a peace that specified Rome's participation in the patron cult of the defeated city of Lanuvium, so Livy says.[11] To invite an alien god's favor or notional transfer to the Roman side, as a good piece of magic, was more than once attested in the earlier Republic and even so late as the early Empire. Such handling of Juno of Veii was most reliably reported.[12] If instances and ritual prayers to go with them were sometimes invented by later writers, they are nevertheless numerous enough all together to support the inference of a cultural proclivity, a way of doing things, that was characteristic of the Romans: at first cautious, involving members of the family, so to speak, whether in war or peace; then, in time, reaching far beyond the boundaries of Latium. The practice (*evocatio*) has an interest beyond politics and therefore beyond the calculated material advantages of a receptive posture. It brought what was someone else's, and once hostile, right into your own home, at the same time both testing tolerance and demonstrating it. Adoption of foreign cults had no historical consequences—that is, no change in action or behavior followed—but the tolerance of which adoption was an index had very great consequences; and that is my point, to be developed further.

The enemy could be Sabine, Etruscan, or Greek—three peoples who were not so nearly identical in culture with the Romans as the Latins. From the Sabines, most likely at a time of victory over their armies in 290, Romans drew the cult of Feronia; from the Etruscans in Republican times, the cult of Veii's Juno, just mentioned, and the haruspices (above) and the science of the augurs, watching what birds did as a predictive. Also borrowed were temple architecture and the dressing up of triumphal generals in the costume of Jupiter, which may be taken as a religious practice.[13] Triumph rituals, with their exotic display and insignia, the Romans of the third century and later loved to elaborate, drawing on the terra-cotta and painted art that they could see about them in their city's temples left over from the days of the monarchy; and modern interpretation has taken it all as very anciently Roman—which it wasn't. But it was certainly made welcome.[14] Etruscan imports all had to do with public life and its dramatic moments, suiting what was said above about the aspects of Roman life that are most fully reported but not of much significance.

Some of the Romans' Greek imports reached them from Etruria only via Latium; some came to them directly from Etruria. They included religious ceremonies and celebrations: the dressing up and parading and feasting of icons, perhaps accompanied by a community feast or chariot races.[15] The latter were an offering to the gods and were attended by them, and their images or altars formed a part of the racetrack's ornament. It is hard to say from which of her two neighbors, to the northwest or southeast, Rome derived these rituals. The same doubts surround various cults, since the credibility of the literary evidence and the interpretation of the archaeological are so contested. Cumulatively, however, the picture of Rome's ready welcome to foreign gods is clear in outline. It is clear, too, from the early date of the Circus Maximus near the center of the city and its very ample dimensions, that what the gods enjoyed was enjoyed by the whole people from the time even of the kings, so that what was obviously in the gift of the uppermost levels of society reached everybody. In that setting, at least, all "the Romans" without qualification were Hellenized.

Greek vases, so amply decorating central Italian graves of the earliest centuries, illustrate the dictum of Tocqueville quoted above. What accounted for them was a matter of intrinsic attractiveness; so far as this pottery is concerned, our museums today bear witness to that simple fact. It applies equally to the expensive celebrations attending the worship of Jupiter, just mentioned. They were delightful. Acceptance or active seeking out of the very gods themselves is, however, not to be explained quite so easily. We cannot agree on how to measure attractiveness in any religious belief nor are we very comfortable in even discussing the question. It would require too much detachment. We can only agree that more openness, and openness of a higher order, is needed to explain the taking in of a god into one's very home, as compared with the purchase of imported art.

The initiating of religious variety the Romans themselves first explained through the familiar story of the books offered to Romulus (or was it the elder Tarquin, or perhaps the younger?) by a prophetess from the oldest of Greek colonies. The senate had recourse to the books often afterward. In the fifth and fourth centuries, thanks to the priests expert in reading them, the state was often saved from some great threat by an appeal to the indicated gods in their Greek homes, not transmitted through a Greek colony: Ceres, Liber, and Libera in time of war and famine, 496; Apollo also in 496, Hercules in 399, and Aesculapius in 291, in times of plague.[16] While the legend about the seer from Cumae seems too good to be true, the occasions when the books were consulted are the sort of thing that quite primitive priestly records might retain, and they are generally accepted by Classical scholars. Appeal to the religion of the Greeks had thus become a routine with its own Roman experts from the first years of the fifth century and the mentions of it continue into the later Republic.

By then, we are among writers in Greek like the annalist Fabius Pictor or those others who were familiar with Greek literature like Ennius, ready to believe in or to invent encounters of some sort between the Roman people of an earlier time, and the other, higher civilization. "Higher": for instance, on the plane of theology which was certainly quite alien to the contemporaries of Marcus Junius "the Bonehead", to say nothing of his ancestors in the days of the kings. Romans then could not imagine a god with any human form, so said the antiquarian Varro, most implausibly. They had to be taught by Greeks in Tarquin's reign. No doubt what the artists of Athens or Cumae had to offer through vase painting and terra-cotta temple ornament did determine what Romans thought gods looked like. When, much later, the Romans turned to the worship of abstract moral qualities or forces such as Trustworthiness, Hope, Victory, Concord, Repose, and so forth, they derived those models also from the Greeks;[17] and, throughout the early centuries of the Republic, though with some interruptions, the building of temples to Greek gods went on, too.[18] True, other cities in the region were active in the same way, though on what scale cannot be known; only Rome's story is relatively well documented. The Hellenizing of religion that is noticeable under the kings thus continued very strongly into the Republic and had, by the mid-third century, quite transformed, not Rome the people, but Rome the city and its public cults. To this familiar story, we may add that the initiative, as the sources describe it, lay with individuals, not by some general vote, and it is safe to say that the result they sought was an admiring reception to support their personal fame. Postcolonial contortions did not forbid the labeling of one culture as superior, and another, inferior. What was Greek was manifestly good, it was well seen, and for this reason the nobility were open to its charms.

Over the course of the long narrative of welcome, the hosts can be seen to grow more educated, more sophisticated. The fact is not surprising. After decades of lavish temple-construction, their first impulse abated and their efforts turned to divinized abstractions like Fides, from the fourth century on, not so much because there was no more money for building but perhaps because there were no more new gods to bring in (a god needed only one home in a city and there were limits to the Pantheon). It is not likely to have been popular demand that in the end divinized Fides and the like; Hellenization at this level was the choice of the cultural elite, an increasingly narrow element measured as a percentage of the population in the centuries beyond those of my concern.[19]

Rome's founding legend offers another illustration of this tendency in Hellenization. Though its development is of enormous interest, only the outline is clear, emerging from the distortions and inventions of late writers like Dionysius of Halicarnassus. He and others were bent on weaving the Roman story into as much as possible of the Hellenic heritage, Homer and all.[20] Trojans (never mind that they were of course not Greek) and Aeneas' flight from his home with his father and son, and then the western chapters of this hero's life and his descendants, had all been introduced into Etruria in pictorial form on Attic vases, and in written form to the settler population of Greek colonies in Campania or Sicily; and this had happened well before the archaic period. Various episodes were then in time recalled locally and refashioned in wall paintings or historical accounts.[21] In Latium, too, in Lavinium, Aeneas was actively worshipped, the archaeological evidence dating to the 300s but pointing to earlier times, while Greek writers reported that the hero's family gods, his *penates* which were also the *penates* of the Roman people, were lodged in the Lavinian shrine; but it is likely that the claim was an invention.[22]

However, not until the end of the fifth century was Aeneas credited with a remote but wonderful role in the founding of Rome. The discoverer of the fact was one Hellanicus, who perhaps knew very little else about the city; and it was a great favor he conferred, since every respectable center of civilization in the West was supposed to be an artificial creation traced back to some almost divine hero.[23] Aeneas and his sons Romulus and Romus, known to Greek historians, pick up only from the mid-fourth century on to the period of something we may call proper history, that is, with Fabius Pictor and his following.[24]

To test whether any of this legendary material was known or interesting to Romans themselves, we have the material evidence. If Aeneas was a founder, then by descent Romans must be Trojans. There is in fact something of this idea to be seen in Etruscan tomb paintings of a date close to 300, suggesting that at least Rome's neighbors saw the connection. More to the point, in Veii at all three excavated sanctuary sites on the edge of the city, votive statuettes of Aeneas have been found, datable to the 320s by the most recent estimate.[25] The dedicants would be the Roman families installed in the 390s after the city was conquered and its ancient population largely displaced; they defined and asserted themselves by this ancestry. Thus it seems safe to place the Aeneas cult and its hero in some special relation with Romans by the mid-fourth century—though, for it to have become established, at least a few decades of prior circulation must surely be imagined.

How or, rather, why it first originated can be guessed from the reminder offered by a Sicilian city in great need of Rome's help: "We are your kin, we too are descended of Aeneas", said the spokesmen of Segesta in 263, seeking alliance.[26] Such a power as Rome had been ever since the 490s, anyone would do well to win over with a brotherly handshake, an assurance of shared history, a bit of tact, in which no Greek would be wanting. It amounted to a welcome into what the Greeks at least believed to be a superior civilization, their own and its glorious past. The Romans would not refuse the welcome.

The legend of a Greek origin had, however, to find a place in the minds of Romans who were brought up to know a wolf cult, and a Lupercal for its services, and a holy day the Lupercalia in February, and Luperci running about the streets to dispense the god's favors (chap. 3). All these elements of belief and self-identity could not be simply discarded. Superior and glorious or not, they were the Romans' own familiar past. Exactly when they first came into being, no one can say, though I suppose it was at a point well before the end of the monarchy. In any case they were very ancient. A sort of graft had then to be contrived: Aeneas' sons must come first, and afterward their descendants in Latium, thus spanning the centuries between the date of Troy, as the learned determined it, and the local line of seven kings on the seven hills. The founding legend in these important preliminary points was (to repeat my conjecture) in place by the mid-fourth century.

Enter the twins. They appear on a bronze mirror belonging to some wealthy woman of Praeneste in the late 300s; as bronze babies they are put to nurse under a bronze mother-wolf in Rome in 296; and most significantly in silver in 269 they and the wolf decorate coins minted in Campania for Rome and spelling out "Romans".[27] In all these three forms of witness we see the hand of the elite, people used to personal luxury, to making gifts to the city, and to handling public contracts. They are familiar with imported arts and ideas—which can only mean, with Greece. What they approve, everyone else must see as stylish and interesting. Theirs is the class most open to Hellenization. They are the instrument of it.

Mention above of Segesta takes the story of tolerance and its effects beyond Rome's city walls. Romans in time ceased to be merely passive hosts to another civilization; it pleased them in Livy's day to imagine that they had actively sought wisdom from such famous lawgivers as Solon for the composition of their Twelve Tables. They remembered their embassies and offerings to famous cities, Delphi included. Perhaps the first of these was dispatched so early as 395. Later, two Greek statues standing at the edge of the Comitium gave rise to the story that, in the midst of the great Samnite wars, the oracle's help was sought and the advice given, to set up images of the bravest and the wisest of the Greeks; and this was done, in the form of Alcibiades and Pythagoras.[28] Only Rome's upper class, of course, would know who these icons might be; the man in the street, the man on the farm, certainly had no interest in such things; but enthusiasm for whatever was Greek among the elite is well imagined, *ben trovato.*[29]

If, besides the Greeks' homeland and western settlements, we look at Rome's own settlements in central and southern Italy, we see quite a broad stratum of society engaged, made up of small landowners. At Veii, prostrate in defeat in the 390s, the victors could do anything they wanted. Their actual policies are not known in the least detail. Classicists are generally agreed that writers of later times, compiling the account of what happened, wanted only their own Roman Siege of Troy and so described the city's conquest. The real facts didn't concern them. At most it can said that a vast amount of property changed hands as a result of the Veii's fall, redistributed among the conquerors according to position and claims. The only sign now to identify who moved in are the clay figurines of Aeneas carrying his father to safety. They were mentioned above: mass-produced items for sale cheap in the usual way at ancient places of worship. But at the same shrines, a number of other gods from preconquest times continued to be honored as well as gods honored only postconquest, when Latin settlers along with Romans left their mark: a mix, thus, of Apollo, Minerva, Jupiter of Liberty, and others.[30] The city's change of ownership registers at least in religion very lightly. The conquerors expressed no cultural mission and therefore applied no administrative machinery to make the site the center of a new and different way of life. The same can be said of many other sites where excavation has been possible, to trace the nature and degree of Romans' tolerance.

The exercise of this restraint in treaty arrangements with neighbors I leave to my eighth chapter. Here, it is way of life and the softer aspects of integration that concern me. These constitute of course the cause and substance of that eventually deep Hellenization to be seen in Caesar or Cicero; but the trait is also to be seen in those very treaties, too, as I think may be fairly argued from the quite different relations between Rome and the Etruscans, and Rome and the Latins, over the course of the fifth, fourth, and third centuries. The difference cannot be explained in terms only of politics or national interest, hence the need to take cultural history seriously.

Rome's own settlements in central and southern Italy were made in cooperation with Latin cities and their people. The two partners recognized marriages from the one population into the other by a right held over from the fifth century, which implies a very comfortable relationship. This prevailed in the so-called Latin colonies established after 338. Their culture was of no interest to the literary tradition, but archaeologists have made interesting discoveries about five of them: Luceria (established in 314), Fregellae (effectively, 313), Alba Fucens (303), and Cosa and Paestum on the coast below the Bay of Naples (both of 273). There is a little information about the Roman citizen colonies such as Terracina also on the coast (329). Their sites are shown at figure 6.1. As at Veii, the coming of Romans brought changes in life but nothing top-to-bottom or programmatic.

At three of the Latin sites, a pit dug at a central point in the city marks the prayers and sacrifices properly a part of founding ceremonies in the Roman tradition: a *mundus* just like Romulus' to designate a sacral space. Excavators also note the sacrifice of a dog at the foundation of the city defenses at Paestum and Ariminum (268), whether or not that was a particularly Roman rite.[31] The custom of anatomical votive offerings, widely shared among all peoples in central Italy, seems to be diffused in southern Italy only, or almost only, through the Roman settlements. To the east on the Adriatic at Pisaurum, after Roman refounding, a number of quite typical Roman deities show up in the material remains.[32] At Luceria the cult of Athena Ilias was established from the start, taken to be a recall of Rome's Trojan ancestry.[33] Thus in their religious life, Roman settlers maintained their loyalty to their familiar helpers. Nothing else would be expected.

That did not invite any disrespect to the gods native to the places where they made their settlements. At Paestum there was a high place in the center previously treated as sacred, with a temple of Athena, her altar, and an altar to Zeus, which was maintained after colonization. There is a similar picture of continuity in cults elsewhere.[34] Burials show some slow change, as Roman in-settlers in time were borne to their graves with the traditional Roman rites and customs.[35]

Since the picture of what Roman conquest meant must draw so much on archaeological evidence, naturally there is evidence of architectural changes. The standard house plan so well known in Pompeii turns up first in a big rich house near the forum of Fregellae, built in the earliest years of the colony; temples of a plan at home among the Romans are built in this and other Latin colonies; in at least one colony (Paestum) the typical provision for neatness and commerce in combination produces rows of shops along the edges of the forum, no doubt for rent from the authorities, each divided into two rooms and all of nearly identical dimensions, "obviously following a modular blueprint".[36] Above all, the entire shape of the city center was marked by the Roman hand for the conduct of government. Small surprise! The very idea of establishing a settlement in the first place was politico-military, necessarily. Control by and for the purposes of rule found natural expression in the copying of the mother city's forum, its Comitium, and Curia in a single flow of construction. I show one of the larger assembly places, almost as big as Rome's: at Fregellae (fig. 6.1).

Fregellae was an empty town when a colony was planted there. The *fabri* had a clean slate to work with. At Cosa likewise no prior settlement prevented the creation of a fully Roman city center. A *comitium* went up next to a forum and, along the sides of this latter, for mass voting, pits were arranged to mark off queues for voters taking part. Such at least is one explanation offered. Pits of the sort were discovered in all five of the best-excavated Latin colonies.[37] They imply some uniformity that the planners at least, who were Roman officials among a mixed population, believed they ought to impose on the heart of the settlement. Very likely the queue arrangements and the *comitium* copied respectively Rome's own Campus Martius and Comitium. But the latter, it should be noted, followed the model of *ekklesiasteria* in Samothrace or Sicily—another proof of the liking for things Greek among Rome's elite.

Whether out of respect for the feelings of the local population or from sheer arrogance, the committee of three that always oversaw the founding of a Latin colony decided at Paestum to discontinue the use of the ancient marketplace for civic purposes and instead to clear a great space for a forum. In the course of clearing, whatever had been there before, perhaps in-

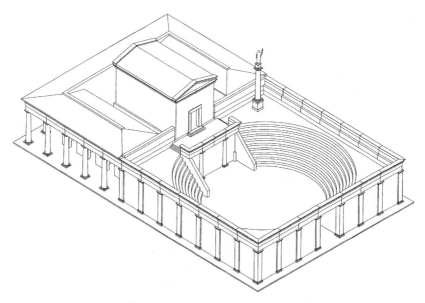

Fig. 6.1. The *comitium* at Fregellae. From Coarelli (1998).

cluding a temple, yielded to Roman needs.[38] The decision reflected Roman priorities. Rule was the prime consideration. Government and its ends must be served first and always, and in traditional ways. But as to the softer aspects of integration, as I called them, above—style and belief, language and arts, marriage and burial—the Romans in their close relations with other peoples were not autocratic. They tolerated a good deal of latitude. It can be seen scattered around colonies and their near neighbors, in the form of non-Latin inscriptions and local coin legends; in tombs and houses and pottery.

Such evidence is indeed suggestive. It is not, however, adequate for useful quantification, for narrative of change, or broad characterization. As a warning, "it is virtually impossible to identify Roman colonial influence on the local Latial material culture".[39] In the interplay of cultural forces perhaps only one thing may be said for sure: the evidence does not support any idea of cultural imperialism on the Romans' part. It does not suffice to show any intent to press their way of life on others around them or beneath them. To the contrary, they show themselves very ready to import, learn, adopt, admire, imitate. So much seems clear at least at the level of the elite.

However, the distinction I have more than once drawn between the softer aspects of Roman civilization and the politico-military leaves the latter still to be discussed in the chapter that follows.

7

AGGRESSIVE

(continued)

The acting out of an aggressive nature on the stage of Roman history was a matter of wars and foreign relations, but also of internal affairs and politics. In the latter, nobles vied with each other for office, century after century, until in the end the power at stake overwhelmed traditional institutions and a monarchy emerged once more. During the period that interests me, however, and indeed until well down into the first century, this competition among clans and their principal name-bearers seems to have had no historical significance. That is, no clan or cluster of clans had a platform in the modern sense, a set of advertised objectives, to give meaning to success or failure at the polls. Like an endless series of professional boxing matches, the story is exciting but at the same time boring, since it offers nothing to think about.

Like aficionados who can quote you the record of fights and fighters in extraordinary detail, so also students of Roman Republican clan-warfare have generated a great mass of biographical information called in the profession "prosopography". It has been at the center of research into the early and middle Republic and beyond, ever since Friedrich Münzer began his very long career as contributor to Pauly's encyclopedia a century ago. That labor of learning was and remains the Classicists' most basic resource; and Münzer in turn was handsomely acknowledged in 1939 by Ronald Syme as a model for his own hugely influential work.[1] From such resources and through such a method, it was hoped that scholars could divine the secrets of Roman policy by observing which *gens*-leader first or most dramatically

87

favored some particular choice; next, by assuming that his clansmen of the time and in succeeding generations would hew to the same line; and then assuming that clans of a more or less similar tradition would join together to claim command of the state. History was hidden in the *fasti* among the ties of descent and kinship, including those by marriage or adoption, a belief that generated an intense interest in Rome's "Who's Who"; but Arnold J. Toynbee's conclusion has very gradually prevailed: "In Roman oligarchic politics, office was an end in itself, not a means to the end of carrying out policies by translating them into measures and securing the passage of these in national assemblies".[2]

If it was not about such great matters as the Twelve Tables or the Licinian land laws, why the competition at all? The answer is simple: office was sought for the sake of a military command and the prominence and applause that could be won only in war. Where elections to command took place, in the Field of Mars, the whole space was sacred to that fearful deity.[3] And what mattered to those ancient leaders in Roman society matters in history. By war they made themselves masters of the entire middle of the peninsula they lived in so that, when they matched themselves against the power dominant in the central and western Mediterranean from 264 onward, they could over the course of three mighty struggles emerge victorious, not by strategic genius—no one would say so—but through simply drowning Carthage in wave after wave of expendable manpower drawn from the defeated and then integrated populations of Italy.

The tendency thus accounting for the defeat of all Rome's neighbors expressed itself in what Roman writers especially enjoyed writing about: virtually annual campaigning. In the earliest Republic this took the form of raids and skirmishes for plunder, vengeance, and (among young males) the coming of age. The better organized campaigns characterizing a more civilized state are annalistic inventions, retrojected, so it is supposed; and this does seem the best way to explain one or two puzzling little incidents in the traditional accounts, and an inscription set up in a neighboring Latin town by a brotherhood of some sort who mention their leader. His is a name known to the Roman tradition. Further, Livy provides examples of small war-bands in operation still into the early 300s and they fit very well with what is known from warrior burials and new or improved city wall-circuits, in proof of frequently dangerous times.[4]

Not very much seems to have been accomplished by Rome's forces aimed at towns in the Tiber valley or nearby Latium in the opening decades of the Republic. Then came an important victory over the league of Latin cities in the 490s and subsequent joint expeditions of larger effect, with the founding of more than a dozen joint colonies taking the story down to the 380s. A second clash with the Latins put an end to their league in 338 after which Rome's colonies were of her own founding alone (Cales the first in 335/4); but allies including applicants from Latin towns were freely accepted as settlers. It was the turn next of the peoples of the eastern Apennines and eastern coastal parts, the Samnites, to face the Romans down to 290, when they and their allies from other parts were subdued. The Greek king Pyrrhus invading Italy was repulsed in several bloody encounters (280–275) and, against the cities that had rallied to his cause in both the south and north, Rome thereafter carried out successful campaigns and colonizing (Beneventum 268; Aesernia 263). So mastery was confirmed and defended.

A map (fig. 7.1) illustrates the familiar tale of Rome's conquests. Whatever its accuracy in detail, it supports the equally familiar picture of the Romans as being forever on campaign. They were at it almost every year.[5] That is conceivable. An economy resting on quite simple agriculture (such as one could still see only a half-century ago in Mediterranean lands) left plenty of freedom from work in the months after spring planting, and so much as was still necessary could be taken up by women or those older men who had fulfilled any military obligation. The call or rather the legal requirement to serve in arms could be answered by the young without insupportable cost to the society, economy, or even the individual family, with a bit of help from neighbors in hardship cases.[6] Whether the recruiter was met with a good will, no one can say. Livy's and Dionysius' tales of eager volunteers take us down to that level of detail in which Classicists have no confidence. It seems idle to wonder what the mass of the population made of it all. Clearly they could be drafted in large enough numbers to make an army every year. Estimates of what that might mean statistically have often been made, only to show that it was quite feasible.[7] Recruits might then return home (if they survived) bringing pay or plunder or the promise of a share in new lands opening up.

The trait of aggression in the nation's character is quite obvious in all this, whether Rome is looked at in its own life story alone or whether it is compared with other peoples of the peninsula. Beyond the obvious, however, a little depth to the analysis can be added allowing a glimpse into the Roman mind, without depending on the coloration that the ancient written histories supply so invitingly.

First, notice the choice of Mars as the god to represent the Roman people on their earliest silver coinage, around 310–300, he being especially associated with warfare and a wolf.[8] The issue was minted from an allied

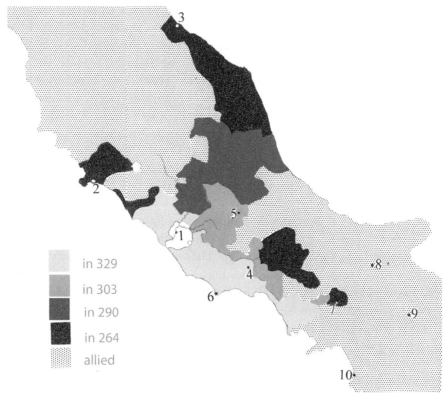

Fig. 7.1. Roman expansion in Italy
Showing Rome (1) and its territory (unshaded) in 495, and subsequently to 264;
on the coasts, Roman citizen colonies; and Latin colonies mentioned in the text:
2, Cosa; 3, Ariminum; 4, Fregellae; 5, Alba Fucens; 6, Circeii; 7, Beneventum;
8, Luceria; 9, Venusia; and 10, Paestum. Drawing, R. MacMullen.

city able to do the job, technically, but the choice of symbolism I take to
be a Roman one and expressive of a self-image in which the customers, the
Roman magistrates in charge of the commission, took pride.

Second: an insistence on Rome's superiority is written into treaties only
from the late third century but represents a claim that I assume was not
then first conceived of: a claim of *maiestas*, "greaterness", which other
states must undertake always to defend. It has been proposed, though also
denied, that the idea can be found in the term "subjects" with which
Carthage in a treaty of 338 described Rome's allies in Latium. It was in any
case distinctively Roman and calculated to drive home the meaning of a

defeat under arms.[9] It was the notional equivalent of making a beaten army pass under the yoke.

Third: genocide. This is recorded only on a rather limited scale in the earlier Republic although on display more grandly in the period post-264, where Ben Kiernan takes up the story and sets it in a larger context. Deliberate annihilation of an entire vanquished people by the early generations of Romans is not something in which Livy and other patriots of his time would take pride, and I assume therefore that instances passed down in memory are all the more credible.[10]

Fourth: it was by deceit and trickery that Romans in 343 gained a rich prize that the Samnites saw as belonging to themselves by right of treaty. Rome's act requires from Livy an elaborate effort of obnubilation.[11] In the Roman value system, we can see one part yielding to another (that is, plain greed), and the incident seems not only credible because it is so much against the grain of the reporter, but an indication of the strength of the winning motive or impulse.

Finally: in the course of their conquests from the mid-fourth century on, the Romans encountered from the landward side a number of maritime states, and won them, and had then to decide how to gain the most from their winnings. Some naval vessels were simply destroyed, some were retained. Compromise with the opportunity for profit led the Romans to depart from their traditional interests and capacities, trying on a naval-commercial role in the seas around them.[12]

In periods of history more reliably reported, there is no need to read a nation's mind in such indirect forms of testimony as these five items; contemporary documents allow direct access. In fact, however, even for ancient Rome, one other kind of useful evidence exists in which to find the trait that interests me: the trait, that is, of aggression. Some of this evidence has been referred to already, available to the Latin and Greek historians and, through archaeological excavation, to ourselves as well.[13] All of it amounts to publicity; it invites applause for war and for the warrior.

First in point of time are temples vowed by commanders if they are victorious, which are then constructed by them or by a son, piously—but gloriously. It was booty that paid for them, just how apportioned is not known, but clearly with the control of war profits largely in the hands of the commander. He might choose not to keep his share for ordinary purposes but for self-advertisement instead.[14] No one would dare oppose the fulfillment of a vow. Vows for a victory took the form of a score of temples in the period from the 490s down to 264.[15] When the traditional gods had all been thanked, new ones were recognized: Victoria herself on the Capitoline hill but only in 296.[16] That was in the course of the Samnite wars when painful successes prompted a surge in construction (temples to Salus, Bellona, Jupiter Victor, Victoria, Jupiter Stator, Quirinus, Fors Fortuna).[17] Victoria was not the only god thanked on the Capitoline: so also was Jupiter Unconquerable in 295. Other triumphant temples were given a lofty site on the Esquiline, Aventine, Quirinal, and Palatine hills, or in much-frequented areas near the Forum and especially the Circus Maximus. With dedicatory inscriptions pricked out in red, they and what they proclaimed would attract notice and the *gens*-name of the donor would be known forever. That was their purpose.

To one side of Jupiter's home on the Capitoline his colossal statue was set up in 293 in thanksgiving for a victory against the Samnites—a work of such a size that it could be seen from miles and miles away—and the donor's portrait, Spurius Carvilius', stood at his feet. As Jupiter's image was of bronze recovered from enemy arms, we may suppose this was the material ordinarily used at the time. By then, statues were quite commonly of donors themselves. Sculptors could even be found to do a triumphant pair of consuls mounted on their battle horses, in 338, an achievement noted by Livy as truly remarkable for the time; but in 306 a consul again showed himself on horseback. Another source, Pliny, adds to the list various non-equestrian statues of the fourth and third centuries. One stood atop a column next to the Comitium, called after its subject Maenius who in this way reminded everyone of his victory at Antium in 338.[18]

And there were painted portraits prominent in temples, too, the first by the father of Rome's earliest historian, Fabius Pictor (proud to bear his ancestor's name), who in the late 300s on the walls of the Salus temple had showed his own clan heroes in stirring scenes; in the Consus temple on the Aventine in 272, a painting of Papirius Cursor commissioned by himself; and in the Vertumnus temple, one of Fulvius Flaccus victorious in 264 over the Etruscans of Volsinii.[19] The style of representation may be guessed from the surviving art of tombs on the Esquiline, to say nothing of many Etruscan tombs, where by the flow of action in panels like a cartoon strip, or like Giotto's, a story could be told and the protagonists identified in writing above their figures.

Fulvius Flaccus, just mentioned, gained some publicity with statues not of himself, but a full two thousand half-size ones pillaged from the city he took by arms: Volsinii. Some were put up in front of the Mater Matuta and Fortuna temples on two bases that still show fragments of the explanatory inscription. Preserved also are the fixtures to secure some of the pillage on the bases, while the rest were distributed around the city for wider viewing.[20] The beaks of Antium's naval vessels were borne home by their captor in 338 to be nailed up on the back side of the Comitium, facing the Forum, there to identify where speakers and assembly presidents stood in later times to face their audience. From Samnites in 310 the profits of war bought gilding for captured shields, which then were hung up for show in the Forum's booths rented to money changers; and in the 290s such a quantity of armor was taken again that its display could be spread elsewhere in the Forum as well as in a triumphant temple.[21]

The general effect of all these advertisements of war is well imagined by Plutarch or his source (whoever that may have been), describing Rome of the third century: "It possessed and it knew nothing of lovely or exquisite things, nor anywhere in it was delightfulness and charm. Instead, filled with barbaric weaponry and bloody plunder, crowned with triumphant memorials and trophies, it was no happy or reassuring sight, nor was it one for the timid or luxury-minded, beholding it".[22]

A generation later, battles could be recalled in a less daunting form: through celebratory tableware which might be used as votives or, shown here (fig. 7.2), as a precious display to be brought out for guests along with the invitation to admire those tanks of ancient battle, the elephants first seen by Romans in King Pyrrhus' army. They were most amazingly to be bested in battle and thereafter to be led shuffling through the hot streets of the capital in the early fall of 275. Of course that event figures in later written accounts; it figures also in art. Damaged plates closely resembling each other and thought to have been all made in or near Rome survive from Corsica, Norchia, and Capena, twenty-five miles north of Rome.[23]

A natural moment to show round such memorial art-objects would have been one of the public banquets paid for out of some commander's share of the booty. Livy's several mentions of this custom belong to the third century, except such early ones as cannot be trusted. Those of the third century deserve belief in the absence of any later memory that they were an innovation.[24] Indeed, grand gestures out of a full pocket by big winners have about them a Greek quality that fits well in a much larger Roman context; it certainly fits well with the militaristic self-glorification seen in the evidence just reviewed. As a further illustration: writing for readers that well knew Augustus' political inventions, Dionysius of Halicarnassus attributes Rome's annual cavalry procession, on white horses, to the celebrating of a great victory won through the grace of Castor and Pollux—this in 496. Livy laconically refers to the procession under the year 304. A chance for the young of the oligarchy to show off their horseman-

Fig. 7.2. The Capena plate in a cleaned-up form. Museo Nazionale di Villa Giulia, Rome, Italy. Photo Scala / Art Resource, NY.

ship and shiny armor is more obviously derived from Athenian practice and the recall of Marathon.[25]

Of all military rituals, the victory parade is of course the best known. Livy provides an early picture of it, when the senate "gave the command for Quinctius [Cincinnatus] to enter in triumph with the ranks of his army. The enemy's generals were led before his chariot, military standards were borne ahead, and the army came next, laden with spoils. Tables are said to have been spread in front of every house, and the troops, feasting as they marched with triumphant songs and the usual jesting, followed the chariot like a band of revellers". To these bare bones of a most natural event, symbolism and elaboration were added layer by layer as time went on, reflected in another description of the year 275 after victories over Pyrrhus' armies far to the south, "before which time you saw only the cattle from the Volsci, the herds from Sabines, Gallic chariots, broken weapons of Samnites, where now you looked on Molossian captives, captive Thessalians, Macedonians, Bruttians, Apulians, Lucanians; or if you looked on the parade itself, you saw gold, purple, statues, paintings, and the luxury of Tarentum; and nothing did the Roman populace look at with greater pleasure than those beasts they had feared, bearing their towers, following with bowed heads the victorious horses in the knowledge that they were captives".[26] Ah! those elephants again, and Tarentum, so expensively Greek. Over the period 509–264 Rome the city opened its eyes, it opened its arms, to some ninety triumphs.[27] In some years there were two. The commander triumphing wended his way from a certain special gate into the heart of the city, very slowly, with obeisances to the gods but to no one else, a proud moment to be savored and often replicated in art. Increasingly he himself was painted and costumed and equipped with white horses just like Jupiter himself, as if that great god had come down on earth. But there is no saying at what point such elaborations were introduced.[28]

One feature of display was enumeration: the tally of everything an army had wrought or won. It could be specified in inscriptions, perhaps (at least later) announced on white boards borne in the parade; representations of captured cities could be carried along.[29] When ancient authors, as so often, specify the number of coins, works of art, pounds of bronze or silver or gold, battalion standards, wagonloads of shields, captives enslaved, enemy slaughtered, or towns destroyed by this or that returning general, the report must derive from claims somehow publicized in these happy moments of homecoming. The point of them was of course to impress specifically and irrefutably, as if to say to the envious, "You doubt? Count for yourself". Indeed some of the figures in the tradition are quite staggering.

This said, we see what was intended: thanksgiving to the gods, especially Jupiter to whom the *triumphator* paid his respects in person at the climax of the ritual, up on the Capitol. It was piety, it was love of Rome; and, as Tocqueville says, "Patriotism is a kind of religion which is strengthened by ritual observance".[30] It was also a great thing for the *triumphator* himself, the summit of a career, an achievement of the particular sort that, far more than any other, would define him forever.

Much more could be said in explanation of triumphs and their place in the public calendar, all of it quite obvious; and much more could be said about the many other ways in which success in war was made known, too—insistently and for future generations, by statues and so forth, as the preceding pages have recalled. But these pages were not offered as art history or history of letters; they were meant rather as an invitation to bring up to the forefront of one's mind one's own everyday experiences that in some way have resembled the Roman scene, so as to apply one's memories empathetically to the Roman experience in the Forum and thus understand what a person might think *and feel,* looking on piles of dirty captured swords and breastplates (the dirt being dried blood, of course), or seeing again the noisy grand processions of the army's homecoming, or marveling at the elogia on shields behind the bankers' tables. Whatever one's business and wherever one stood in the most frequented parts of the city, surely it was war, glorious war, that met the eye or ear. What was expressed and at the same time inculcated in citizens, this they had collectively chosen as their national character.

The empathy required in this exercise is no more than we might bring to bear on the story a friend tells us about some recent problem, or what we may see on the stage, Shakespearian. It is a mental operation entirely familiar to all of us. In reading history, however, the effort has a particular value since it allows penetration beyond the evidence of *what* happened, to *why:* that is, to motivation, which historians of course want most to determine. It is a further benefit, that all the material described above allows engagement with Roman realities through evidence little tainted by novelistic invention. We may rightly distrust the literary tradition. In contrast, we cannot doubt that the various monuments in the city, and the rites and celebrations most applauded, constituted a continuing education in what it was to be Roman.

Romans when they are better known to us (let us say at and after the time when Polybius commences his account) confirm in the outlines of their conduct what sort of people they were. They were very much of the character inferred, above, from the furnishings of their city and their behavior in it. Although what moves them to a chosen course of action is now more fully and believably treated, yet motive must still be inferred from action. They are bellicose, quite in love with the fame to be won in war.[31] Livy for all his faults understood this and wanted his audience to understand also, in the only way possible, that is, empathetically; and for this reason he adds color to his narrative with a broad brush, in lots of novelistic touches to agitate and engage his readers emotionally.[32] Historical truth lay in what readers could sense in themselves.

This sort of experiential discovery of past realities finds no place in the usual academic style. It doesn't allow of probative application. To put the idea in simple words, and as an example: declaring that the chief cause of an event was love, where someone else says it was hate, can lead to nothing better than a shouting match, because the two alleged causes cannot be quantified and then compared.[33] There can be no rational engagement between the debaters—which is why academic treatment of Roman aggression, in the determination to be "scientific", will ever dwell on the symptoms and outcome of that aggression, not on its springs. These can only be felt; and the feeling must be evoked by such data as can be trusted.

8

~~~

PRACTICAL

(continued)

The trait of practicality defined at the beginning of chapter 4 continued to shape the collective behavior of the Romans in the opening centuries of the Republic.

National character like individual character is (to repeat once more) best known from what people do, not from what they say about themselves, and there is in any case no one of those days to tell us, "This is how we are, we Romans, a down-to-earth, problem-solving, uncomplicated folk". Introspection even in a better-documented period was not something Romans much indulged in (and watch out when anyone describes himself as simple!). We have, however, an early event that is quite useful and revealing. It is the First Secession of 494 in response to continued bad times, when the chief sufferers in the city staged a walkout and extracted from their oppressors, the big property-owning class, not only some of the changes they sought but novel institutions for themselves corporately: chiefly a tribunate of the people and a tribal assembly, as was described above. These successes were won without bloodshed or other great risks; the structure of law, as opposed to abuses, remained in place, unchallenged; and, since the tribunate and assembly are fixtures in subsequent history and their origin is not placed in any other moment, the outline of these events may be accepted as fact. The same may said of the second walkout in 449 following on prolonged agitation that led to the Twelve Tables. It looks like real history—in outline at least and so long as we disregard some of the very silliest pages in the Latin literary tradition, with which the account concludes.[1]

In these episodes a broad cross-section of the city is involved, although no doubt their own leaders were propertied themselves. It is almost fair to call the actors "the Romans" without qualification. Over the next couple of centuries, however, the whole people in action play no further part. Instead, it is the people at the top who take over the stage, whether patrician or plebeian: a Claudius, a Junius, and so forth. "Roman history" is theirs—as we could not say if there had continued to be more general walkouts, more popular rejections of the leadership that led to institutional change.

How decisions were actually made within this upper class cannot be learned from the narratives that survive. These are untrustworthy at any level of detail, as Classicists so often complain; and the writers who composed them had no interest to spare for the process, anyway. The fact is strange; yet in 1831–32 Tocqueville must have been continually aware of the two great political parties then taking on their definitive names and historic shape in the United States before his very eyes, without his ever actually *seeing* them; for he never alludes to them.[2] So also in the whole run of ancient Roman annalists, so far as we can tell from their surviving texts, no page was given to decision-making that took place before the open meetings of the senate and assembly. Perhaps power arrangements made in more or less private settings lacked the drama or dignity that deserved a record. I must simply assume that Roman nobles often ate their evening meals with each other and did much business there, as noble lords in nineteenth-century Britain and sheikhs in the modern Middle East are shown to do.

In what terms they talked, with what aims and assumptions, may be indirectly inferred from the suicides of two disgraced noblemen in the First Secession—a dark match for the shining deaths sought by other, heroic noblemen on behalf of their country in Roman legend.[3] The stories serve to show, not actual events, but a value system in place in oral history to be retold to generations that touched the writers of the late third century. It was a system by the rules of which great exertions and sacrifice for fame were clearly expected of the leadership class; and my conclusion—beyond cautious!—leads into the question how such intense and potentially destructive competition could be contained, for the good of all involved.

It was certainly in the interests of the *gentes*-leaders that it should be contained, and much of it obviously fitted well enough within the narrow confines of the Comitium, where control was easy. Elections of major magistrates in the centuriate assembly had unlimited space outside the *pomerium* but it was perhaps not needed since voting took place at, and as the commencement of, the war season in March, and by men in army order. It is not clear if anyone took part except those recruits actually being enrolled to fight, therefore in their assigned units and ready to obey: one legion, two legions, sometimes in the first half of the third century as many as four, but never so much as a quarter of adult male citizens. The Haves as the cavalry voted first in a bloc, pointing the way to the right choice.[4] Military discipline and the openness of voting certainly did not favor fractious behavior; the great majority of the participants, in their late teens and twenties, were of an age to respect their elders; and most, too, were a day or many days from home, feeling strange and the more easily managed. What counted to win was therefore not electioneering, as I imagine, but membership in a very small and diminishing number of eligible families entitled to the serene naming of agreed candidates as a fait accompli, a done deal.[5] All of which would imply prior negotiations among the leadership behind closed doors. Breaking ranks to solicit votes in the streets could only be seen as reprehensible demagoguery. In fact, it was made illegal in 358.[6] The more normal *modus operandi* was eminently practical.

In this conclusion, the place and importance of the oligarchic value system fits very well indeed. The elders of the major clans sought, each one, to ensure to their rising younger members a chance of adding glory to their name in some victorious battle, and they enhanced that chance by restricting competition for office and working together to keep out challengers. Only through the natural attenuation of their own ranks were the older dominant *gentes* in the course of time to be challenged; and those newly risen clans generally adopted the oligarchic *modus operandi* once they themselves were in a position to choose. It only made sense to do so.

If such were the rules of public life, the trait of aggression in the Roman character was well served, at least in a Darwinian sense; that is, the leadership class did not tear itself apart in rivalries nor weaken its authority by appeals to the mass of the population. Well served also was the chief instrument of ambition, armed force; and, besides, in armed force lay the safety of the state. To decide on war, therefore, and to assemble the troops that would be needed (meaning annually) must engage authorities at every level in the most important efforts.

Historians would give anything for a close look into the operation of the draft and assignment to ranks and fighting units. Almost nothing is known about all this except the crucial role of numbers. The art of counting was once raised to a high level by the so-called "hydraulic societies" in ancient Mesopotamia and Egypt. It served them for purposes of taxation. In Rome the same art was quite characteristically applied to the inventory of battle-ready men and the economic base that supported them and their equipment—the base in landed property, *iugera,* of about 0.65 acre or 0.25 ha. The Romans' choice of what to count reflected the fact that they were a fighting and farming folk.

I defer for the moment the measuring of land. Of male citizens, the census began with the urban and rural tribes into which the population had been divided under the kings. Division can have served no other purpose than to provide a tally of those fit for armed service (possibly also for corvées). Next in the procedure, all those who assembled in the Field of Mars were called to the favorable attention of the gods by various priests, sacrifices, and rituals, and were then duly numbered.[7] With what accuracy? Julius Beloch, the father and founder of ancient Roman demographics, looking at the sources, judged "the traditional numbers of citizens in the first century of the Republic unacceptable", and went on to wonder whether "it is in itself likely that in a semi-barbarous Rome statistical data of this sort would be recorded at a time when in Greece no one would have dreamt of such a thing".[8] His question is useful, not because it makes much sense—civilizations must just be allowed to be different—but because it points to the importance of national character. The ancient Greeks (who simply defined "civilization" for Beloch and the later nineteenth century) chose to give their minds to art and philosophy. The Romans in contrast saw value in an accurate knowledge of their strength and were very likely joined in this by Latin cities, too; for certainly by the third century these latter were able to say how many citizens they had. At that point, the use of a census in preparation for war is well attested. It may be assumed in much earlier times among the Romans. If doubters should persist, they may be fairly asked when the Roman system can have come into existence if not in the time of the kings, and what could have led up to it, and what would have been the point of so laborious a thing if it had not actually worked.

As to its very existence, about which Beloch was so skeptical, this may be assumed without defending the totals assigned by the literary sources to its operations; for the ancient historians simply could not handle figures. Classicists are agreed about the fact, lamenting the statistical contradictions and self-evident absurdities they find everywhere, as for example in Fabius Pictor's estimate of Rome's population or Livy's casual mention of double or even treble levies in times of special danger.[9] Discussion continues nevertheless, driven by modern ideas of demographic analysis. If the figures offered to us cannot be trusted, can good approximations be reached indirectly? The answer must lie where Beloch first pointed it out, in the multiplying of the Roman state's known acreage by the probable density of habitation. As to area, it does indeed seem certain that records would have survived even in Fabius Pictor's day to show at least whether a neighbor state or people had come into a formal relation with Rome—that is, had been made an ally or a colony—and what the date of that arrangement was; and the approximate boundaries of neighbors appearing in the narrative of Rome's expansion can today be traced on a map, as has been done many times since Beloch without ever departing very much from his results. By his method of approximation modern scholars have reached some agreement on how many citizens Rome had at various times.[10]

The research purpose is analytic. Of course we want to know how big Rome's draft pool was, so as to indicate the difficulty or ease of fielding armies in comparison with other states. That, however, is our own purpose, not the Romans'. For the Roman leadership it was rather a concern not to spend more of their authority on conscription than on directing their armies against the enemy; in other words, a concern for fairness, or at least the perception of that. They couldn't have revolts on their minds all the time (and, for what the evidence is worth, Livy does sometimes report complaints about the draft). Conscription would be accepted as fair that demanded no more than one in two young men from each village within a *curia* which was a unit within a tribe; or more likely, much less than one in two young men; and they must be assigned in absolutely even quality throughout all the legions.[11] Each unit of population subject to the census had to know and report its numbers and produce its quota. There is no reason to suppose, additionally, that the grand total of all males in all villages together would have been sought, though there is no reason to think it might not have been recoverable, with some digging into the family papers of censors.

These being the practical considerations, as I imagine, they had to be fitted into the size of the fighting force decided on by the senate, which appears to have been at first a single "drafting" (*legio*) of six thousand men, and then two legions a little smaller that constituted an "army" for a pair of consuls, and then perhaps regularly after 326, four of these legions.

It is no special claim for the Romans' practicality that they wished to win at war, and that they took note, as all peoples did and do, of weapons and modes of fighting that seemed best able to secure victory. These matters were in fact of the greatest interest, witness the prevalence of arms and armor in burials of the sixth century and earlier.[12] The archaeological evidence can be looked at today to learn how they were used. They imply a mix of du-

eling with long spears or short, or with swords; and no doubt everyone protected himself with as much metal armor as he could afford. What is of most
interest, however, is individual and small-unit tactics, about which Classicists are agreed to find no clear picture in the written record.

In the archaeological evidence, in the Republican period, the chariot
from which warriors alit to fight disappeared. They were not taxied but
rode into battle and then, it is commonly thought, at least in early times,
they dismounted. But not always, as time went on. A bronze fourth-century plastron to protect the upper front body was taken by a Roman from
a Faliscan foe and at least shows the use of such armor for a rider who
would have no left hand free to hold a shield; therefore he must have
fought mounted; and similarly in a painting from Apulia in the same period or early third century, where the rider had a plastron and lance,
though also a companion who rides with a big round shield and a sword;
and in Lanuvium of the 470s, an entire set of fine armor was buried with
a long curved sword suited to a slashing attack, an ax, spear, and two
javelins. Among all these articles, the absence of greaves and shield is taken
to indicate a cavalryman.[13] From very nearly the birth of the Republic,
then, the Romans seem to have lived and fought at the center of a great region in which mounted warfare had come into general use, with a variety
of arms and armor, ultimately on a Greek model, to which the Roman
conformed without contributing anything of their own—unless it was
their invention that *equites* should be subsidized by the state.[14]

As to foot soldiers and their equipment, changes can be seen but there
are complications. In Greece the hoplite style of combat found to be most
effective was hand-to-hand with helmet, greaves (or at least one on the left
leg), spear, and big shield, in close formation so that your comrade on the
right protected your exposed side. This was the phalanx, in varying depth
of ranks. But hoplite and phalanx did not necessarily go together and there
is no archaeological evidence to say they did. Instead, all the items of defensive equipment are of course wanted in battle and are discovered in
burials or otherwise, or in art, in various Italian sites with which the Romans would be familiar; but we are left to wonder how they were most
commonly used in the field.

There is some help in sixth-century Etruscan art (and it is relevant to
the Romans on the assumption that warfare is not like most other skills
but actually a matter of life and death, so that effective alternatives spread
quickly from one people to another): reliefs on Etruscan bronze vessels
show what are clearly lines of differently equipped soldiers, whether bearing round shields or rectangular; other vessels show elongate oval shields

and long thrusting spears borne by some soldiers and it is supposed their manner of engagement was in individual duels with their long thrusting spears, while in the same groups, others have short spears for throwing. Some depictions of soldiers as full hoplites at the turn of the fifth century show what was known but not what was in actual use: tombstone reliefs from Clusium where three soldiers follow one behind the other, wearing kilts, greaves, and crested helmets and carrying short swords and big shields; but with a flautist among them to identify a funeral procession in the Etruscan mode, and in file, not ranks, therefore not real hoplites.[15]

Only in time, over the fifth and fourth centuries, is there material reflecting Roman styles: helmet, breastplate, long sword, and oval shields like a *scutum* rather than the Greek-style round one, for example in Daunia (Apulia), a later fourth- or early third-century depiction of an infantryman with sword and big oval shield. A Capuan painting of the fourth century adds another picture of a kilted, helmeted soldier with a long spear and big oval shield.[16] Of the heavy throwing spear, the *pilum*, of which literary sources speak, not even rusty traces have been identified.

In sum, the material evidence tells us that in the first two centuries of the Republic some foot soldiers bore shields of one size or shape, some of another, and spears for thrusting or to be thrown; and sometimes, perhaps ordinarily, troops with a certain kind of equipment were positioned together. To say more we are thrown back on written evidence; and this can be trusted only for the second century when we reach down to Polybius and those old veterans from whom he had learned.

"It is appropriate therefore to begin with Polybius", G. V. Sumner suggested long ago; for in Polybius we will find what we do not find in other sources for the early and middle Republic, at least not sources of any credibility: battle descriptions of light-armed and heavy-armed forces, and cavalry, and thrown spears or javelins, and heavy spears used as pikes.[17] Troops not further distinguished but apparently en masse run forward in a fierce charge; in another engagement the light-armed fall back upon the heavy-armed whose ordered ranks they completely disrupt; again, blocks of men form up in a column to a depth of many ranks in a phalanx, as he calls it. As a good study discovers in Greek hoplite combat, it "was much more varied and dynamic in its nature" than scholarly reconstructions generally suppose.[18] And from the 250s to the opening phases of the Hannibalic war, what we have in these scattered mentions is as much as we can learn of what combat looked like in that period.

It must be confessed, however, that we haven't learnt much beyond the existence of differences among kinds of troops in their arms and armor, and the fact that they were brigaded together, and that sometimes they ran forward all together or tried to stand firm in a mass; and we have the names of categories of troops implying something about how they fought: *hastati* (the *hasta* being a heavy spear), *triarii* ("third-rankers", Polybius' "light-armed") and *principes* ("first-rankers" who are the most heavily armed), all three Latin words transliterated by him as terms of Roman military art.

One thing more Polybius tells us about, and it is especially interesting: a movement characteristic of Roman army formations, which he had not observed anywhere else in all his travels and experience, and which allowed ranks to open up to receive not only light-armed skirmishers, if overwhelmed, but a heavy-armed line as well (made up of "standards" by which he means what Romans called "bundles", *manipuli*). In this maneuver we see something of the practical inventiveness that I look for; further, good evidence of a fallback provision being made into a part of training, so as to prevent great losses in flight; and we see provision for a defensive line to protect a recovery or orderly retreat, in the form of pikemen (*triarii*).

Enter Livy, a century later, to introduce under the year 340 a disquisition on Roman military usages and equipment at that time and earlier, too. Earlier, he says, Romans fought in phalanxes like the Macedonians,[19] and there are reasons beyond his text for crediting the Etruscans with the use of the formation, passed on or somehow otherwise adopted by the early Romans; but (4.59.11) when the Romans instituted military pay in 406 they changed to formation by maniples. Now, how could there be pay when there was not yet any currency? Livy's pages of explanation are densely packed with such details that make no sense, the more one tries to understand them, although serious efforts to do so go back to at least 1844.[20] We can only say that changes in drill, formations, and ranking indeed took place. Sumner points to terminology, where *hastati* in Livy are no longer armed with a heavy spear but rather with a heavy javelin that could be thrown, and *principes* have been pulled back from the very front to a middle line.[21] It is also clear that change did not all take place in some single great reform. The process was piecemeal and, as I assume, experimental, to test what worked.[22]

Fortunately, to focus only on what concerns me, it is enough to conclude that the units of army organization were reconstituted sometime in the 300s to provide both massed firmness and flexibility. And that was a good thing. An entire line or set of lines could open without breaking so as to admit comrades who were struggling, and then could close up once more. A particular sort of heavy throwing spear, a *pilum,* was adopted by the Romans as it had been quite widely in Italy of the earlier fourth century, and with it, a larger shield, the *scutum,* that protected the entire body; and these serviceable items remembered as Samnite were adopted in the course of Rome's wars with that enemy.[23] Whatever made sense in combat was thus accepted from whatever quarter. The cavalry "soon learnt to copy Greek arms" says Polybius (6.25.11), describing a new smaller shield; "for the Romans are a match for any people at changing their practice to emulate what is better".

He offers one other useful comment, too, about Rome's military capacities and their effectiveness, when he measures them against Hannibal (3.89.9): "among the advantages on the side of the Romans was an *inexhaustible* supply base and *manpower pool*". With these italicized words, I turn to the devices that Roman genius could invent and apply so as to make, in the course of conquest, not unforgiving enemies out of the defeated, but partners for the future in ever larger wars.

The story, many times told, is notable for the variety of treatment afforded to enemies; yet it is a variety in service to the essentials. The Romans could have followed the example of the most brilliant of the brilliant Greeks in the making of an empire, imposing not only taxation and conscription but their own form of government as well, and their own alphabet, even their own weights and measures. Instead they showed sense: they settled for the control of force. Declarations of war (which meant in effect all foreign policy) and the supreme command were to be theirs, and they might claim armed support from others according to terms agreed on.

The terms were the key to success. It was the good fortune of the Romans to have lived even into the earlier years of the Republic as neighbors and cousins of other Latin-speakers, and to have shared with them more than one important cult along with a range of practices that made up their way of life. In Latium, sharing took the form of the recognition of rights among the citizens of all the city-states, by all others: the rights governing marriage, business (including property-owning), transfer of residency, and escape from deadly feuds (the *ius exilii*). How such reciprocity first developed is unknown; the result, by the turn of the fifth century, was at any rate familiar to the Romans as to all Latins. It broke down the idea of citizenship into constituent elements inviting partial incorporation. Applying this novel idea to whole states, not individuals, opened up a practical solution to problems of supremacy that Romans encountered, and mastered.

There was nothing novel in those of Rome's treaties that did not touch matters of sovereignty for either signatory, as for example with Carthage or with Praeneste in 499 when Praeneste went over to the Roman side from the Latin, in a time of troubles. That time, however, pitting Rome against the Latin cities as a league, ended in a great victory for Rome and the Cassian Treaty that was agreed between them, in 493. It is a reminder of the sorry state of the surviving written record that, while this important document could still be seen and read in Augustus' day, Livy at the relevant point in his narrative never mentions it, instead confessing that "you can't make out how things happened in each year of such remote antiquity and authorities"; and the ineffable Dionysius of Halicarnassus, after pages of invented speeches, concludes only that the upshot of that great victory was "the old friendship, alliance, and oaths".[24] Just what was agreed must therefore be inferred from conduct, subsequently; and the earliest evidence then is the establishing of settlements of new landowners by the Romans and Latins jointly in the territory of conquered states and peoples, under the name "Latin colonies". In these, on the model of settlements by the Latins themselves before their defeat, everyone was equally a citizen of a newly defined sovereign city-state enjoying with any other sovereign city-state the various rights mentioned above, of marriage and so forth. More than a dozen of these colonies asserted the rule of the Latin-speakers united in their League, conjoined with Rome, and in locations carefully chosen for their strategic value, until in 340–338, when relations between Rome and the League degenerated into war once more.[25]

In the interval before that great rupture, Rome continued to fight and win and spread its hold over central Italy, and in the course of all this instituted two new features in its treaties. To its close Latin neighbor Tusculum, soon after 381, it agreed to give its full citizenship, even enrollment in one of the rural tribes through which voting rights were determined, to be exercised by Tusculani who chose to migrate to Rome; but their community continued just as it had been, self-governing.[26] They were thus incorporated but not incorporated, allies when they were at home, secured by treaty, but able even to hold office if they moved to the larger city and were there registered. They could appeal to the centuriate assembly against an unjust decision by a consul. Whether at home or at Rome, however, they were obliged to provide both recruits and war taxes just like any ordinary Roman citizen—were thus "burdens-bearing", *municipes,* as the Roman etymologists said, looking at the word *munia.* Considering that Rome's Latin allies had for long provided troops in jointly declared wars and had financed those contingents themselves, Tusculan status may not have been more onerous than before, and its land and local independence remained secure.

Further, to Caere soon after its defeat in 353, citizenship was extended but without the right to vote. The city was Etruscan but on especially friendly terms before the war, and was the more readily admitted to the status of *municipium.* Admission, however, had its limits. Its inhabitants were not enrolled in tribes but were instead listed only in their local ledgers. And at the moment of incorporation a city of this status later might see its territory reduced.[27] Both Tusculan citizenship and Caeritan, but especially the latter, served as templates to be imposed on other hostile or unruly city-states and peoples.

After a last great war with the Latins in 340–338, referred to above, the old Latin colonies dating from pre-493 and the newer joint ones thereafter in conjunction with Rome, were at Rome's disposal, along with the city-states that had formed the league and a few peoples like the Sidicini. To control them all, Roman settlers were sent to selected cities such as Cales (the first, 334) to overawe the region or to control a main road. But these cities, modeled on the earlier Latin colonies and therefore called "Latin", were somewhat different: possessing rights in the four respects mentioned above but neither members of the League (which was dissolved) nor sovereign entities at all. They commanded their own fortunes only within their own four walls. They were otherwise parts of a Roman state, willy-nilly. In the years before the outbreak of the Punic Wars, Rome founded close to twenty Latin colonies, Beneventum and Ariminum being the last two (in 268). Each had an initial population of 2,500 up to 6,000 males, among whom a majority, who had been Roman citizens, were now demoted to "Latin" status, while natives of the locale were raised to that status, all together making a united community; and there is no sign of division among them along lines of origin (it was quite different in Greece's western colonies where, in some, a wall divided the new from the old inhabitants). Michel Humbert in the fullest study of the subject supposes there was a deliberate policy of amalgamation or rapprochement at work here, to make a union out of former enemies.[28] What induced Roman citizens to surrender their birthright was no doubt the offer of land; besides, being at some distance from the capital, their participation in voting would have been next to impossible, anyway; and what was an inducement to the natives, at least the aristocracy among them, was the assignment of large amounts of land in reward for their support, whether that support had been as collaborators before defeat or was to be counted on afterward.

At a few points in Rome's expansion in and after 338, eight outposts were established strictly for Roman citizens on coastal sites (Ostia and Antium being the first) and only for quite small numbers: no more than 300 families. They had exactly the same rights in their new home as in their old. They were expected to take care of themselves as quasi-military outposts and, in at least three, their town plan resembled an army camp's; if they were exempt from service in the legions, this was only fair, since they were set down in exposed and uneasy places. In Minturnae, the Romans left in place a wall marking off their section of town from the natives in the other half. The arrangement was a departure from that seen in Latin colonies.[29]

It mustn't be thought, while noting grants of citizenship to so many of their former enemies, that Romans were a lovely generous people. I suppose nothing of the sort. Their conduct was dictated by practical considerations, out of the good sense to see that "greaterness" under continual challenge, in a body politic suffering from a low-grade infection that never relented, could never really be enjoyed. It could only be asserted. Of this truth there were certainly reminders. From among the peoples who had been subdued in war and had thereafter been made Romans, angry protests against their condition arose again and again. Citizenship had been imposed on them by force, and with it, painful obligations to say nothing of the affront to their pride.[30] It was therefore the Roman concern to minister to infection and if possible even prevent it in the first place by carefully calibrated concessions and adjustments.

Exactly how these were debated and turned into action is unknown. The four models of settlement—*municipia* with full rights like Tusculum or without voting rights like Caere; notionally "Latin" colonies like Cales; or maritime citizen ones like Ostia—were not always the first choice. It was more usual to confiscate a defeated city's land and give it out to Romans individually. Such harsh treatment was of course most common in areas where Rome's poor were happy to be settled, close to the capital; but there was a limit to the numbers of the Roman landless and to the consequent demand for a new home set among the angry former owners. Further from the capital, other considerations came into effect. In general it is clear that the oligarchs in charge of making decisions had no officials through whom they could rule from a distance, nor as individuals had they the means to administer some seized estate at a great distance from Rome. It was rather in the capital that their lives were centered and had meaning. Let others, then, enjoy what power and privilege could be found in the provinces; let the three-man committees for colony-founding set off to do their job; but it couldn't be of much interest to the great *gentes*. The composition of the committees is almost never reported. At best, patrons might steer the rewards of a victory to their own clients; but the evidence for this is not of much use.[31] The only control exercised over the affairs of conquered cities in what can be called an empire, in the fourth century and later, was most likely invited by the cities themselves, when their local

magistrates sought to comply with Roman law, and prefects in a committee of three were sent out to them from Rome to preside over assizes.[32]

Property law was predictably of huge importance to the Romans, witness the provision attributed to Rome's earliest lawgiver, that whoever disturbed a boundary mark should be consigned to the gods for punishment
(meaning, kill him ad lib.).[33] We must assume that not only Roman
landownership was registered in the community's mind and memory from
earliest times, and then eventually by local officials in ledgers, but that this
was the practice throughout settled Italy. Consequently Roman conquest
and the inventory that followed had good records to work with; and, if
boundaries were to be fixed anew, in disregard of the old or in previously
unoccupied land, this could be done by surveying in the Roman fashion,
using the Roman foot and its multiples. The first multiple was the
"plough-gang" still known in Dr. Johnson's day (for the Romans, it was an
actus of 120 Roman feet), the distance an ox can take a furrow before it gets
a rest; next, a square of that dimension; next, a *iugum/iugerum* (as much as
a yoke of oxen could plow in a day) measuring one by two *actus* (120 × 240
feet); and the largest unit, the "hundred" containing that number of family plots of two *iugera* inside a square twenty *actus* on a side, to be seen in
329 at Terracina.[34] By such means the whole of state lands could be inven-
toried, though I assume this was done only as need for distributions arose.

Marking off land was left to the standard army's two hundred engineers, *fabri,* able to repair equipment and supervise construction. This is
what Livy tells us (1.43.3) in a confused disquisition on the army under
King Servius Tullius. There is no saying to what date his information really
fitted; but the large number of such experts suggests how important their
duties were seen to be. Open territory they laid out in strips such as have
been traced around Privernum and Falerii after 340, at Terracina in 329, or
around Luceria in 314.[35] The archaeological evidence supports an earlier
date for the first organization of the *fabri;* their skills and instrument (the
groma) were taken from the Greeks via the Etruscans, so the Romans can
claim no credit there; but the application on a grand scale was to be one of
the wonders of the Empire, eventually identifiable in Tunisia, Croatia,
Spain, Greece, Hungary, Syria, France, perhaps Germany and Britain, and
most and best in Italy, over hundreds of square miles. All that is of course
a later story.

A little can be learned about social structure from the size of plots given
out: most of them at Luceria measuring ten *iugera* (2.5 ha, 6.5 acres) with
some larger ones also, marked off inside strips that were sixteen *actus* wide
and very long. In Livy's account of the distribution of Veii's territories sev-

enty-five years earlier, seven *iugera* were enough to attract and satisfy new settlers; and at a date in between, we saw above (chap. 5 at n. 61) that 500 *iugera* might be thought of as a huge estate. By the mid-first century we hear of landowners with some hundreds of thousands of *iugera,* though not all in one piece, of course.[36] That too is a later story—how wonderfully profitable aggression had proven!—giving a sense of the proportions of change from the fourth century to Caesar's lifetime. But even so early as the end of my period of study, it has been estimated that the Romans controlled two-thirds of the good arable land in the peninsula, through state ownership or ownership by colonies.[37]

What they controlled they improved for use. Swamps they drained by canals and tunnels in the same fashion as the Latin folk to their one side and the Etruscans (the teachers in these arts) on the other. In Etruria the tunnels they could use as models might stretch for several miles.[38] Leaving aside the Romans' legend of their entry into the besieged Veii by a tunnel, there is a reliable mention of Manius Curius Dentatus in 290, after his conquests in Sabine country and no doubt using his army engineers and the labor of captives, draining the Velinus lake into a little river, thereby to open up a lot more arable.[39]

In Etruria excavation has cleared or identified and approximately dated a great deal of civil engineering besides drainage works, from which the Romans borrowed for their own projects: in particular, canals to divert rivers or spread their force in flood and so to allow the crossing of valleys; huge cuttings to smooth out the steeper stretches of roads; detours and switchbacks for the same purpose; stone paving that would insure passage for carts in the rainy season—all this from the sixth century on, and manifestly known to the Romans in due course of conquest, since we can see them taking over Etruscan roads and bridges for their own use.[40] As a practical matter, in aid of their *maiestas,* the Romans had to have all-weather access to the furthest reaches of their empire and were as ready to borrow construction techniques and infrastructure, as to copy others' weapons and modes of fighting.

The state's oversight of roads was asserted, though minimally, in the Twelve Tables, to regulate their width and protect their paving; and to the same period, the mid-fifth century, the Via Latina can be dated, joining Rome to Monte Cavo and the cult center of the Latin League's Jove. In the other direction, the Via Curia was extended by Manius Curius Dentatus perhaps in the same year as his draining of the Veline lake near Reate/Rieti.[41] Between these two dates, the Via Salaria was paved in the fourth century, and the famous Appian Way (begun 311), the Valerian (306) with a connection to Alba Fucens, the Caecilian around 300; and there were others.[42] Financing and construction were in the hands of consuls, censors, or aediles, the latter attested for the 260s.[43] They learned from experiment that second-rate stone wouldn't hold up and the thing had to be done all over again; the line had to be extended from time to time and branch off into new areas; but in the end they did the job to the satisfaction of subsequent history: that is, their work lasted and lasted. It was counted in the first century by a Greek observer as one of Rome's greatest claims to glory. Tocqueville with characteristic wit paid tribute to the durability of "those long artificial rock formations that we call Roman roads".[44]

Roads and colonies went together. Sometimes the colony came first and the road was directed through its center; sometimes the road came first and the new town was built to straddle it.[45] Inside, straight lines and square corners were the rule, just as they were in the surrounding territory. Greeks and Etruscans and then the Latin league had long favored these features in laying out their towns; for good measure the Etruscans and then the Romans added rituals that determined orientation and made it holy and blessed.[46] In these matters as in others that have been pointed out, the Romans saw no reason not to copy what worked, and then to improve on it in their own way, as in town planning: through the use of their familiar units of measurement, for instance, at Fregellae in 328, where housing blocks are two *actus* wide; at Venusia in 291 and Ariminum in 268, two by three *actus;* at Hadria in 289, one and a half by two. Toward these metrics and conventions, the Romans can be seen advancing gradually: in their earlier urban planning, down to 338, they laid out construction as the terrain made convenient rather than programmatically.[47]

The military *fabri* who laid out a new town knew it should have a big open rectangle in the middle, and adjoining, a *comitium* on the familiar model, a round space inside a square with a senate hall next to it; and this is what is found at Alba Fucens, Fregellae, Cosa, or Paestum, "the canonical model spread abroad from Rome in every 'Latin' colony".[48] At Paestum the spaces for sixteen or so shops along the two long sides of the forum were identical, "obviously following a modular blueprint"; in Cosa the residential spaces were standardized, squares that were fractions of an *actus.*[49] There is in Fregellae a house of the form so entirely Roman, dating to the turn of the third century, with atrium, *alae, tablinum, cubicula,* all these familiar in Pompeii.[50] What had proved satisfactory was not to be redesigned needlessly.

Practicality in planning a city must put the water supply near the top of the list. Wells were the usual answer. By the fourth century the capital had evidently outgrown the possibilities, leading to the first aqueduct undertaken by the builder of the great southward trunk road, Appius Claudius in 312. His two public works were almost the first to take their name from their author. They insured his fame, which was the point of the undertaking, naturally.[51] The Aqua Appia entered the city at a substantial depth and no doubt cost a lot of money. So also the next aqueduct drawing from the Anio River to the north, and paid for by Manius Curius Dentatus and his fellow censor in 272 out of the spoils of war against Pyrrhus. In the course of aqueduct construction that remarkable invention, the arch, comes to light, carrying the Appia on its shoulders; and it is found in a number of structures of about the same date and thereafter.[52] The invention of cement (which was apparently not the Romans' own but learnt by them from others) made a pair with the arch, as crucial to the history of Western architecture; but it didn't come into the Romans' hands for a century or so after Appius Claudius.[53]

And that story I continue a few pages below.

9

WRAP-UP

This essay originated in my difficulties with the prevailing historical reconstruction of a certain part of Classical Antiquity: nothing less than the first five hundred years of Roman history. In my dissatisfaction with the consensus and its reliance on the literary sources I am certainly not alone. Classicists including the very best have rejected such evidence as just not believable. They have done so even at some risk of making themselves unloved, or worse. At best they may be dismissed as "hypercritical".[1] More still have questioned this or that particular ancient writer or piece of the narrative but their reservations have never disturbed the orthodox very much. The orthodox continue to believe that there is some more or less detailed account of those many centuries awaiting recovery from the surviving evidence, despite all its difficulties—some recoverable truth.

But I don't think it can ever be recovered from the sources traditionally written and traditionally read in modern times.

To explain: in data-rich areas of historical inquiry, such as the period in the nineteenth century that I am familiar with, disputed points are either too tiny to matter and for that reason no one rests on them in argument, or they are too enormous to be disposed of with any certainty; so argument goes on, not about particulars, but about accumulations of data and their comparative weight. For example: where and why did World War I begin? Only children will point to a certain archduke's violent death. No serious answer is to be sought in any single cause like that. That is not how things really happen on any scale deserving of study. Instead, we look at a whole set of factors and their interplay, at a high level of generalization, as they affect behavior; and this looseness of thought is tolerable because it is acknowledged to derive from an adequate supply of information that no one doubts. Whatever can be doubted has been discarded and there is still plenty left over to work with. What results is one particular sort of truth. Call it "modern".

How modern historians decide to discard or accept a particular item in the first place is no great secret. They apply methods and standards which they would call common sense and which I have called courtroom wisdom.[2] In trial settings we are familiar with the careful consideration of witnesses, human actions, motivation, behavior; and the process (though perhaps on a different scale) is just what is involved when we test and accept items of evidence for modern history. What diaries, letters, official or commercial archives or newspapers do we have to work with? From these we go on to interpretation.

This latter, like courtroom inquiry, may sometimes appear a sloppy business—certainly nothing like mathematics. No, it is much harder. Its difficulty lies in the number of variables that must so often be taken into account, and in their uncertain character that requires taking account also of still other variables, and so forth; with the result that we can only sum up our thoughts in abbreviated form as "probabilities". It is a familiar fact in debates among modern historians (a very curious fact, none the less) that when one person declares an explanation to be "probable", the other person need not ask for more argument but, instead, may make the case for a different one; for it is understood that probabilities are discerned or arrived at by the recall of factors too many and too tedious to list, or simply beyond human powers to list in their entirety, and the supply of agreed-upon information is generally enough to advance discussion. What was it that drew the poet William Blake, with other men of a similar place in society, to his preferred church? What explains the flowering of letters in America's Southern states in certain decades of the last century? The answer offered may not be accepted but neither is it challenged in detail. From this process will emerge no more than a qualified winner, at first, presented to the audience, the readership, the public, to be accepted by more persons or fewer, so as to be agreed and to be pronounced a consensus, or to be rejected and let die in silence—*Totschweigen* in German academic lingo. Whatever the final outcome, the foundations of argument are not the problem. Rather, it is the weight that is assigned to one or another force or forces perceived to be at work in the making of some result; in short, interpretation.

By contrast, in data-poor areas, the very tiniest pieces of evidence may really count. Consider how "Trafalgar Square skeleton forces historians to rewrite the story of Roman England", the headline of a recent newspaper article.[3] One single discovery can make a big difference; notionally (as here) a hundred thousand lives are affected, that is, they are to be differently understood, over a stretch of at least several decades across an area the size of Switzerland. By the same token, if the excavated burial were to be judged a hoax, this same population and everything they did, notionally, would disappear like a dream.

This is why the Trafalgar Square discovery is headline news, at least for ancient historians, and why its assessment had better be right. Call in the experts, then, to rule on the archaeology, the likely date of the thing, and on perceived similarities with other finds elsewhere; for it is archaeology that is in question.

It might instead have been philology. It has been noticed, for example, that one ancient annalist believed Romulus to have ruled in the tenth century while another put him in the eighth. Either way, there are very significant human consequences, notionally. How, then, did such writers approach their art so as to arrive at such discrepant results—one of which must be wrong, or both? How did ancient writers think? Call in the most relevant specialists. If it is the reading of a damaged document of some sort, a paleographer or papyrologist is needed to winkle out a smudgy word or two and see its meaning; or it may be in an inscription on stone or a coin legend. But whatever it is that needs to be carefully looked at and sized up, "Let the cobbler stick to his last", as the Ancients themselves advised us.[4] Each kind of evidence from the past demands particular skills long formed in the right postgraduate degree program, in the right learned journals, governed by the sort of questions that define each discipline; each can add some tiny increment of information, well evaluated, well presented, ready for use in the understanding of the past.

Then last, to find the sense in it all, sizing up all the notional consequences, call in the historians. It is their craft. May not other specialists pick this up naturally in the course of practicing their own particular craft or discipline? May it not be learned, for example, from the close study of Livy? What an idea! We might as well look to Galen for lessons in open-heart surgery. The interpreting of history, like so many other arts in our civilization, has very greatly improved over the course of the last century or so. Its improvement may be credited largely to the richness of the data base itself, such as is available at least for modern times; for this has not only invited but almost necessitated more and more sophisticated analysis.

At the same time, however, richness of data has taught restraint; for, properly considered, it suggests or rather, it continually shows us the interconnectedness of things across differences of class, region, occupation, or manner of life; so, in whatever way we reconstruct the past in our pages—finding the key in this or that action or actor, in this or that historical force or circumstance—our choice demonstrably affects and is affected by everything else adjacent. We cannot modify, then, or amplify or embellish what is known, or render our reconstruction more significant or less lacunose by our conjectures, without introducing changes all around. Any historical scene so lightly conceived, so capriciously compounded of guesswork that a single archaeological discovery could "force historians to rewrite the story of Roman England"—anything of that sort should be quite unthinkable. It certainly is among modern historians. Yet in data-poor periods such conjectural constructs are almost the rule, for easily understood reasons, and most obviously where the amount and quality of evidence are least satisfactory.

Lack of restraint is the problem, "a rage for saying something where there is nothing to be said" (as Dr. Johnson put it, in his criticism of an over-ingenious scholar). For illustration, I point once more to Livy's pages and the general written records on which we depend so very much for our reconstruction of early Rome and its story. They are shot through with every sort of fiction, spin, caprice, art, contradiction, variant accounts, and physical impossibilities. So say the specialists—and it is theirs of right to make the charge. It is their craft. Surely, then, no one would waste any ink on such impossible material, except to say, "We cannot know, *non liquet*". To the contrary, however, unrestrained reconstruction remains in fashion, supported by much learning and justified by the insistence that this or that chosen part of the literary tradition can be made to tell the truth even if, granted, nobody can trust the whole body of it.

Where these are the problems in method, a different approach may work better. We may look beyond the traditional written accounts, to unadorned and unmediated patterns of behavior. How the Romans acted as a people over time reveals a character that can be known, themselves serving as their own unconscious witnesses and providing confirmation in tendencies that are credibly attested.

It is, for example, not hard to accept their bellicosity, jostling for arable and pasturage as they were, and confined by the Sabines on one flank, by the Etruscans on another. It was easiest for them to push in amongst their like, the Latins—but not to exterminate them. Some less hostile outcome had to be worked out, agreeable to the dictates or sympathies of a shared way of life. Nevertheless, the Romans' expansion continued without pause.

Of course warfare was nothing they had invented, witness the walls surrounding every community in Latium that had the resources to construct them, or the scores of stone-built fastnesses scattered about Samnite lands, before ever the Romans offered any threat. War was not the Romans' invention yet it was their love, we may say, or their preference or proclivity.

And a *settled* tendency at work continuously over any length of time need not be a *marked* tendency, in order to produce differences of significant historical magnitude.[5] I would suppose everyone is perfectly aware of this; but it is a truth so commonly and casually applied in understanding our neighbors, we may undervalue its usefulness in understanding the course of nations. It can be seen at work in and for the Romans, in the increasing size of territory they controlled; it can be seen in the map of Italy (fig. 7.1) to be read and animated in one's mind's eye almost like a comic strip, so as to follow their movement from one area of shading to another, always in the direction of empire and "greaterness", down to the mid-third century.

There is a second illustration, not of aggression as a national trait, but of practicality. At the close of the previous chapter, evidence was offered of the Romans' very simple good sense applied to construction, where whatever was being built was built again and again; and from the repetition emerged models or modules, subject to the improvement that testing might suggest. Every project could be made easier, for instance, through the use of an agreed set of metrics. The device was no invention of the Romans. Their genius showed rather in its application which, if it had been more complicated and intellectual and theoretical—in short, more highbrow—scholars would more readily acknowledge. Who, however, can see genius in the *actus* and its fractions and multiples, all derived ultimately from the weary plodding of a plow ox? Can the Roman mind at work compare with the Greeks', which discovered entasis and the mathematics of proportion? *There* was genius. The Romans had nothing to match it, unless what is measured is historical significance—meaning, whatever determines the action of a lot of people in some respect they take seriously. By this standard, however, the Roman's claims can be seen staked out across all those many parts of the Mediterranean world that I mentioned in the preceding chapter: in Syria near Damascus, in Italy near Padova, in Tunisia and Hungary and so forth. Here for centuries to come they marked the land by their inventory and their methods of exploitation.

Uniformity, simplicity, and repetition obviously made for economy of effort. As Tocqueville said, "it is acknowledged that when a workman is engaged every day upon some detail, the whole commodity is produced more

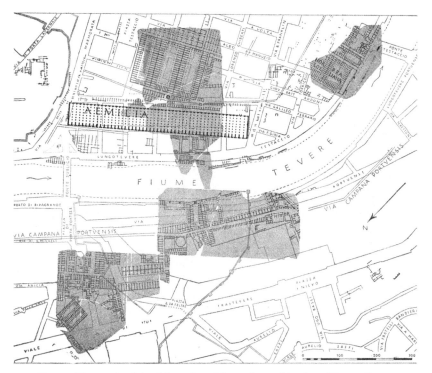

Fig. 9.1. The *porticus* [*Aemi*]*lia* or [*nava*]*lia* on the marble plan of Rome. From Carettoni (1960).

easily, quickly, and cheaply".[6] Once the potter's mold is prepared, votive figurines can be turned out every single day by the dozens or, with a stamp, cups and vases can be decorated by the thousands; or by surveyors, city plans or whole huge landscapes can be laid out according to some single plan. The principle is the same: a module or template is repeated as necessary, better the tenth time than the first, and often to produce results, it may be, of truly historic proportions.

I instance at Rome the "*porticus Aemilia*" of two stories some 60 meters by nearly 490 (ca. 300 × 1,600 feet) divided laterally into fifty barrel-vaulted bays on the ground floor (fig. 9.1).[7] It was at the time an eighth wonder of the world, you might suppose, at least for its gigantic size; but it was never so admired. It is in fact barely mentioned. It was too utilitarian; merely practical. What makes it interesting, however, is the lavish use of cement—rubble bound by mortar throughout this vast project—still to be seen in the walls and dated to 174 or perhaps a generation later. The trick of construction lay in movable, reusable wooden forms or templates,

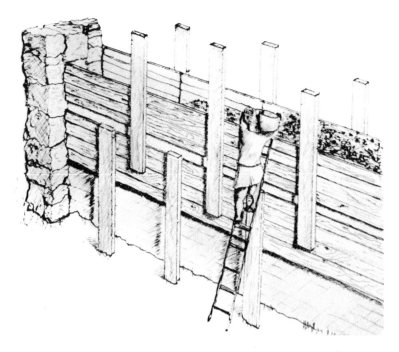

Fig. 9.2. *Opus caementicium* in production. Drawing, R. MacMullen.

or shutters as architects call them, which could be entrusted to quite un-skilled labor for any size of building. By this means the built world in and around cities everywhere was gradually transformed over the succeeding centuries.

I show here three levels (fig. 9.2): nearest the ground, a completed con-crete section; above it, concrete being left in forms to harden; and, in the upper third, concrete being poured to fill the forms. The latter are simply a module in wood, just as the "hundred" (the surveyors' *centuria*) is a no-tional one used in land measurement, and the *comitium* is an architectural one for public assemblies. What was characteristically Roman about tem-plates was the lack of imagination about them, the high order of organiza-tion directing them, their everyday usefulness, and their display of applied as opposed to theoretical intelligence. In all these aspects I see practicality. As to its role in the shaping of a civilization, that story needs no telling.

These two of the four traits of Roman character that I focus on—ag-gressiveness and practicality—take me to the mid-third century and then well into the second. The other two of my four choices I don't need to il-lustrate, nor need I follow them all into the bright light of the first century:

to the period of Cicero or Augustus. Here in these great men's home was the hub of an empire; from here their rule extended everywhere; here every other language besides Latin was spoken, most of all, Greek, and by all races, all finding their place without disturbing the ancestral Penates and Luperci. Here were the forums, the aqueducts and baths, held out to other cities for imitation. Here were the Romans everyone knows.

But for a moment it is instructive to detach oneself from these familiar figures, so as to see them and their setting from a distance (the greater, the better), asking how it was that they eventually turned out just as they did. Answering, at the end one should be able to say, "Such was the only possible outcome because *that's who the Romans were*". The answer would at least be a form of understanding that a modern historian can live with.

NOTES

PREFACE

1. The types I mention are prominent in my *Sisters of the Brush* (New Haven 1997) and *Sarah's Choice* (New Haven 2001) with Sellers (1991) 122, for the businessman; as also in Tocqueville (1836) 1.57f.; 2.209, 215.

2. Tocqueville "the first social scientist", in Elster (2009); and Tocqueville (1836) 2.221 (*mores*) and 255–62: more than circumstances and more than laws, it is a people's "habits, opinions, manners" (262) that serve as the base and shaping force of any society.

3. *Democracy* 1.17. It adds very little to my argument, that ancient writers also thought in terms of national character (however misleading the word "national" may be): for example, Livy in many passages, Oakley (1997–2005) 2.264, or Lucian speaking of the Paphlagonians (*Alex.* 9) or Tertullian's report, "It has been said that the Thebans are born dull and brutish, while the sharpest people in wisdom and speech are those of Athens. . . . So widely diffused is the idea of ethnic individuality"—*De anima* 20.3, *tamque vulgata iam res est gentilium proprietata;* and he goes on to instance such opinions in the comic poets, Sallust, and others, cf. Waszink (1947) 283–85; further, with many examples, Giardina (1997) 34ff., 99, 202, and good summary comments, 38.

4. Hofstede (2001), e.g., 13 on national character.

5. Carandini (1997) 39.

6. Watson (1975) 16; cf. Syme (1960) 315, "The Romans as a people were possessed by an especial veneration for authority, precedent and tradition", etc. Rüpke (1990) 14 suggests, "Der Versuch einer Gesamtinterpretation ermöglicht das Verständnis isolierter, haüfig schlechts überlieferter Details"; but he then turns away from the idea. "Any broad application of mentality-history" must be rejected since national character is constantly changing.

7. Hofstede (2001) 8, 33, choice of "aggressive" or "conservative" by some analysts as traits useful to analyze; or Wallace (1990) 291, "It is not parody to regard Rome as a warlike and conservative society"; or Forsythe (2005) 153 deciding among possible interpretations by invoking "the Romans' . . . practical political thinking"; MacMullen (1980a) 15 and passim on "national character"; and below, chap. 1 n. 12.

8. Hill (1961) 3 referring to "H. A. L. Fisher's view that history is merely 'one damned thing after another'" ("histoire évènementielle" as the French Annales school would call it).

CHAPTER I

1. Ascribing it to an early king Ancus Martius, Ennius in the second century told of a harbor for foreign traders at Ostia in the Tiber's mouth, but Livy 1.33.9 tells not of a port but only of saltworks. Torelli (1999) 29 accepts (without citation) this regal-period foundation, as others have done; but there is no archaeological support for either settlement or saltworks in the regal period nor even before the late fourth century. See Salmon (1970) 71; Poucet (1985) 155; and Zevi (1996) 3ff., with support from G. Calza; also Smith (1996) 180 quoting J. Heurgon.

2. Watson (1975) 4; a third example of characterization, below, n. 12; Briquel (2000) 50 on the Via Salaria; and the nature of early Rome, Johnson et al. (1961) 9: "The code [of the Twelve Tables] is concerned with subjects peculiarly suited to an agricultural and pastoral community, which had hardly any industrial interests or commercial activities or cultural avocations".

3. Cf. the Cicero passage (*Acad.* 1.2.8f.) with the acerbic pages of Palmer (1970) 8ff. and 22f. Palmer here deals and dispenses with Varro's numbering of the members in the Alban or Latin League, a figure of thirty to be found nevertheless in most modern accounts of early Rome, as e.g., in Momigliano (1989) 85; and further on Cicero's use of the antiquarians' favored etymological reasoning, Rawson (1972) 37, 42, despite some distrust of it. Antiquarians pursued ends and data different from the historians', sometimes with significant effect on the historical record, cf. e.g., Coarelli (1983) 50. While Livy himself did not draw on Varro by name (but see Oakley [1997–2005] 2.43), other historians did, very much; and notice in Livy many "pseudo-antiquarianisms", as noted in Gustafsson (2000) 29.

4. On Curtius, Livy 1.12f., with Varro's three additional alternatives, Bremmer (1993) 165f.; on Olus, cf. Alföldi (1965) 216f. conveniently gathering the sources which apparently begin with Fabius Pictor, subsequently picked up by Varro (*L. L.* 5.41) and others, who must have approved the aetiological pun even if they do not spell out the name of the king; and on chronology, Pallottino (1987) 227.

5. On statistics, cf. below, chap. 3 n. 32; on the imaginary coinage and its role in fines and army-muster classes in the regal period, Crawford (1985) 17f. On the totality of anchorage, cf. Ungern-Sternberg (1988) 241, after a review of all written sources pre-500: "even by an optimistic estimate it is evident that no *coherent* picture of the monarchy period, from these sources, can be reconstituted" (emphasis

added). One might think of the variant accounts of Titus Tatius or the interval and relation between Demaratus and Tarquinius I, not to mention the stretching out of the span 750–509 among only seven kings.

6. *Antiquissimus,* Livy 1.44.2; on Fabius' date of writing, Oakley (1997–2005) 1.22; and Ogilvie (1971) 7, the ancient historians "did not seriously investigate or question the credentials of the traditional version of Roman history which had become established by the time of Pictor". I would restrict the statement to the Latin writers, recalling the tale Pictor invents to explain the origins of the Second Punic War, which Polybius 3.8.1–11 rehearses, concluding (3.9.1f.) "its senselessness is obvious without comment". I would take this as an indication of Polybius' general opinion of Pictor. Further on Livy, below, chap. 5 nn. 3f.

7. *Falsus in uno, falsus in omnibus,* which my friend B. Frier calls "a fairly standard (although controversial) jury instruction as to the testimony of witnesses" and which Boswell in *His Life of Samuel Johnson* quotes simply as a common maxim in his time (1744, or p. 98 in the Modern Library Edition); also Dickens in *Bleak House* (chap. 57, "Fast and loose in one thing, fast and loose in everything"). On the annalist, cf. Wiseman (2008) 18, "Livy was a good storyteller".

8. Only as a sort of jeux d'esprit ("curious to speculate") Momigliano (1963) 107 imagined what we would have if we had only archaeology without "the literary tradition". He shows little appreciation of the possibilities. True, he was writing long ago and at an unfortunate juncture in archaeological publication in which E. Gjerstad figured prominently.

9. Cornell (1995) 73; Michels (1953) 36f. and passim; 45f. on Varro used by Augustine's *City of God* 18.12, where the Luperci "go up and down the Sacra Via"; and (41f.) on Dionysius of Halicarnassus, *Rom. Ant.* 1.80, where "the youths living near the Palatine proceed from the Lupercal and circulate about the village"; Momigliano (1966) 533, where Latte is cited but also, *contra,* E. Gjerstad. The short Varro-passage is judged by critics to be in parts incomprehensible, where it reads, *Lupercis nudis lustratur antiquum oppidum Palatinum gregibus humanis cinctum*; and Latte does not acknowledge Michels' finding that in fact none of the twenty relevant texts has the Luperci making a circuit around anything. Smith (1996) 155 reads the texts as I do; also Flobert (1985) 112; others misunderstand the Latin to mean *cinctum* by the Luperci, cf. e.g., Munzi (1994) 355.

10. Cornell (1995) 222, quoted; to the same effect, 408, "history by definition cannot exist without written documents" (a strange idea); and some further chewing at how to handle the two kinds of evidence in Carandini (2000) 147.

11. For "free association", see below, Linderski's words in n. 27. For a piece of standard day-by-day or week-by-week political narrative quite plain in the ground, see for example the siege of Paphos, Maier (2008) 63–97, or better known, that of Masada.

12. "The Romans were notoriously conservative in the way they maintained ancient cult practices" (Cornell [1995] 25); Dumézil (1987) 98, apropos religion, "un trait certain du caractère romain en toute matière . . . c'est son conservatisme".

13. Cato, *De agr.* 1.2, *ubi ad villam venit, ubi larem familiarem salutavit . . .* ; 1.5, the *vilicus* and family *feriae serventur* (and again, 138); 143, the *vilicus'* wife's duties; other ritual observances, 138–42, including for the dead, and the earliest indication of their rites, *parentalia,* far to the south in the Roman colony of 314, Luceria. Cf. the inscription protecting a certain sacred grove which bans burials there, and their rituals, *ne parentatid,* Riccobono (1941–43) 3.224 and *DE* 4, 3, 1971 s.v. "Lucus" (A. Pasqualini, 1972), with the date suggested by A. Degrassi, "shortly after 315/4".

14. *Aulularia* 25f.; further, 385, offerings.

15. Poets' evidence in Orr (1978) 1560–64; on the Penates, Wissowa (1912) 161–66; on the archaeology, Orr (1978) 1576, "hundreds of portable altars" in Pompeii from late Republican times; but none earlier than the end of the second century, Fröhlich (1991) 69; in Ostia from A.D. 100, Bakker (1994) 8–17. Cicero's great grief at his daughter's death and elaborate plans for a villa of mourning (as it may be called) with a temple, *fanum,* and gardens, all explained in full to his most intimate friend, see *Ad Att.,* 12.18–43, and Shackleton-Bailey (1966) 5.404–13.

16. *Parentatio,* "to make an offering of appeasement" to the deceased (Oxford Latin Dictionary); Michels (1967) 134; and 217, the calendar date.

17. For example, Colonna (2005) 485 on what was later called the *silicernium;* Bergonzi and Bietti Sestieri (1980) 50–54 on vessels and food remains and (76 no. 32) terra-cotta stoves to heat food; Holloway (1994) 120 on libations at Castel di Decima near Rome, seventh century; Tagliamonte (1996) 80, at Aufidena into the fifth century; Bartoloni and Cataldi-Dini (1980) 145, continued contact in a seventh-century Esquiline hypogeum; for the Quirinal votive material, my thanks to Elizabeth Colantoni for an as-yet unpublished paper delivered in 2006, though Zeggio (2000) 332, to which she refers, prefers another explanation; in Smith (1996) 88, at Osteria dell'Osa near Gabii, 850 tombs of the period Latial III (770–730/20), where "it would appear from the evidence . . . the graves were revisited after burial, so even the funeral was not the final act"; and Ampolo (1984) 75, 77ff., and 89 on *parentes,* ancestors in the Twelve Tables.

18. For graveside cult from Numa's time on, see Degrassi (1963) 408, 413; observation of the Ninth-Day rites for the deceased with aspersion of wine, in the Twelve Tables, Riccobono (1941–43) 1.68; and for ancestor worship in Rome of Late Antiquity, MacMullen (2010) 595–600.

19. *RE* s.v. "Heros" col. 1126 (S. Eitrem); Stillwell et al. (1976) 316; Calame (1990) 154; and MacMullen (2009) 37–40 on Philippi, and on Geneva, 93f.

20. Ampolo (1980) 166; Poucet (1985) 122, 135; Gros and Torelli (1988) 62–64; Holloway (1994) 53f.; Smith (1996) 101; Carandini (1997) 59, 62–68; Pensabene (1998) 7f. with fig. 1 on which I base my fig.1.1, and traces of a late fourth-century or early third-century shrine; an altar in the center of one hut, 11ff., which was sixth century and was found and sacralized in 294; 18–23, huts around the "casa Romuli" datable to ninth to eighth centuries; further, 64–69 and 74–76, noting that there were several sites considered by the late-Republican sources to be the house of Romulus (making any modern choice problematical); Pensabene (2000)

74f.; Carandini (2000) 131; and Carafa (2000) 69. Pensabene (2006) 335, 337, is careful to point out that there is no reason for identifying the heroon of the site with the legendary Romulus, as later became common. For the miniature huts, see comparable ones elsewhere in areas near Rome in, e.g., Danner (1993) 94.

21. Dionysius of Halicarnassus, *Ant. Rom.* 1.79.11.

22. On many signs of the "wish to conserve ancient holy places" in the southwest corner of the Palatine, see Pensabene (1998) 13; Glinister (2000) 58f. (Palatine) and passim; Ampolo (1980) 166; Holloway (1994) 81ff. on the best-known example under the Black Stone paving in the Forum; and extraordinary numbers of seventh-century votive gifts piously buried at Lavinium, next door to Rome, in Rüpke (2007) 27 and 154.

23. Wissowa (1912) 161f.; Cornell (1995) 102, "the cult of Vesta . . . securely dated to the second half of the seventh century"; also G. Cifani's unpublished paper, with my thanks to the author for sharing the text; and Carafa (2000) 70f., distinguishing between evidence of cult, and built facilities a bit later. For Vesta in Latium, see e.g., Beard et al. (1998) 1.51.

24. Rüpke (2007) quoted, 157.

25. MacMullen (1981) 42, 49ff., and passim; Glinister (2006) 12f., all gods heal; on body-part votives, Rüpke (2007) 155ff.

26. Body-part votives widespread, from early fifth century in Rome, Cristofani (1985) 23, though in the south, only decades later; North (1995) 144, fourth-century evidence and later, widespread in Italy, e.g., to Diana; Beard et al. (1998) 1.11f.; and Rüpke (2007) 157ff., like Beard et al., noticing how little of such religious practices appears in literary sources.

27. So, Beard et al. (1998) 1.1–6. To avoid "scholarly fantasy", it is best to renounce any possible confident knowledge of Roman religion older than the third century, cf. Linderski (2007) 510, 596 (quoted).

28. Carafa (2000) 68f. dates the conservation of votive material to ca. 625, and the earlier shrine to 750–725; Colonna (2005) 581 dates the beginning of the temple to the 580s, the completion toward the end of that century, so also Cifani (2008) 80 or Albertoni (2008) 14; but Danti (2008) 27 mentions architectural material found in the foundations, datable to the latter date (530–510) and Holloway (1994) 8ff. would prefer the earlier fourth century for the temple's final construction.

29. Apollo's cult area in the second half of the sixth century, Donati and Stefanetti (2006) 122, citing F. Coarelli; 81, the god honored with his first temple in 432; Herakles' shrine in the sixth century, the Great Altar in the Prata-Flaminia, Wiseman (1994) 4 or Colonna (2005) 582, "Servian"; perhaps datable as early as the seventh century, cf. Gros and Torelli (1988) 28 and 74. On the popularity of Herakles, Colonna (1981) 413, quoted.

30. On the archaic temple in the Cattle Market (Sant'Omobono) cf. Mura Sommella (1993) 225; Holloway (1994) 10, 68–80; for the less likely proposal, temples of Mater Matuta and Fortuna, cf. Gros and Torelli (1988) 28; Naso (2001) 231f.; Rüpke (2007) 127; and *RE* s.v. "Matuta" col. 2328 and *OCD* 1360, with men-

tion of the Satricum temple of comparable date (ca. 550) to which Livy's story (5.19.6) would refer Rome's original temple, delapidated and renovated in 396.

31. On Vertumnus, Colonna (1981) 163 and Colonna (2005) 537f., a pre-Tarquins date. On Vulcan, Linderski (2007) 538f.; Glinister (2000) 58; acceptance of an archaic date by Gros and Torelli (1988) 29—this, "hypothesized", Holloway (1994) 86, but assured by Carafa (1998) 105 (actually, eighth century).

32. General popularity of Mars, Dumézil (1987) 252f.; known at Satricum in ca. 500, and venerated by someone probably later in Rome, Aronen (1989) 37; Sabatucci (1988) 87, Mars' festivals and cult among Latins, Samnites, etc., and at Rome (88–90) supposed to have been one of a primitive triad, with Jupiter and Quirinus, in the "arcaico stato romano", before the Jupiter-Juno-Minerva group; his festival supposed to have been celebrated "from the very earliest times", Donati and Stefanetti (2006) 32; Mars and Numa mentioned together, Festus 510L; but Palmer (1970) 166 dates his first Roman temple to 388.

33. On the auspices and the circumstances of reversion to the senate, see Livy 1.31; further, D'Ippolito (1998) 32, though very little is known about the rites, cf. Willems (1878–85) 2.173f.; and for the quotation, D'Ippolito 34, going on to say, "The state was the historical outcome of the federation of *gentes*".

34. Coarelli (1986) 185, the calendar in a fixed form by or before late sixth century, as indicated by what deities were included or not; Beard et al. (1998) 1.6, noting so-called red-letter days in the calendar as "maybe earlier" than the Republic, and no *dies festi* "proven to be post-regal".

35. Romulus' *lituus* preserved on the Palatine, *CIL* 1, 2, the *Fasti Praenestini* p. 234, on which perhaps can be based an *ante-quem* date of 390; in the Curia of the Salii, as suggested by Pensabene (1998) 9, 11, 67; and a bronze of ca. 580 in Etruria to show its shape, Cristofani (1985a) 251.

36. J. Linderski by letter kindly supplies the references for the use of a flint knife by the fetial priests at treaty-swearing (Serv. ad Aen. 8.641; Liv. 1.24.8; 9.5.3); cf. Serv. in *Aen.* 1.448, the Jupiter priest must shave with a bronze razor because that metal is suited to cult acts; Livy 1.32.12, *hasta praeusta* in Bayet (1971) 9, and of cornel wood (20) as, on the Palatine, the tree believed to be sprung from Romulus' spear; prohibition of wine, seventh century or earlier, Ampolo (1980a) 31; and *far*, Sabatucci (1988) 60f.

37. Mycenaean model, *Enciclopedia dell'arte antica, classica e orientale* (Roma 1958–) s.v. "Scudo" 7.143; *RE* s.v. "Salii" col. 1886.

38. Schäfer (1980) 351f., 362–72; Sabbatucci (1988) 95f.; and Torelli (1990) 95–98.

39. E. A. Meyer (2004) 37, the approach seen as superstition by Polybius.

40. The Twelve Tables reflected rules of life long settled in the community, so, Holloway (1994) 170 or Cornell (1995) 107; Cic., *Leg.* 2.59, "as boys we had the Twelve Tables by heart like a formula to be memorized"; peculiarities of language, and especially *brevitas,* 2.18 and E. A. Meyer (2004) 60f.; inscribed in bronze, 26 n. 29; and the translated bit in Johnson et al. (1961) 12.

41. Holloway (1994) 81–90, whose dates I follow; Coarelli (1986) 167–88, with

an earlier dating, 172; Ampolo (1980) 167; Colonna (2005) 490; and text conveniently in Riccobono (1941) 26–75. The pillar is often called "the Lapis Niger" itself which is rather the area of pavement above it—the Latin being misunderstood, e.g., by Momigliano (1963) 107, Colonna loc. cit., Dumézil (1987) 99, Grandazzi (1991) 137, 186f., or Humm (2005) 602, 606.

42. The *vicus iugarius* runs up into the city from the Produce Market, *Forum Holitorium,* past the Saturn Temple on its east side. Cicero warns of oxen, *Div.* 2.36.77 in Dumézil (1987) 101.

CHAPTER 2

1. Raaflaub (1996) 297 points to the importance of a people's integrating other peoples, and so amplifying its military power, as a "well known precondition" for Rome's empire.

2. *RE* s.v. "Palatium" 7f., 16: *Palantion* in Arcadia named as Evander's home by Fabius Pictor (he the first?); all the hill called *Palatium* not *mons Palatinus* till Augustus' day.

3. J. C. Meyer (1983) 17 (local differences), 91–111 and passim; Cornell (1995) 48–57; and Colonna (2005) 483, 533.

4. Aulus Gellius 13.4.4.

5. Chap. 3, below, at n. 19.

6. On the two Luperci groups (one, Quinctii or Quintilii), see Sabbatucci (1988) 96; 94f., the Salii Palatini and Collini, serving Mars and Quirinus respectively; 34f., on the *montani* excluding the Quirinal hill; 101ff. or Colonna (2005) 583, the four regions of Numa's reign; Sabbatucci (1988) 340 or Smith (1996) 156, on the Septimontium ritual; on its probable invention by Varro, Fraschetti (2007) 328; on the three Tribes, their basis unknown, supplying their own cavalry contingents, Palmer (1970) 5–8, 153f., Ampolo (1981) 53, Poucet (1985) 102f., or Cornell (1995) 114, everyone agreeing that the Tribes were not ethnic units; as to later Tribes created by Servius Tullius, some bearing clan names, see Gros and Torelli (1988) 72.

7. Ampolo (1981) 64, 66f.

8. Holloway (1994) 10f. rightly concludes that the identification is not proven, but it is often offered as a fact; 70, the inscribed fragment (. . . UQNU . . .) which Colonna (2005) 535 dates to the end of the seventh century; Holloway (1994) 80, the succeeding pair of temples dated to the fourth century or later though presented as seventh century by Gros and Torelli (1988) 28, or mid-sixth, p. 38; and Holloway (1994) 90, the "international" quality of the finds.

9. Simone (1981) 93; Naso (2001) 231ff.; and Colonna (2005) 534 and Cristofani (1996) 16 on a Latin "accent" in Etruscan of Sant'Omobono and Palatine texts; for Etruscan names at other Roman sites, cf. Colonna (2005) 534, Cristofani (1996) 16 and 45 (Capitoline), and Smith (1996) 103 (Quirinal).

10. Colonna (1981) 63, Vertumnus cult in the vicus Tuscus; Cornell (1995) 224 or Torelli (1999) 17 on *nomina Etrusca* in the early *fasti.*

11. Izzet (2000) 42; Holloway (1994) 71; and Glinister (2000) 58.

12. Smith (2000) 139; earliest pottery, Holloway (1994) 69 or Delcourt (2005) 82; felines, Holloway (1994) 170; altar, 75.

13. Livy 1.34; Dionysius of Halicarnassus, *Ant. Rom.* 3.46.3; 3.47.1f., "driven out by the natives"; and Cornell (1995) 124 adds the concurrence found in Polybius and Cicero, while doubting (with no reason given) any relation between Demaratus and Tarquin; the Corinthian roots made clear in Bickerman (1969) 396; the story outlined by Winter (2005) 241–47 to make Demaratus Etruscan (Tarquinii as Tarquin's "ancestral home"). But I notice the story as given us is taken as usable history by, e.g., Potter (1979) 71, "the ring of truth about it", or Waarsenburg (1995) 235.

14. Vulci is near the coast nearly 100 km northwest of Rome. On the famous François tomb, the best date seems to be ca. 300 or little earlier, cf. Coarelli (1983) 43, Mansuelli (1968) 8 or Alföldi (1963) 214, 225 (and 58, on Demaratus, the sole reference, where the reference, in Polybius 28.19.f., concerns a different Demaratus!); a cautious resumé of the narrative and hypotheses in Pallottino (1987), passim, or Cornell (1995) 138–41; ascribed to events of the mid-fourth century by A. Maggiani in Cristofani (1985a) 310. On Homeric figures at Vulci, see Roncalli (1987) 101f.; on the wide popularity of the subject in Etruria at the time and the Tarquinii tomb, Maggiani (1983) 83f.

15. The Etruscans' debt to Greece is too large a subject for a note, but notice Strabo 5.2.2, that Demaratus raised the level of the arts in his new home by bringing with him a team of Greek artists and artisans. Among moderns, see e.g., Cristofani (1987) 16f., 42f. or Gros and Torelli (1988) 47 on architectural terra-cottas, city wall-construction, etc.

16. Esquiline, eighth/seventh century, Bartoloni and Cataldi-Dini (1980) 126 or Momigliano (1989) 68; Holloway (1994) 82, Attic ware under the *lapis niger.*

17. Chap. 1 at n. 31; Etruscan origins are suggested, not convincingly, for other Roman deities, e.g., Robigo, Gianferrari (1995) 138, or Neptune, cf. Sabbatucci (1988) 245; Smith (2000a) 30, on temple-planning and ceremonial matters (which belong to later times).

18. Naso (2001) 231, three-celled as also the Regia and the second Mater Matuta temple; modeled on Etruscan domestic architecture, Gros and Torelli (1988) 79; Ionic-style antefix-fragments of later sixth century in Capitoline foundations, Danti (2008) 27.

19. Colonna (2005) 582, regarding Vulca—who perhaps never existed, cf. Holloway (1994) 10. In any case, Varro's attributing to Vulca the anthropomorphizing of the Roman gods is obviously false, as has been more than once pointed out, given the depictions of Greek gods in that form on pottery universally in use in central Italy in earlier centuries.

20. Ionic-style antefixes on the Regia, Colonna (2005) 490, cf. the Gorgon ornament in the Sant'Omobono temple, Holloway (1994) 76; at the shrine of Apollo (the Apollinar) in Prata Flaminia, Donati and Stefanetti (2006) 122, an altar in the first half of sixth century; and Diana installed by the sixth king, so tradition said,

on the hill beyond the *pomerium* (Aul. Gell. 13.4.4); for *kouroi,* cf. Cristofani (1985) 17.

21. Kleiklos, Colonna (2005) 534; Cristofani (1987) 15f. on service routines and storytelling; and Greek drinking-vessel terms in seventh-century Etruscan, with many other terms from the seventh century, Simone (1972) 504, 508, Colonna (1973–74) 142f. and Cristofani (1987) 16.

22. Wine and olives, Ampolo (1980a) 31, 33, or Colonna (2005) 580, with tell-tale pottery forms, e.g., 577, in a house not far from Rome (Ficana, seventh century); or *oinochoai* in Satricum, cf. Bartoloni and Cataldi-Dini (1980) 131f.; funeral banquets, Ampolo (1984) 79; symposia in Latium from ca. 670, De Santis (1985) 195, also finding viticulture in Rome at end of the eighth century, 213.

23. Cristofani (1987) 46; in Latium, Smith (1990) 109f., e.g., at Gabii.

24. For "heroic" burial styles similar in southern Etruria and Latium to those of Eretria (post-750), see Torelli (1989) 34. Livy 1.35.8f. reports the invention of the *ludi Romani* and *Magni* and the construction of the Circus Maximus. There is no archaeological evidence for the structure but Gros (1996–2001) 1.346 dates it to the Tarquins together, instancing scenes of races in Etruscan sixth-century friezes, to which I assume Ogilvie (1965) 149 refers when he mentions unspecified "archaeological evidence for the construction". No doubt relying on Livy, Coarelli (1981) 327 dates the Circus to Tarquinius Priscus, and Smith (2000a) 29 allows a track for races at the site in the archaic period.

25. See Ampolo (1980) 168 or Torelli (1999) 3.

26. Colonna (1981) 162, luxury ceramic manufacture; Colonna (2005) 521; "symbiosis", 514; Romans in inscriptions, Momigliano (1989) 81, cf. the Roman at Volsinii, Colonna (2005) 526.

27. Identical molds for pottery, see Colonna (1981) 162; for plaques, cf. Romana Fortunati (1993) 255, 261, and Smith (2000) 144; panthers, in Bartoloni (2006) 68, the date apparently first half of the sixth century; chariot parades at Veii and Rome, cf. Holloway (1994) 75; and Colonna (2005) 681f.

28. Pottery, cf. Colonna (2005) 521; architectural ornament, Colonna (2005) 490; Gorgon motif, Carlucci (2006) 5; large terra-cotta figures for temple roofs, Lulof (1997) 88–94, 103; and on Mater Matuta cult, see Smith (1996) 219 and Torelli (1997) 165, 168.

29. House plans and stone, see J. C. Meyer (1983) 142 or Colonna (2005) 586.

30. Colonna (2005) 523; on rich chamber tombs in vogue for a part of the seventh century in most of Etruria and Latium, see Cristofani (1987) 44f.

31. Rasmussen (2005) 84 and Lulof (2006) passim.

32. Colonna (2005) 681f. On the Orientalizing period, it may be enough to refer only to De Santis (1985) 195ff.

33. The change noted by De Santis (1985) 196 or Torelli (1989) 37 and attributed to a conscious act of the aristocracy (including that at Rome) by Colonna (2005) 504–15, 580, 585f., pointing to the Twelve Tables; but Ampolo (1980) 186f. and (1984) 78–82, followed by Smith (1996) 187, points to the too-long time-lag between the archaeological evidence and the evidence for Rome's sumptuary legislation.

34. Holloway (1994) 88f.; see Smith (1996) 140, that in sixth-century Latium, Greek imported pottery constitutes ca. 1 percent of what is found, showing the rarity of import.

35. On intermarriage (*ius conubii*) with the Sabine Claudii but perhaps also with Valerii and other *gentes,* see Mastrocinque (1996) 43; in the *fasti,* many *gentes* from both Latin and Etruscan centers are shown by names like Auruncus (cos. 501, 493) and Nomentanus, or Tuscus and Aquilii (Etruscan), but also Sabinus (cos. 487), cf. Ampolo (1981) 58–62.

36. "The snatching of the Sabines" was said to explain the names of Rome's thirty Tribes, hence the number of the snatched, though there were several versions of the tale, and larger numbers reported, as in Dionysius of Halicarnassus, *Ant. Rom.,* 2.30.6 and 2.47.3. Thirty was "the usual figure", Ogilvie (1965) 80. For imported eighth- to seventh-century luxury artifacts found in the Sabine city of Cures, see Ampolo (1996) 92; on the Sabine *lingua,* see Peruzzi (1990) 254f. citing Suetonius and Gellius; on the Sabine chief, Titus Tatius, Colonna (2005) 564; and, on the *tribus Claudia* formed for Attus Clausus = Appius Claudius, ibid. 249; the Sabine language is Oscan, Cornell (1995) 43, but very close to Latin (and Umbrian, says Peruzzi 1980, 126); further, Momigliano (1966) 553; and for a Sabine word entering Rome as a name, "Nero", cf. Sabatucci (1988) 100, 115.

37. On Varro, Titus Tatius, Quirinus, etc., see Donati and Stefanetti (2006) 144; also Palmer (1970) 165f., disposing of any Sabine Quirinus; more comprehensively, Poucet (1985) 92ff., 97, 143, 165; and Prosdocimi (1996) 230, 233. Momigliano (1966) 553 saw a "fusion" of the two peoples and their language, witness the two Luperci sets, but Ampolo (1981) 53 dismisses the idea of one Luperci set being Sabine. For later Sabine clans immigrating, cf. Mastrocinque (1996) 42f. and below, chapter 3. J. C. Meyer (1983) 129ff., Dumézil (1983) 123 on Quirinus, and Colonna (2005) 564 hold out for the (variously dated) king legends and early Sabinization.

CHAPTER 3

1. Pierson (1938) 673f., "les Dieux s'en vont".

2. Weems (1850) 7, 10 (chap. 1); chap. 2, the hatchet story.

3. On Augustus and Romulus, cf. Carandini (2000) 131, or Starr (2009) 368; on the cult arrangements, see chap. 1, above, at notes 18ff. and Carandini (2000) 131 and passim. Showing his own belief in the historicity of Romulus are Carandini (1997) xxivf., 119, with nearly thirty collaborators among whom are many that may not share his views but do nevertheless supply buttresses to support them; further, Carandini (2006) 83–87 and passim; and Carandini (2007) 25f. Using strictly philological criticism, Fraschetti (2007) seems to me to have demolished Carandini's reconstruction, and his arguments are not well answered by Carandini (2008), comparing e.g., 448 which simply repeats one of the challenged assertions, cf. above, chap. 1 n. 6.

4. Quoted first on Romulus, Momigliano (1989) 94; quoted second, Cornell

(1995) 61, cf. 68, "Romulus certainly known in Rome before the end of the sixth century", a view roundly reasserted in Cornell (2000) 47, citing support (J. Bremmer, the story dates from the early sixth century, Carandini preferring the era of Romulus himself, the mid-eighth century); also Carandini (2006a) xxi and D'Alessio (2006) 291, pointing to the Lupa as the terminus *ante quem* for the Romulean legend.

5. "Not definitive", quoted from the director, C. Parisi Presicce, for the Comune di Roma, on the decision of February 28, 2007, *La Repubblica* July 9, 2008; expressing, however, "strong doubts" about its antiquity, Parisi Presicce (2000) 19f.; and A. La Regina, superintendent of cultural heritage, *La Repubblica,* February 12, 2007, and July 9, 2008, supporting the much later dating on the basis of many lab tests repeating those of the expert commissioned earlier, A. M. Carruba; further, Lombardi (2002) 612 on the publication of the report expected from Carruba at the time of Lombardi's book.

6. Lombardi 612, finding (602) that thermoluminescent tests indicate a sixteenth-century date for the bronze's latest restoration (which of course indicates nothing about the original work); Formigli (1985) 38f., 46, on technique, very clear and full, indicating the small scale only of "cire perdu" for "la piccola plastica etrusca"; Gale, Giardino, and Parisi Presicce (2005) 133, 137 on the origin of the metals; and Isman (2007) on various experts' views. Mattusch (2007) 14 asserts without substantiation that the lost wax method "is attested for some large bronzes". *Contra,* Carruba (2006) 30 on the three best-known pieces—Arringatore, Chimaera, and Mars of Todi—to which add a fourth, an urn lid of Perugia in Cristofani (1985) 293, all these founded in segments (and all other one-piece sculptures are smaller than a half-meter, in Cristofani's catalog).

7. See Hoving (1996) 92 on Gisela Richter; and similar attributions by experts in style, vs. science, in e.g., Mills and Mansfield (1982) 45ff.

8. Quoted, Bonfante and Whitehead (2007) 3. The recent view of Dardenay (2010) 38, that doubt about the traditional date is too serious to allow use of the evidence, adds nothing.

9. Cristofani (1985) 290f., "The animal's posture makes it impossible that she was suckling the twins", "it can only be intended as a votive offering . . . apotropaic"; compare Neppi Modona (1977) 146f., the small bronze Etruscan male-wolf in the same fierce posture, a votive offering to the netherworld; further on the Lupa, Wiseman (1995a) 63; and Livy 10.23.11, a text suggesting to Carandini (2000) 103 that there was a twinless bronze as old as the Republic.

10. Seventeen Republican examples in Dulière (1979) 2, Nos. 29f., 33f., 38, 45, 49, 53f., 176–80, 186, and 191f., show the sharply turned head, "geste de sollicitude maternelle" (40); likewise in another ca. 160 examples in the catalog up to the early Middle Ages—as against a small number of imperial coins and gems with the wolf in profile (being impossible to show in the traditional way due to the small scale). The importance of the head posture is noted by Cristofani (1985) 291, and the purpose of the Wolf as a votive object. Notice also Varro's mention of a wolf goddess, Luperca, Wiseman (1995) 1; and the belief (among many other alterna-

tives) that a Lupercus was a minor deity protecting the flocks from wolves, and the Lupercal his sanctuary, in *RE* s.v. "Lupercus" col. 1835 (Marbach) or Pensabene (1998) 104.

11. Adam and Briquel (1982) 48, quoted; a work without parallel in any Etruscan setting (36), done for a Praenestine lady (57); declared a fake by Gerhard (1840–97) 5.172, Dulière (1979) 1.73, and Parisi Presicce (2000) 19f., but defended by, among others, Adam and Briquel, Wiseman (1991) 1, Cornell (1995) 63f., Wiseman (1995) 5, Wiseman (1995a) 69, Carandini (2000) 102, Capelli (2000) 233, Carafa (2006) 309, and Dardenay (2010) 35. My fig. 3.2, incidentally, is presumably that published in the *Monumenti dell'istituto di corrispondenza archeologica*, cited by Cornell (1995) xi, for his page 64, and shown again by Wiseman more than once, with an incorrect attribution. The identification of Pan is specially argued by Wiseman; both standing males are seen as shepherds by various scholars, Wiseman (1995a) 69f., though Dardenay (2010) 36 sees Pan in the left-hand figure. Wiseman (1995) 1 would see the twins as the Lares and, (1995a) 71, would relegate the wolf to "a wild beast to symbolize the Feralia", a view so unlikely, it seems to me to invalidate most of the structures and identifications he has proposed for the whole mirror scene.

12. The coin issue with the legend POMANO (*rhomanon* in Greek) is dated to 297 by Parisi Presicce (2000) 21; to 296 by Dulière (1979) 1.19; 2.76; and to these or somewhat later dates by Humm (2005) 321; but better, to the year 269, cf. Classen (1963) 450, Crawford (1985) 31; Pensabene (1998) 68f., or D'Allessio (2006) 314, cf. also ibid. 287, where Coarelli and others are referred to as favoring a fourth-century dating for the foundation legend. Classen (1963) 448 and 557 shows how a local Roman story was fitted into Greek knowledge of Romulus and Rhomos (*sic*) by the mid-fourth century (the spelling also in Plutarch, *Romulus* 6.2); and D'Ippolito (1998) 62 ff. reviews the text evidence to show the story, twins and all, emerging first in Fabius Pictor and his Latin *Annals,* next in Ennius, and later in Greek writers.

13. Quoted, first, Classen (1963) 448, 457; second, on the *lagobolon,* Wiseman (1995) 5. Many would still agree with Cornell (1995) 68, that "Romulus was certainly known in Rome before the end of the sixth century" (unsubstantiated); and Plut., *Romulus* 6.1, describing Faustulus as *suphorbos.*

14. Plutarch, *Romulus* 6.3; passages in Livy such as 1.22.3, *agresti Romani ex Albano agro, Albani ex Romano, praedas in vicem agerent,* leading to war; MacMullen (1974) chap. 1 on pastoral life in the Principate; and on modern Epirus, Campbell (1964) 25, 29, and passim.

15. On the Parilia of April 21, see Beard et al. (1998) 53.

16. Livy 10.27.4; Plut., *Romulus* 3.15, also shows the female wolf to have been once sacred to Mars and the source of the fact to be traced through Fabius Pictor to Diocles of Peparethos of the second half of the fourth century, cf. Chassignet (1996–2004) 1.XLVII and 19. Further, Livy 3.66.4, the Aequi and Volsci are imagined calling the Romans wolves. As to the wolf as apotropaic, cf. above, n. 9; on the Lupercal, Delcourt (2005) 150, with a fuller account in Steinby (1993–2000)

s.v. "Lupercal" (F. Coarelli), the cave site known and restored in Augustus' day; but the chamber in the depths of the Palatine, perhaps for dining and recently glimpsed by a sort of periscope, seems quite clearly not to be the grotto referred to by Dionysius of Halicarnassus, *Ant. Rom.* 1.32.4f. and 1.79.8, *pace* Carandini and Bruno (2008) xiiif. and 11.

17. Spindle whorls and other signs of wool production in Latin burials, e.g., on the Palatine, Bedini and Cordano (1980) 98f.; Zeggio (2000) 332, Esquiline; Smith (1996) 63 (Osteria del'Osa); Colonna (2005) 485; weapons in early Samnite burials, Tagliamonte (1996) 52, 72; in Latin burials, including Rome's, Bergonzi and Bietti Sestieri (1980) 56, bronze spears; Bietti Sestieri (1980) 88, bronze swords; Bedini and Cordano (1980) 101, 109f.; Bartoloni and Cataldi-Dini (1980) 133–36, 146; Bietti Sestieri (1985) 143, 145, tenth-century Lavinium; arms as indicators of rank, Bietti Sestieri (1985a) 168, at Gabii, and at Decima also, Bietti Sestieri (1985b) 185, and in Latium overall in the later 600s, Bietti Sestieri and De Santis (1985) 206, as also Torelli (1989) 34; Torelli (1990) 95–97; Smith (1996) 82, 92 (Decima, chariots, etc.), 110f., emphasizing use of arms, some quite unserviceable but showy, to assert one's greatness; Colonna (2005) 205f., 485, 487, "the warrior nature of the ruling classes", 568f., 574, a war chariot in a woman's tomb at Praeneste; 596, seventh- and sixth-century arms in burials of Sabine lands up the Tiber valley; and on seventh- and sixth-century Etruscan burials (arms of all sorts), see Saulnier (1980) 9f. 50, 64, 69f.

18. City walls are little attested in southern Etruria but common in Latium, e.g., of the eighth and seventh centuries, cf. Bietti Sestieri (1985a) 153f.; Torelli (1989) 36f.; Cornell (1995) 199, 201f.; Smith (1996) 77f., 81, 86, 130, 134; and Colonna (2005) 534.

19. On defenses between the northeastern Palatine and Velia/Carinae, see Smith (1996) 21, 77, 86, 81, interpreted as separating the two ("the settlement was still not unified"), and 153; also Donati and Stefanetti (2006) 129, dating the first wall to the eighth century; for more precise dating to about 725, with its Porta Mugonia, subsequent destruction, then rebuilding in ca. 600 and again in ca. 560, cf. Holloway (1994) 101 or Carafa (2000) 70f.; and "none of these [three successive] walls could have been a defense wall. They were too low and too lightly built . . . a primitive *pomerium*", perhaps, cf. Holloway 101 and Smith (2005) 94.

20. Written sources can be used to suggest separate fortification of each of many early little heights and settlements, see Cornell (1995) 200. The "Servian" wall is of the fourth century or later, cf. Smith (1996) 153, Smith (2000a) 27, or Holloway (2000) chap. 7, summed up at 101. It is still shown as a grand solid line around the whole city of the seven hills, in e.g., Gros and Torelli (1988) 27 fig. 19 or Carandini (2000) 189 map C (and the "Romulean" wall all around the Palatine shown in map B on the preceding page, described pp. 275f., is equally imaginary). M. Andreussi in *LTUR* 3.319–24, relying on studies of the 1930s or earlier, would defend a regal period excluding the Aventine section; Colonna (2005) 583 notes another flank excluded on the Esquiline.

21. Colonna (1988) 56f. offers one of many estimates of the city's size, relying

on the literary tradition for a total of noble proportions (further, n. 28 below).

22. Pascal (1981) 288 and passim; Sabbatucci (1988) 128, 329; Smith (1996) 172 ("perhaps a sort of purification ritual"), 175; Carandini (1997) 317–20; and Beard et al. (1998) 53.

23. *Populus,* cf. Palmer (1974) 6 or Smith (2006) 200; *hostis,* cf. Watson (1975) 154, in the Twelve Tables, *adversus hostem aeterna autoritas,* though perhaps the semantic change *peregrinus* = *hostis* dates only to the fourth century, Gargola (1995) 199; and ibid. 26, on the *pomerium* separating *domi* and *militiae.*

24. Carafa (1998) 105, on Vulcanal datable finds of second half of the eighth century, including arms, with a connection drawn to Livy 1.375, very appropriately (though Livy can only have made a lucky guess at the rites); and 107, 166, Salii in the Praenestine *fasti.*

25. There are difficulties with this flow of names, e.g., disagreements among sources, which I leave aside (e.g., Nomentum). On Gabii, see Livy 1.9f. to 1.54 and Dionysius of Halicarnassus, *Ant. Rom.* 2.33.2 to 4.63.1; further, Cifani (2005) 220. Momigliano (1989) 66, with others, may be right in crediting the survival of the Gabine treaty into the first century.

26. On ninth- to eighth-century Roman domination over nearby Decima, Laurentinum, etc., see Bietti Sestieri and De Santis (1985) 202. Ogilvie (1965) 214, contrasting the dig reports, judges the traditional Signia story "apocryphal" and, for Circeii, offers only complicated possibilities to reconcile archaeology, which best fits with a *colonia* date of 393, and the written source which requires a date pre-508; but Taylor (1960) 53 accepts the possibility of a colony at the site, even though cut off from Rome by Praeneste lands. On Ficana, see Sacchi Lodispoto (1983) 99 and Cifani (2008) 207.

27. For example, the war against Gabii is explained by Livy (1.54) in one excellent anecdote which he lifted from Herodotus 5.92.6, a second less known (3.154), and, as "told by Livy . . . many of the stories are not really Roman but Greek stories reclothed in Roman dress", Ogilvie (1971) 7; but, seen by Ogilvie (1965) 209, the absorption of Gabii by Rome is nevertheless acceptable as a fact.

28. Beloch (1926) 178, regarding the area of the Roman state, strangely ignores the Polybius text; cf. Map 1 and support for it, 141–79; see further, Ampolo (1980) 168 on comparative size of mid-sixth-century Rome vs. Latin, Etruscan, and Greek cities, conveniently again in Cornell (1995) 204–7; the map and area estimates repeated in Cornell (1995) 205f.; and Colonna (2005) 522f., 531ff. on comparative size, Rome vs. Etruscan and Latin centers from the ninth century on.

29. Polybius 3.24.4 and 11f. on states *hypekooi* to Rome, by which Walbank (1957–79) ad loc. understands "an alliance recognizing Rome's military leadership based on a series of separate treaties"; also Last (1928) 859ff.; the treaty perhaps preserved in the Capitoline temple, as suggested by Bremmer and Horsfall (1987) 70, and accepted as real by Wagner (1984) 213, Torelli (1999) 17, with bibliography, and Forsyth (2005) 122f. more recently.

30. Bietti Sestieri and De Santis (1985) 202; Ampolo (1988) 76 or Raaflaub (2005) 13, the Tiber is still seen as Rome's frontier in the Twelve Tables and into the

fourth century; but cf. Humbert (1978) 56, "across the Tiber" in the Twelve Tables means only beyond Rome's holdings in that area; and the southern Etruscan defense-works, in Cifani (2005) 217 and fig. 9, certainly imply some Roman presence or threat in the area close to the city; cf. also Colonna (2005) 523.

31. G. Cifani in his paper to the Ninth Roman Archaeology Conference 2009, "Archaic urbanism in Central Tyrrhenian Italy and its social significance", notes the "rapid economic growth" in the sixth century to be explained only by "an economy based on war booty"; and on the territorial gains, cf. Ampolo (1980) 81f., with a table given again in Gross and Torelli (1988) 80 and Cornell (1995) 207.

32. Dionysius of Halicarnassus, *Ant. Rom.* 2.37.4. Ampolo (1980a) 25ff. discusses ratios of land to sustainable population; 29f., the Roman total proposed for the sixth century is ca. 35,000; accepted with variants higher and lower in Cornell (1995) 205ff. and Smith (1996) 154 and (2006) 174, where one low estimate is of an army of 9,000. The figure for adult males is ordinarily multiplied by four for a total population, see e.g., 28f., though Ampolo cites other scholars who prefer a percentage of two-sevenths to represent adult males, and though Cornell (1995) 207 prefers something less than 30 percent. Regardless, Livy 1.44.1 sets the figure at 80,000 quoting Fabius Pictor much later, on which see e.g., Raaflaub (2005a) 21 ("vastly exaggerated"); and Dionysius of Halicarnassus 4.22.3 adds another 4,700 for good measure, which would indicate a state with a third of a million.

CHAPTER 4

1. Livy 1.52.4, *minime Romana;* Polybius 36.9.9 on Romans' *proairesis;* and Aul. Gell. 3.8.8, quoted in MacMullen (1997) 116, a passage that Broughton (1951–52) 1.194 seems to accept as a real letter from the consuls to Pyrrhus.

2. *Pace* Cornell (1978) 110, "The fact is that an independent or autonomous Latin culture never had a chance to emerge" (where by "Latin" he means Roman).

3. Cf. above, chap. 1 n. 33.

4. Gros and Torelli (1988) 28 or Steinby (1993–2000) 1.310, the Comitium originally quadrangular and oriented, a *templum inauguratum* (Cic., *Rep.* 2.11); its date, later 600s, cf. Ampolo (1980) 166, or perhaps much earlier in use if not in built accommodations, Carafa (2000) 69.

5. Readied for use by a layer of beaten earth, see Gros and Torelli (1988) 68; earliest paving ca. 700–650, Smith (1996) 102 or Carafa (2000) 71; a second paving, De Santis (1985) 196; Torelli (1989) 37; Colonna (2005) 533; Ammerman (1996) 127; Carafa (2000) 68; and dating the first pavement ca. 640, Gros and Torelli (1988) 78, with more and better ca. 600.

6. Ampolo (1980) 166; Smith (1996) 101; in the Republican period, Aldrete (2007) passim.

7. On the Forum Romanum, Smith (1996) 101 and (2000a) 24; Holloway (1994) 86, quoted; on fill to confront flooding, an estimated 20,000 cubic meters in the seventh century, Wiseman (2008) 2; in the Forum Boarium 30,000 (more than a million cubic feet) brought in toward the beginning of the fifth century,

Colonna (1981a) 46; and Ardea's walls, where I suppose a workday of six hours producing six cubic feet of earth per man per day brought from the nearby slopes, over a span of a fortnight, and thus recalculate the one hundred men working for six years, as supposed by Colonna (2005) 579. He compares other walls elsewhere.

8. Coarelli (2008) xviif. and 4, "curioso"; on the "Servian" wall, see above, chap. 3 n. 20.

9. On these various well-known structures, all archaeologically attested before 600, see Ogilvie (1965) 214; De Santis (1985) 196; Smith (1996) 101 and 156f.; Steinby (1993–2000) 1.288; and Colonna (2005) 490, 584.

10. The Capitoline temple, Gros and Torelli (1988) 77; Colonna (2005) 581f. or Albertoni (2008) 14 accepting the tradition of construction begun under the first Tarquin in the 580s and not finished for fifty years; the "Tuscan" plan not known earlier than the Mater Matuta temple, Colonna (1988) 63; datable pottery of 530–510, Danti (2008) 27; the Diana temple, Colonna (2005) 582.

11. By roads, I mean the paved kind of the Appian variety, but for paved streets including the Sacra Via, see Colonna (2005) 534 and Gros and Torelli (1988) 66f.

12. Pallottino (1972) 37, "any choice today among points in time or events as the date of 'the foundation' would be a mere abstraction without the least relevance to the historical truth"; but this scholar's common sense has had little effect. On steps toward unification, see above, chap. 3, on the Luperci, Salii or Suburenses.

13. *Gentes* from Latium were incorporated into the senate in the seventh century, according to tradition, with support from Livy 1.30.2 where we have mention of *gentes* whose first consul is also known in the *fasti,* Tullii (500), Quinctii (471), Geganii (492), Curiatii (453), Cloelii (498), and a *magister equitum* of 494, Servilius; other references to Livy and Dionysius of Halicarnassus in Palmer (1970) 132f. In confirmation of an early clan presence, notice the clan names borne by the older *curiae,* Gros and Torelli (1988) 67f., or Smith (2006) 85, and the clan names of some voting *tribus,* Smith (1996) 196.

14. Ninth-century kin-group patterns, cf. Bergonzi and Bietti Sestieri (1980) 48, 61, 64, 70; Torelli (1989) 34f., on family groups, clans, which stress lineage, in burials in the Alban hills and in parts of Rome; at Gabii, Smith (2000a) 32 citing Bietti Sestieri, or Colonna (2005) 567f., comparing the arms in other Latin sites and on the Esquiline with poor around rich warrior burials, constituting or showing a gens; all archaeological evidence strangely denied by Smith (2006) 155, perhaps because burial patterns are anepigraphic? On show-off arms, see above, chap. 2 n. 32.

15. Quoted on Rome, Waarsenburg (1995) 182; on "C", 147, 293, 298, 310, 317, 321f., "corporate clan", cf. 315, "interpretation of such larger clusters as gentilitial, as opposed to family, burial complexes [here as elsewhere in Latium] is generally accepted".

16. Waarsenburg (1995) 232–37, 321; 322f. on *aes signatum* and its setting; further on the setting and changes down to 600, Colonna (2005) 569ff., 580–86, and Pesando et al. (2005) 67ff.

17. Double names begin in eighth century, standard by the sixth in Etruria

with signs of this in Latium, cf. Colonna (1977) 176, 180f.; tied to self-trumpeting of princely tombs, 188; Momigliano (1989) 99; and Smith (1996) 192, adding the Satrican inscriptions to the Etruscan ones.

18. Luperci colleges, chap. 2 n. 6.

19. Rich houses close to the Regia, see Gros and Torelli (1988) 81; also Holloway (1994) 55 (made possible by landfill); and Carafa (2000) 71 (dated ca. 525).

20. Broughton (1951–52) 1.13; Dionysius of Halicarnassus. *Rom. Ant.* 5.40.3f.; Livy 2.16.4f.; Ogilvie (1965) 272f., supporting an earlier date for Appius Claudius' immigration; and Cifani (2009) 312 n. 2 supplying more bibliography. For *ius conubii* and clans of foreign origin, see above, chap. 2 n. 35; Aronen (1989) passim on the Sabine Valerii; and Smith (1996) 190 arguing that, if *clientes* were protected against fraud in the Twelve Tables, they counted as citizens.

21. Varro, *Res rust.* 1.10.2, *dicebantur,* and a comment by Oakley (1997–2005) 677, "this seems to be an antiquarian construction based on" later practice. Much has been made of the fact that the plots would not have supported a family, therefore access must have been granted to common land, etc. For the history of the discussion, see Palmer (1970) 27f. and Gabba (1991) 184; also Colonna (2005) 570. The Romulean *bina iugera* are sometimes treated as history, e.g., by Momigliano (1989) 100, Colonna (2005) 570, Cifani (2009) 312f.

22. *XII Tab.* 4.5, trans. Johnson et al. (1961) 10; Cifani (2009) 311f. Smith (1996) 26 denies the *gens* inherited jointly; rather, as single members; but I see no sign of such a thing, nor is it clear how it could be administered.

23. Cifani (2008) 185, and (2009) 320f., 323f.

24. Besides much material in previous chapters, it is enough to quote Torelli (1989) 34f., on "the importance which particular family groups had gradually assumed within society from the middle of the eighth century onwards, thus destroying the original economic and social homogeneity which is reflected by the cemeteries of the previous phase".

25. Monarchies in Latin and Etruscan cities: e.g., Livy 1.3; 2.9; 4.17.8; and beyond the literary tradition, at Caere, Giardina (1997) 51.

26. For Romulus' thirty *curiae* and three *tribus,* see Livy 1.13.6ff., Dionysius of Halicarnassus, *Rom. Ant.* 2.7, and Varro, *Lingua Lat.* 5.55 quoting Ennius. All these passages fit together, but the Romulean date is rightly rejected by e.g., Ogilvie (1965) 80; and on less than thirty *curiae,* notice the so-called "old" ones in Varro, *Lingua Lat.* 5.155 and their number, four, in Festus 186 (p. 180, ed. W. M. Lindsay), *veteres* "of Romulus' creation"; further, Palmer (1970) passim, e.g., 76f. for more *curiae* names, a total of seven "Old", which derive both from places and *gentes;* 83f., on assemblies; 131, on the "Old" to which (138, 189) three more are added in the early Republic, making thirty; on cults, 71, 80 and Sabatucci (1988) 24, 60ff. Mommsen (1969) 3, 1, 9 and 90, took a tricky phrase (Gell. 15.27.5), that voting in the Curiate Assembly was *ex generibus hominum,* to mean that *curia* members were all in some *gens.* He is followed by Momigliano (1963) 111 and Cornell (1995) 116. Palmer (1970) 69–75 studies the usage carefully and concludes the phrase instead points to old, original villages—which I accept.

27. On the Curia Hostilia, cf. Ampolo (1980) 166 (dated ca. 600), Gros and Torelli (1988) 78 (dated ca. 640), Torelli (1989) 37 (dated 600), or Colonna (2005) 579 (dated ca. 620). A good summary in Poucet (1985) 105, that a monarchy, senate, *tribus,* and *curiae* are all "highly probable" by the reign of the first Tarquin, but we can say no more.

28. Torelli (1999) 16f. on the Satricum inscription with Publicola's name and "condottieri" followers.

29. Dionysius of Halicarnassus, *Ant. Rom.* 4.22.3, with other figures according, 4.19.1; and Livy 1.44.1.

30. On Rome's area of rule, see above, chap. 3 at nn. 29ff.

31. Livy 7.25.10, trans. B. Radice; Brunt (1971) 510, estimating 216,000–270,000 troops from Italy, another 48,000–60,000 provincials in 43; and at the time Livy was writing, there were still twenty-eight legions plus large numbers of auxiliary troops in arms, therefore many times the number he is in awe of.

32. Arms: chap. 3 at n. 17.

33. Torelli (1989) 35f.; Waarsenburg (1995) 92f., supposing hoplite fighting from 650/625, although the equipment (not the massing) had been common much earlier; 95, 108, 170f. pl. 25f., sword and spearheads, eighth and seventh centuries; Torelli in Gros and Torelli (1988) 70 on "a falangist revolution", with Waarsenburg (1995) 92 on the sudden reduction of arms in graves post-650 (of which I can't see the relevance).

34. See Ducati (1927) 1.201 and fig. 222, on Vulci in 625–575; the convincing treatment of the art and phalanx in Etruria offered by Spivey and Stoddart (1990) 128–31 with fig. 76, a Greco-Etruscan amphora of ca. 530; 129f., hoplite arms of eighth to seventh century in Etruria; as also (129) at Rome; also at Lavinium or Gabii, Colonna (2005) 558, 569; and Cristofani (1987) 64, on bronze depictions of fully armored warriors glorifying the individual fighter, not a hoplite class. Cornell (1995) 184 seems confused in asserting the adoption of the hoplite phalanx in Etruria and Rome by 675 or earlier, while (435) quoting Spivey and Stoddart in support of his view, though they deny it (loc. cit.).

35. See Ogilvie (1965) 83, on Livy 1.15.8; 152 on 1.36.7; Palmer (1970) 30f., 34; and Wiseman (1994) 11, dating the *celeres* to the late fourth century or later.

36. Cornell (1995) 176 on the Tribes, and quoted; Smith (2006) 177, 188, on Tullius' four Tribes.

37. See Colonna (2005) 511 (cavalryman's armor, Lanuvium in the 470s) and 647 (horse armor, Eretum). Ogilvie (1965) 288 points to evidence of warriors, "mounted hoplites", riding to battle and then fighting on foot; and Cascarino (2007) 29 imagines these latter also.

CHAPTER 5

1. Clans were as old as the *luperci* (chap. 2 n. 6) and are attested archaeologically from the period of the kings in neighboring societies just like archaic Roman,

with their princely tombs (chap. 4 nn. 14f.; n. 19 on princely homes in Rome); so there can be no doubt of their early prominence.

2. Livy 1.59.6, the coup by the *primores civitatis;* foremost, Brutus and Lucretius, the prefect of the city (§12), with the senate filled up by *equites* called, with their descendants, "enrolled", *conscripti* (2.1.10f.); for Dionysius of Halicarnassus emphasizing *patricii* as opposed to the populace or masses, *demos,* throughout his account, see *Ant. Rom.* 4.73.1; 4.76.3f.; 4.78.1; 4.81.1, *patricii,* "the illustrious, the grand"; 4.82.4; 4.84.4; M. Horatius agent of the king, 4.85.3; and Broughton (1951–52) on the four *gentes* named, giving a consul and several tribunes of the people down to 423 (Junii), five consuls to 457 (Horatii), six to 429 (Lucretii), and ten to 437 (Valerii).

3. Cornell (1995) 11, "It is quite wrong to dismiss the story of (e.g.) Virginia as fiction simply because it cannot be shown to be based on fact. It cannot be shown to be fiction either"—which would explain the writer's acceptance of Romulus as a historical fact (above, chap. 3 n. 4); and the interpretive principle is applied, e.g., at 275 ("no evidence that they [annalists] invented", therefore we have the truth). In quite another context, the logic of the statement ("simply to accept as not untrue even what is not proved true") is confronted head-on by Ungern-Sternberg (2005) 82.

4. Luce (1977) xixff., elsewhere making plain that the target of interest is not the historicity of Livy's account but its literary methods—though necessarily touching on its reliability. See, e.g., p. xxi, "For five chapters Livy reproduces the version of the historian Valerius Antias (38.50.5). At a point roughly two-thirds of the way through the story he interrupts to inform us that there is absolutely no agreement among the authorities he has consulted, including Antias, on even the most basic facts he has just told and that he has no idea whom or what to believe (56.1). After discussing some of the knottier problems for two chapters, he returns to Antias' account in order to finish off the story"; and Diodorus Siculus on Republican Rome is generally seen as no better, cf. Poma (1984) 116. I may instance, out of a hundred differences in names and dates between this latter author and the better known, Rathmann (2005) 429, on the founding of Luceria. For even broader disparagement of the literary tradition by philologists, see Wiseman (1979) 24f., 52, and passim and (2008) 18; Mitchell (1990) 236, "Livy had little or no reliable information about anything before the third century", etc.; Cornell (2005) 60, too long to quote, but by a defender of the tradition; or Humm (2005) 261, "the problem of the sources is obviously crucial . . . where these are few, late, and little to be trusted, peu fiable". Cf. from a law perspective, Jolowicz (1952) 10 on the Struggle of the Orders: where "details belong for the most part to the period of traditional history, and what is said by the historians is, at least in part, mythical, the difficulties of reconstruction are increased by a tendency to read far back into the mythical past reforms which, in fact, took place comparatively late" (a point made by many scholars in the succeeding sixty years).

5. Develin (2005) 294.

6. Pais (1920) ii, reacting to the reception of his *Storia critica di Roma*

(1913–20); regular use of the word, e.g., in Richard (1978) 37 to brush off the opposition, or Develin (1985) 14, Cornell (2005) 61, Humm (2005) 17f., Cifani (2009) 313, or Dardenay (2010) 12, to brush away any doubts about Dionysius Halicarnassus and Plutarch.

7. Fraccaro (1957) 65, in debate with L. Pareti.

8. Momigliano (1989) 90, quoted; Oakley (2002) 452. For some of the problems in the written sources, see recent indications in Sandberg (2000) 130 n. 33; for the late 500s in particular, a range of confidence showing in Grandazzi (2008) 1.77 on Porsenna, "about whose occupation of Rome for a time, there is today unanimous agreement", in contrast to Cornell (1995) 217, regarding Porsenna, where we have "no more than speculation . . . but no reason in principle why the tradition should not be a romanticised version of events that really happened".

9. See Cornell (2004) 115f. on the Romans' skimping of coverage of the early Republic; Marincola (2009) 16, on the hourglass shape of Fabius' coverage of Roman history; Peter (1967) 1.5–39 or the slightly expanded listing in Chassignet (1996–2004) 1.16–54, where a majority of the citations and much more than a majority of the pages of Fabius Pictor are devoted to the period pre-509; and, for the Taormina *dipinto,* Manganaro (1974) 392, fig. 2; 394, the text; 398, "Philinos" to be inserted; the date moved up by Blanck (1997) 248; distribution shape confirmed by Dionysius of Halicarnassus 1.6.2 saying of both Fabius Pictor and Cincius Alimentus, "what followed the city's founding they ran over superficially"; and note also Gnaeus Gellius writing ca. 130 and in his Book 15 (out of ninety-seven!) reaching only to the year 389, his work being exhaustively used in turn by Dionysius and by Licinius Macer, cf. Raaflaub (2005a) 2; and Macer served as Livy's principal source for the Republic, see Ogilvie (1965) 272, 336. True, Pictor and Macer and others survive only in scattered quotations, and Cornell (2004) 116f. offers reasons for caution in estimating coverage from such fragments. A specific improvement in the record that survived for use by the late writers can be noticed as the fourth century goes on, cf. Oakley (1997–2005) 1.39, or around the turn of the fourth to the third century, cf. Cornell (2004) 120—despite the alleged loss of records (Livy 6.1.2). Cornell, however, here contradicts his earlier view (1989, 289) that very elaborate narrative indicates it is "historically authentic".

10. On dated temples, see above, chap. 1 at nn. 28ff. for the regal period or, e.g., the Castor temple, Ampolo (1990a) 487. On the Twelve Tables, see chap. 1 n. 40; on the treaty, the *foedus Cassianum,* Humbert (1978) 68 and 92 on Cic., *Pro Balbo* 23.53, and Livy 2.33.9, along with a fragment of Cato, Ampolo (1988) 80; also Cornell (1995) 299 and H. Galsterer in *Neue Pauly* 4.581. On the *fasti consulares,* see Broughton (1951–52) 1.xi, "I am inclined to accept almost the entire list of eponymous magistrates", i.e., consuls; with some doubts about the fifth century, A. H. McDonald and S. R. F. Price in *OCD* s.v. "Fasti" 588; Ogilvie and Drummond (1989) 18f.; Oakley (1997–2005) 31f.; generally trusting of *fasti* for the period pre-264, even pre-366, Richard (2001); trusting, back to 473, Eder (1990) 28; more skeptical (as I agree), Holloway (2008) 120–24. Linderski (2007) 638 is reluctant to dismiss a recent argument of R. Bunse, that it was not two consuls but

a *praetor maximus* and two *praetores minores* who ran the state from 444–367; but the disturbance to well-settled beliefs among the later Romans seems to me far too great to consider this. On the *fasti triumphales,* less reliable until the third century, see Ogilvie and Drummond (1989) 19; on conflicts with other sources, see e.g., Pais (1920) vi, ix, xiiif., 46 (all, with Livy), and 56f., in summary, or Humbert (1978) 182; but cf. Cornell (1989) 290f., making a case for a more trusting dependence.

11. On historical frescoes, the most famous were painted by the elder Fabius Pictor in a temple dedicated in 302 (Valerius Maximus 8.14.6 and Pliny, *Nat. hist.* 33.19). Very fragmentary paintings in an Esquiline tomb show figures of various sizes, mythic or heroic with names written above including a Fabius, see e.g., Hölscher (1978) 347ff. and Abb. 2; of disputed date, early third century, or first half, or generally third, so, Bianchi Bandinelli (1970) 114f., 403, and fig. 117, Cornell (1995) 390, or Holliday (2002) 83–90, or Baldassare et al. (2003) 46; or possibly first century ("a faithful copy", Bianchi Bandinelli 11), so, Croisille (2005) 160, 167, and fig. 117. On memorials, Degrassi (1987) 522; Cornell (2004) 119; Farrell (2005) 424; on portraits, Appius Claudius Caecus' the first, see Humm (2005) 46f. and Holloway (2008) 116f.; on narrative ballads centuries earlier than their only mention, Poucet (1985) 62 and Herzog (1988) 73, scholars representative among oral-tradition or "oralture" specialists, in their skepticism of that genre: "it was not meant to serve in the investigation of the true past" (*Wahrheitsfindung*). In very valuable pages, Oakley (1997–2005) 1.16–65, discusses the sources from 509 to ca. 225, but (1.23f.) indicates a faith in oral tradition which he doesn't defend and which I think could not stand up, unless he means only the vague outline or emotional coloration of recollected events.

12. Appius Claudius Caecus, consul in 307 and 296, was the first and oldest hero eulogized in *CIL* 11.1827 = Degrassi (1937) *Elogia* p. 19 no. 12 and p. 59 no. 79, cf. e.g., Livy 10.18 to explain the inscription's *complura oppida de Samnitibus cepit,* etc.; Humm (2005) 51–56, indicating no faith in the survival of an original inscription. *ILLRP* pp. 178f. no. 309 gives us the career of Scipio Barbatus cos. 298, where (in ancient spelling which is not likely to have been invented by the recutting on his sarcophagus, but with differences from Livy 10.12.5 and the *fasti triumphales,* Pais [1920] 65) his offices are recalled and how he "took Taurasia, Cisauna, Samnium, and subdued all Lucania and carried off hostages" (also *CIL* I², 2, 377 nos. 6f. dated to the third century, A. Degrassi; the date defended, 2, 4 [1986] 859, against those who doubt the recutting, among whom, more recently, is Cornell [1995] 466); accepted as texts, though of late third century, by Humm (2005) 362, or recut ca. 190, Wiseman (2008) 7.

13. For speeches surviving, see e.g., Franke (1989) 171 on the best known, that of Appius Claudius Caecus; more fully in Humm (2005) 63, adding that of Menenius Agrippa in Livy 2.32 and Florus 1.17.23, with Ogilvie (1965) 312f. For various observations on oral tradition relevant to the Roman version, see the classic Vansina (1985), e.g., at xiif., 99f., 104, 168, 189; further on falsifications, examples in Henige (1974) 197f. or Raaflaub (2005) 66; specifically on the Roman version,

Ungern-Sternberg (1988) 248, "the problem of historicity in the oral tradition can only be addressed with the greatest caution"; further, 250 n. 68, on Cornell's championing of Roman legends as evidence; and as the best of authorities, Oakley (1997–2005) 1.23f., concluding that later writers "drew on the collective, and accepted, oral memory of the nation". On early Roman literacy, cf. Poucet (1985) 63f.; Cornell (1995) 104f., 421; and E. A. Meyer (2004) 37, where scholars "agonize" over the problems.

14. On the sources for the early Republic, a place to start is Dionysius of Halicarnassus, sharply skeptical and critical of earlier writers especially the Greek, e.g., at *Ant. Rom.* 1.73.1, cf. Delcourt (2005) 53f.; in a large body of modern scholarship, see Oakley (1997–2005) 2.38 on *lectisternia* and (2002) 453 and passim; further, Gabba (1991) 10, 12, 94; Cornell (1995) 13 and Cornell (2004) 120, on the input from the *Annales Maximi* for ca. 300 and afterward; further, Holloway (2008) 109f.; Poucet (1985) chap. 1 passim, e.g., 61 on official or priestly records, "documents historiques, probablement squelettiques"; similarly in Holloway (1994) 1; again in Fraschetti (2007) 327, noting "the well known meagerness of epigraphic material" in early Rome and "beyond that, the extremely late emergence of Roman historiography" toward the end of the third century; but of course some of even this bare-bones official-appearing documentation may be invented or misreported, cf. e.g., Ampolo (1981) 55; further, Ogilvie and Drummond (1989) passim, skeptical or unbelieving across the board; specifically (19) on the *fasti triumphales*, *pace* Cornell in the same volume (292), who supposes that the more elaborate an account, the truer to history. There are to be added the annalistic mentions of colonial foundations whose dates are quite often to be confirmed archaeologically, as e.g., at Narnia, Lackner (2008) 128.

15. Cornell (1995) 13; Oakley (1997–2005) 1.25, 28.

16. Texts on shields, Cornell (1995) 210f.; more examples, Holloway (2008) 16, but of doubtful historicity; an inscription on a bronze corselet with the consular date (241) and the boast to explain the piece, "at the capture of Falerii", confirming the *fasti triumphales*, cf. Zimmermann (1986) 37–40; Donati and Stefanetti (2006) 96, a treaty on a bronze tablet; in temples, Ampolo (1981) 54f.; and Oakley (1997–2005) 1.34, collecting various other examples.

17. Cato frg. 77 (Gellius 2.28.6) and Cic., *Leg.* 1.6 (*ieiunius*), in Chassignet (1996–2004) 1.1 and XLI; a full evaluation in Frier (1999) concluding (177f.), "ancient authors . . . proceeded to reassemble mentally a probable form of the chronicle . . . from which it was an easy step to the recreation of its history" (read, "invention").

18. Among various indicators of the bad quality and small usefulness of Greek writers for historical information about Rome, pre–Fabius Pictor, see esp. Polybius 12.3–28 and 12.4b–c on Timaeus and others; similarly, Dionysius of Halicarnassus, cf. Delcourt (2005) 54. The same author (*Ant. Rom.* 1.6.1) found no history of Rome in Greek earlier than the first half of the third century; and this, only a sketch, cf. Gruen (1992) 26. Greek writers paid very little attention to the date of the earlier ones they relied on, an illustration being Dionysius' characterizing "Cephalon of Gergis" (*Ant. Rom.* 1.72.2) as "really ancient", *sungrapheus palaios*

panu, the person in question being a pseudonym for Hegesianax no further back than ca. 190, cf. Gabba (1991) 12. An exception, but adding nothing to Roman knowledge except a misnomer, is Aristotle's mention of the city's capture by the Gauls (but "Lucius" for "Marcus"), cf. Bremmer and Horsfall (1987) 63.

19. "Fog", Holloway (1994) 1. In a spirited defense of the truthfulness of the Roman literary tradition, Lendon (2009) disregards its changes with the data base and seems otherwise unpersuasive regarding the Republic; but (I would say) the attempt makes no fit at all with the Monarchy, e.g., at 44: we may trust what we are told because "in fact the tradition about early Rome, as we receive it, is quite consistent"(!); yet on the same page a large fact found throughout the tradition is cited only to reject it (regarding Demaratus, cf. chap. 2 n. 13, above; more generally, above, n. 13). A better-reasoned defense of the historicity of the written sources is offered by Cornell (2004), who, however, is quite ready (p. 124) to dismiss a very important scene in Livy as "the product of rhetorical invention" and perfectly anachronistic, though appearing to explain motivation.

20. Livy 3.47.5, on his own sources' inauthenticity, where he speaks of the mid-fifth century and must draw on them, "if by chance the ancient writers contain any truth" (*forsan aliquem verum auctores antiqui tradiderint*); and on estimating probabilities, Forsythe (1999), e.g., 47 or chap. 3 passim.

21. Forsythe (1999) 60f.

22. On the avenging of the Caudine Forks in Livy 8.38–8.40, see Forsythe (1999) 68f. ("very little, if any at all, can be accepted as historical"), with Oakley (1997–2005) 4.585 concurring; and these two titles may serve to show a good range of notices about contradictions, variants, and embellishment in the Roman historians. For Spurius Cassius, see Ogilvie (1965) 337f. and Zevi (1988) 130f.

23. Above, chap. 1 n. 36 and Harris (1979) 171 on fetial dress, etc.; on a reference in Plautus and instances past 200, ibid. 166–69; on the institution attributed to Servius Tullius by Cicero, *Rep.* 2.17.31; as to lustration of army, see Gargola (1995) 16; that fetial rites were gradually disused in the old form, see Ogilvie (1965) 110, but continued in a bogus form, 127f., by denominating a bit of land near the city as "hostile", at which the rituals could be aimed. "The Romans liked such fictions", says Taylor (1960) 75.

24. For the chickens text, cf. Mommsen (1969) 1.84f. and Bruns (1909) 2.77; Palmer (1970) 88; Crawford (1971) 133, depictions datable to 260–242; and Linderski (2007) 14, 169f. on *pullarii.*

25. D'Ippolito (1998) 72, commenting on a Livy text for 390; Wiseman (2008) 306, dating the surviving *fas/nefas* days to the fifth or fourth century; yet the Twelve Tables recognize *dies fasti,* Riccobono (1941–43) 71, tab. 11.3; ibid.1.62 (where a patron who cheats his client is consigned to divine punishment as *sacer*).

26. On the importance attaching to what priests said, the only source is the literary tradition, where they are always in charge, but generally obliging; North (1990) 51f. supposes secular officials were "in control" (52) but at the same time, not (53); better, Gargola (1995) 15; and on the importance that the nobles attached to religious control, especially the *auspicia,* see Oakley (1997–2005) 2.20f.

27. Above, chap. 1 n. 33; Linderski (1990) 36f.

28. Taylor (1960) 6; below, chap. 8.

29. Cf. chap. 1 at n. 33: and in D'Ippolito (1998) 36–41, interesting pages on the principal institutions of the regal period.

30. *Sacer,* see above, n. 25. Richard (1978) 161, 164, 167, insists *clientes* were not citizens because they couldn't sue at law; but, besides preferring the authority of Dionysius over the Twelve Tables, he rests his case only on Magdelain (1971) 106, who makes the assertion without the least support.

31. In Riccobono (1941–43) 1.38–40, Table 5.4f. and 7a, the estate (*familia*) left without an heir or in the hands of a madman reverts to the nearest agnate relative and, if such be lacking, to the clansmen (*gentiles*); see also Gabba (1991) 184 and Cifani (2009) 311ff., 315. But clan ownership does not rule out ownership by private individuals or families.

32. Although Beard et al. (1998) 1.67 deny these *gens*-cults before the late Republic, in fact a number are well attested, e.g., the one supported by the Sabine Valerii on the campus Martius which, in the mid-third century, was partly taken over as public *ludi,* cf. Aronen (1989) 19–21, 27; also the Hercules cult supported by the Potitii and Pinarii on the Capitoline, taken over in 312, cf. Smith (1996) 199 or F. Coarelli in *LTUR* (1993–2000) 3.16; cults of the Fabii in at least the fourth century, 200f. and Coarelli (2006) 45; others including *gentes* settled in Rome since the fourth century, Farney (2007) 42–46; perhaps some of those mentioned by Macrobius 1.16.7 or *CIL* 14.2387 (the Iulii in Bovillae, second or first century). For repudiation of *gens*-cults, Bruns (1909) 1.76.

33. See D'Ippolito (1998) 40f. Humm (2005) 459 offers two reasons to discard the text, both of which can be contested. For capital punishment in the centuriate assembly meaning *maximus,* cf. Riccobono (1941–43) 1.64, Tab. 9.1.2, Cic., *Sest.* 65, Richard (1978) 549, and Bringmann (2007) 14; for the hours of use for litigation, see Riccobono (1941–43) 1.28, Tab. 1.6f.

34. Recent work with bibliography, Holloway (2009) 71ff.

35. The Comitium was used to pass laws, which was very rarely attempted in the *centuriata,* cf. Sandberg (2000) 134. For steps up to the (later so-called) Rostra, of ca. 500, see Coarelli (1983–85) 1.132, 137, Momigliano (1989) 75, Carafa (1998) 132, Colonna (2005) 584, or Coarelli (2007) 53; for the square shape and orientation to points of the compass, a *templum,* see Coarelli (1983–85) 1.139; a level plaza, 1.150f.; a circular shape post-293, 1.148f., or more precisely at the beginning of the First Punic War, Coarelli (2007) 53 and (2008) 57—so also Morel (1989) 487; inaugurated and square, Gros and Torelli (1988) 28 or Steinby (1993–2000) 1.310. Earlier, Coarelli had dated the circular shape in or soon after 290 but only completed in 263, cf. Coarelli (1983–85) 1.149ff.

36. A plan is often shown in Coarelli's works, e.g., Coarelli (2007) 52 fig. 15; dimensions, Coarelli (1983–85) 1.148 (40 × 40m) and fig. 39; the larger possible crowd total at 5,000 in MacMullen (1980) 456; around 4,200 in Scheidel (2006) 217, splitting the difference between my figures and Mouritsen's (below, n. 42).

The triangular shape suggested by Carafa (1998) 152 fig. 25 for the Comitium post-370 seems to me impossible, as also to Coarelli although Patterson (202) 217f. seems to prefer it; in the reduced, circular form with a diameter of thirty meters, room for "several hundreds, standing, if not rather more than a thousand", Thommen (1995) 364; regarding participants standing not sitting, see Forni (1994) 1.21 or Carafa (1998) 123. Of the encumbrances, the statue of the augur Naevius was ascribed to a king, the Graecostasis, much later, the bronze shrine to Concordia dated to 304, the statue of Marsyas and Greek hero statues at the beginning of the third century, plus those of the Sibyls, of Camillus, and others, see Coarelli (1974) 70 and (2007) 54. The Maenian column postdated 338, see Coarelli (1983–85) 1.134, 149f.

37. Citizen numbers in Ampolo (1980a) 28ff.; Raaflaub (2005) 21; on speakers first to face the Forum, Forni (1994) 1.21 or Thommen (1995) 362f.

38. *Clientes* were citizens, above, n. 30 and chap. 4 n. 20; *patroni* had clear legal obligations understood before the end of the monarchy, Watson (1975) 102ff.; on *curiae,* Palmer (1970) 80 and 138 (dining halls; the number thirty by the end of the sixth century); 83, *curiae* meet in the Comitium. *Pace* Carafa (1998) 103f., 176, the passages from Dionysius, though confusing the Comitium with its adjacent or enclosed *vulcanal,* show the latter as a regular meeting place, not the Forum. Coarelli (2007) 56 notes that "various witnesses situate the [Vulcanal] in the Comitium near the Graecostasis".

39. Livy 3.17.4 of the year 460, where the *populus* gathers in the Forum only for an emergency, by implication not the normal meeting place (*comitia interim in foro sunt);* quoted is Coarelli (2005) 25 characterizing the suggestion of Mouritsen (2004) 41. Humm (2005) 607f. accepts the dimensions of the Comitium but simply dismisses the evidence of Plutarch and Cicero on the turn toward the Forum, in 145 or 123.

40. Mouritsen (2004) 32, 40 places only the election of "lower magistrates" in the Comitium but Coarelli (2005) 25f. misreads him to include *all* elections. The use of the Comitium for legislation is agreed, cf. Varro, *Res rust.* 1.2.9, and Cic., *Laelius de amicitia* 96 cited by Coarelli.

41. Coarelli (2005) 26; Mouritsen (2001) 19f. looks at the circular later phase of the space in which notionally 3,600 to 4,800 might fit, though he is doubtful of so high a figure; quoted (32) on the "tiny proportion".

42. Mouritsen (2001) 21ff. and 32 would lower my own estimates for the late Republic, and may be right; Develin (2005) 300 suggests their retrojection, and "relatively few would ever vote in regular circumstances". The population estimates for 290 can be derived from Beloch (1926) 217 and 621. I note the rejection of the low percentage by Coarelli (2005) 26, since "everything we know about Roman *libertas* (understood as citizenship) shows that, on the contrary, the right to vote was exercized [!] by the whole citizen body"—this view (like Humm's, above, n. 39) asserted without evidence or discussion.

43. The Jupiter temple was dedicated 509 and that of Castor begun 496 and

dedicated 484, cf. Holloway (1994) 1, 7f.; Zevi (1988) 121f., 125, 127, and Colonna (2005) 582, temples of Saturn 501/497, Mercury 495, Ceres 493, and Semo Sanco 466; lastly, the temple of Apollo in 431, Torelli (2006) 578.

44. On the economic downturn, using the tradition, see Brunt (1971a) 50; using the archaeology, J. C. Meyer (1983) 162, Poma (1984) 74ff., Cornell (1995) 66, D'Ippolito (1998) 49 (rejecting a denial of the downturn), Colonna (2005) 1.326, 493, 504, 506f., 511–13, Patterson et al. (2004) 6, or Raaflaub (2005b) 192, where Latium's and especially Rome's economic retreat is dated in the later sixth and first half of the fifth century or later still. For a cap on burial expenditures, see Riccobono (1941–43) 1.66ff., XII Tab. 10.3, 6. *Pace* Colonna (2005) 585f., the idea that restrictions on funerary *luxus* in the Twelve Tables is reflected in the cutback in grave goods, earlier, is rightly rejected by Ampolo (1984) 80ff., followed by Smith (1996) 187. The phenomenon antedates the law by several generations.

45. Riccobono (1941–43) 1.27, tab. 1.4, *proletarii* as distinct from *assidui;* 32f., tab. 3.1–5, chaining of debtors; 52, Tab. 6.1, *nexum;* 61, Tab. 8.18 on interest limits (12 percent).

46. "Residents", above, chap. 4 n. 13; Riccobono (1941–43) 1.63, Tab. 8.27, *sodales;* Waltzing (1895–1900) 1.35, a traders' festival under Mercury at the time of the dedication of a temple to him in 495; 1.36, the guild thus initiated, Livy 2.21; and 1.62–65, more on early guilds, under Numa and so on down to 367 (Livy 5.50.4).

47. See Oglivie (1965) 309; but he himself credits the general outline of the tradition.

48. On the shrunken curiate representation, cf. Taylor (1966) 21, Sandberg (2000) 133 ("possibly toward the end of the fourth century"), or Humm (2005) 201; as to the *comitia tributa* which I set in the wake of the first secession, Ogilvie (1965) 310, 381, would set it in 471 but grants that a tribal assembly must have been invented in 493 to elect the tribunes of the people (which is a quibble). Other conjectures have been proposed.

49. Cornell (1995) 178 reflects a scholarly consensus long established: "it seems certain that they [Tribes] were connected with the census . . . probably from the very beginning". The earliest history of the *tribus* is, however, full of questions. It seems unlikely that those outside the city would bear *gentes*-names, as they do, if they had been created after 494. Cornell (2000a) 70 dates the first ones to Romulus; other scholars, to Servius Tullius, e.g., Smith (2006) 177, while Alföldi (1965) 306f. preferred a date some decades post-495. Among others, Taylor (1960) 47 notes the check in new Tribe creation in 495, at a total of twenty-one, till 387, *pace* Alföldi. More detailed speculation, e.g., Humm (2006) 46, seems to me idle. For voting by Tribes in the *concilium plebis* just as in the *comitia tributa* (of course not by *curiae, gentes*-dominated, despite some scholarly conjecture), see Sandberg (2000) 133f. or Develin (2005) 309.

50. Assemblies by Tribes with patricians presiding must be inferred, since not to do so would be "bizarre", Oakley (1997–2005) 2.182. Mitchell (1990) 187f. or Humm (2005) 422–28 are among many who suppose, I think rightly, that the dif-

ferent sorts of tribal assembly were different only as regards the magistrate presiding.

51. Dionysius of Halicarnassus, *Ant. Rom.* 10.57.5, says those drafting the Twelve Tables drew "from the Greeks and from their own unwritten customs". On orality, M. von Albrecht is quoted in E. A. Meyer (2004) 37; 71, where laws are seen as spells, *carmina;* and quoted on patrician domination, De Martino (1979) 1.47.

52. Silence in Livy on law; disdain in Dionysius of Halicarnassus, cf. Poma (1984) 160.

53. Identification of *patricii* with *patres* in certain texts, the view of many, or with *gentes,* De Martino (1979) 1.53; and there are many other debates. Mitchell (1990) 90 summarizes the consensus (before arguing for his own views); or see Richard (2005) 110 on *patricius* defined pre-509. On the marriage ban, see Ungern-Sternberg (2005) 79, with Linderski (2005) 223f. explaining special marriage rites by which patricians held on to some priesthoods.

54. For plebeians where they shouldn't be, see e.g., Mitchell (1990) 5, 19f., Forni (1994) 1.430f., or Raaflaub (2005b) 199; at 189, proper emphasis on the rise of rich plebeians.

55. As for example, Cornell (1995) 265, "Mommsen was absolutely right".

56. Brunt (1971a) 47; Mitchell (1990) 18; Oakley (1997–2005) 2.23. And I quote Richard Savage (*The Bastard* 1.8).

57. On the close relation, in points a virtual identity, between priestly and jurisdictional powers, see above, n. 26 and Jolowicz and Nicholas (1972) 89. The opening of the pontificate came in the same year as the opening of other priesthoods to plebeians by the Ogulnian law.

58. See Ungern-Sternberg (2005a) 324.

59. On the early dates in the tradition, cf. Manzo (2001) 48, 63–93 passim; good texts for the patrician gobbling up of *ager publicus* are Livy 3.1.2f.; 4.48.2; 4.51.5; 6.14.11; and 6.39.10. Humbert (1978) 62ff. lists the years of agitation and accepts that they reflect a large truth, though some portion is invention; to the same effect, many others, e.g., Brunt (1971) 28 or (1971a) 51; and, on patterns of landownership close to Rome seen in excavation in the fifth and fourth centuries, fitting with the tradition of the Licinian-Sextian law (but of course not proving it), see Tomei 668ff.

60. Classicists like Forsén (1991) 14–50 or Cornell (1995) 461f. cite many scholars who deny the historicity of the Licinian land-law; add e.g., Gabba (1991) 186f. or Oakley (1997–2005) 1.676f., who sees in Livy 6.36.11 "an antiquarian construct" regarding allotment size for the poor, two *iugera.* But the number fits quite well with others in Livy that he cites. Accepting the tradition more or less entire are Jolowicz (1952) 14, Brunt (1971) 30, or Manzo (2001) passim; and Patterson et al. (2004) 6 cites other scholars to agree with, that the settlement patterns so far excavated fit with a rise post-367 of a new class of owners. The archaeology is of course very thin, a problem now generally expected for the fourth and third centuries, cf. e.g., Cambi (1999) 116.

61. Livy 10.13; on such "wooden" items as trustworthy, above, n. 14; confidence in the fact, perhaps connected with 367, expressed by Forsén (1991) 76, 81; its credibility in Oakley (1997–2005) 1.655ff. with persuasive reasons for believing the reference (quoted, 1.656), especially valuable for defense of the figure 500 *iugera* (1.659); but two *iugera* were seen as impossibly small by the poor, who then got seven in 393, cf. Manzo (2001) 96f. on Livy 5.30.8, with other colonial grants in Oakley (1997–2005) 677.

62. On these various laws "which the patricians tried to disregard", cf. Jolowcz and Nicholas (1972) 24f.; on the Valerian of 449, Badian (1990) 397, stressing that most law from the mid-fifth century on was made in meetings of the plebs and, being confirmed by the senate, was law for all; Cornell (1995) 277f. in agreement; ibid. 341 on the Publilian law, and (preferable) Humm (2005) 121, 190, 426f.

63. For the 1 percent figure, I work from 292,000 in the year 265 (Livy); cf. Brunt (1971) 27–32 cautiously accepting of the census figures in Livy et al., as likewise Frank (1933–40) 1.21f.; a slightly different view in Beloch (1926) 217 (270,000 citizens in 263). Percentages for major elections which were notionally 100 in the year 500 dropped precipitously in 338, and further, thereafter, cf. Scheidel (2006) 218.

64. For good remarks on how to look at and think about Roman politics (though focused mostly on the later Republic), see Burckhardt (1990) 95 and passim.

CHAPTER 6

1. On *haruspices*, see Livy 5.15.1 and Mitchell (1990) 68f. J. A. North in Beard et al. (1998) 20 doesn't explain how he knows (not just conjectures) how they came to Rome in the early Republic.

2. See above, chap. 2 n. 35, and add the member of a clan early disappearing from the record, "Genucius Clusinus", misread as "Clepsina", cf. Ampolo (1990) 210f. Notice also names of *curiae* and *gens*-traditions recalling Latin towns, cf. Palmer (1961) 132f.; and "at least five patrician families . . . claimed Sabine descent", Farney (2007) 79.

3. Early mention in the Twelve Tables 5.8, Riccobono (1941–43) 1.41, with interpretation by Sherwin-White (1973) 322f.; also the tax on manumission of 357; on *gens* membership, Nicolet (1980) 23; and for estimates of the numbers involved in the fourth century, quite limited, see Humm (2005) 220, or quite large, Harris (1990) 498f.

4. Above, chap. 1, n. 26.

5. Quoted (condensed) from interesting paragraphs in Tocqueville (1836) 3.70, 94ff.

6. Above, chap. 1 nn. 13ff. North (1989) 581 confronts the problem of "Roman-ness" in religion versus Etruscan or Greek or other influences, but doesn't pause for reflection; and Cornell (1978) 110 denies there ever was "an independent or autonomous Latin culture"; but for the right word, see Linderski (2007) 596 quoting and commenting on A. K. Michels.

7. The *cinctus Gabinus,* cf. Guaítoli (1981) 153.

8. Harris (1979) 170.

9. See Wissowa (1912) 250, on the Aventine temple and cult; 289 or Torelli (1999) 93, on Venus-cult by 295 (Livy 10.31.8f.); on Juno at Lanuvium, Livy 8.14.2f., Sabatucci (1988) 39 and Schultz (2006) 209, comparing, at Tusculum, Palmer (1974) 7 and 21 and Humbert (1978) 268; for Vestal priestesses at Lavinium and Alba, cf. Beard et al. (1998) 51. On Mars at Aricia, Falerii, Trebula Mutuesca, Praeneste, see Dumézil (1987) 214, 252f., 418; on Juno, 425; on Minerva, Donati and Stefanetti (2006) 39; on Jupiter Imperator, Palmer (1974) 21 and especially Manichetti (1994) 26f.; or again, Mater Matuta in Rome and Satricum, or Castor and Pollux in Rome and Lavinium, Smith (1996) 219 and 222.

10. Livy 8.9.6 with Dumézil (1987) 108f. and passim.

11. On Lanuvium, Livy 8.14.2 and Dumézil (1987) 430.

12. Veii, in Livy 5.21.3ff.; Macrobius 3.9.7ff. and Palmer (1974) 47f.; apparent confirmation in archaeology (a break in cult evidence), Gustafsson (2000) 47, 71, although cult then resumed once more, Blomart (1997) 102; in Isauria, the inscription of A.D. 75, *Année épigraphique* 1977, 816; at Falerii in 241, Lenski (2008) 233f.; and evocation of Carthage's patron goddess in 146, recalling the earlier evocation of 249, cf. Palmer (1974) 47f., 129, or Blomart (1997) 105. Donati and Stefanetti (2006) 97 point to the transfer of Volsinii's Vortumnus statue to Rome after the defeat of her home city in 264.

13. On Feronia, cf. Donati and Stefanetti (2006) 144; for "Tuscan"-plan temples, cf. Colonna (2005) 586.

14. See Pais (1920) xxiv suggesting a triumph-= element only adopted in the 290s (by a slip, misciting Livy 10.47.3); also Versnel (1970) 299 concluding that what we know as the Roman triumph ("Etrusco-Roman") is probably a fourth-century product, with recall of earlier rites; more persuasively, Bonfante Warren (1970) 60f., pointing out what great amounts of ancient Etruscan terra-cottas and wall paintings must, to Roman antiquarians, have shown everything that was grand and spectacular in dress and accoutrements; and Rawson (1990) 171 noting paintings of Roman triumphs of 272 and 264 to be seen much later, along with Fabius Pictor's. I am not aware of any evidence for earlier triumphal rites that might have been known to the writers we rely on. In 201 the Romans were borrowing still more features for triumphs from the Etruscans, so says Appian, *History* 8.66. Of course, many scholars have said in the past that the Roman triumph (meaning essentially all features) was on display as early as the eighth century, seventh, etc., and the conjecture, unsupported, supports the notion of "Etruscan Rome".

15. Castor and Pollux came to the Latins from Etruria, and thence to Rome in 484, along with a so-called Tuscan temple plan, cf. Gros and Torelli (1988) 84, where Wissowa (1912) 268 withholds judgment on direct or indirect importation and Palmer (1974) 79 favors derivation directly from the Campani; for the dating of the Castor temple confirmed by excavation, cf. Donati and Stefanetti (2006) 21 or Guldager Bilde and Poulsen (2008) 21. Minerva is brought from Greece to Etruria and thence (as Minerva, not Athena) to Rome, Sabatucci (1988) 110; Venus

cult is imported in the same manner, Dumézil (1987) 452f.; and other Greek deities were widely worshipped in central Italy in the seventh and sixth century, as also at Rome, e.g., Diana/Artemis, Wissowa (1912) 250f., or Hercules, cf. Lulof (1997) 103; others, later, e.g., Mercury in 495. A few temples considered not native (however the Romans may have conceived of the distinction) were worshipped beyond the *pomerium*. On chariot racing being Greek but via Etruria, cf. Thuillier (1975) 564ff.; on *lectisternia,* a fulsome description of the first, in 399, Livy 5.13.4f., with Wissowa (1912) 276, 304, or Oakley (1997–2005) 2.38; on sacral parades and games from 496, according to Dionysius of Halicarnassus and Fabius Pictor, see Palmer (1974) 100; games even under Romulus, and staged also by the Latin League according to tradition, Sabatucci (1988) 274f., 310, 334.

16. Comprehensively in Oakley (1997–05) 2.38; on Ceres etc., cf. Wissowa (1912) 51, 297, or Palmer (1974) 100; on Apollo in 496, cf. Wissowa (1912) 293; on Venus Verticordia, cf. Donati and Stefanetti (2006) 43f.; on Aesculapius, ibid. 9 and Sabatucci (1988) 19f.; on Hercules, cf.Wissowa (1912) 274, 276; and on consultation of the Books in plague time in 431, cf. Gustafsson (2000) 39 (Livy 4.25). For credence in the consultations as history for the fifth and later centuries, cf. North (1989) 616, 618 or *OCD* 1401.

17. Varro, in Augustine's *City of God* 4.31, says the earliest imaging was in the 580s, whence the inference that it was to serve the Jupiter temple; but whatever the more primitive Romans may have once thought, they were already exposed by the seventh century to Greek images in pottery and textiles, as Cristofani (1985) 19 points out, rightly rejecting Varro's reconstruction as antiquarian (Wissowa 1912, 32 and Colonna 2005, 582, accept it). For *lectisternia* as a cultic innovation on the road to anthropomorphization, see Beard et al. (1998) 1.63 (verbatim from North [1989] 578). For the Concordia temple of 367, see Wissowa (1912) 328 and for the Temple of Victoria of 294, Beard et al. (1998) 1.69 or Pensabene (1998) 11, the idea inspired by Alexander's success in war, it is supposed, and, p. 68, "the cult of a divinized abstraction such as Victoria was a sign of Hellenization"; for the Fortuna temple of 293 in Trastevere, see Livy 10.46.14. Wissowa (1912) 330, 333, or North (1989) 616, find fifth-century temples of Spes, Quies, Virtus, or Pudicitia plebeia, in Livy, which are dubious; Salus and Fides publica are more easily accepted in the end of the fourth and mid-third century, cf. Hölkeskamp (2000) 227.

18. Saturn and Mercury in Colonna (2005) 582; 583, the Greek temple plan with surrounding columns, for Jupiter on the Capitoline, introduces the style favored thereafter for Castor; and see above, n. 15, on temple building.

19. For the fifty-year pause in Greek temple construction, see e.g., Wissowa (1912) 50 or Poma (1984) 74; on an upswing in the fourth century, cf. Wallace (1990) 279f.; for the narrowing of Hellenization, MacMullen (1991) 419–28.

20. On Dionysius of Halicarnassus, see e.g., Delcourt (2005) 114; in Dillery (2009) 81, Dionysius draws invention from Fabius.

21. For Troy's legends in sixth-century Etruscan painting, cf. Bremmer and Horsfall (1987) 18 or Giardina (1997) 65; for Troy (end of seventh) and Aeneas (end of sixth) known in Etruria, cf. Zevi (1981) 148f.

22. See in Moscati (1997) 76f. a venerated cenotaph with a seventh-century burial beneath it and a row of thirteen altars in front; further, Humbert (1978) 183; and a full, excellent description of the site in Holloway (1994), dating the hero's tomb (138) by pottery of the late 300s, in works of restoration (which does not give clear indication of how much earlier the tomb was identified with Aeneas).

23. Hellanicus of Lesbos knew Aeneas as the founder and name-giver (from a woman of Troy, Rhome), cf. Dionysius of Halicarnassus, *Ant. Rom.* 1.72.1f., Gabba (1991) 12, Cornell (1995) 64, 66, or Delcourt (2005) 84f., 87. Dionysius' text is discounted by Gruen (1992) 18 for no given reason, but he says quite rightly (10) that "Greeks assumed that all cities of stature could be traced to their Hellenic roots".

24. The "Romulus" whose grandson founded Rome appears in a Greek writer, Alcimos, around the mid-fourth century, cf. Delcourt (2005) 92. "Romos" in "Cephalon" (cf. Dionysius of Halicarnassus, *Ant. Rom.* 1.72.1) dates only to ca. 190, cf. chap. 5 n. 18. Timaeus (ca. 260) knew of the Romans identifying themselves as Troy-descended, cf. Polybius 12.4b, and from ca. 240 (Livius Andronicus) "the Aeneas theory holds the ground", for Gabba (1991) 14. Ennius, *Annals* 1.31–48 knew of the Aeneas tie; on Naevius, cf. Holloway (1994) 193.

25. See Roncalli (1987) 101f. on the François tomb paintings, the date of which may be the third quarter of the fourth century, Torelli (1984) 229 and A. Maggiani in Cristofani (1985a) 310, or a little later, Alföldi (1963) 214, 225. The Veian figurines at one site date to the fourth or more likely to the first half of the fifth century, so, Vagnetti (1971) 88, matched (181) at the other two sites, while M. D. Gentili in Cristofani (1985a) 280 prefers a date of sixth/fifth century; but these early dates are disposed of by Torelli (1984) 228, (1988) 68f. and (1999) 25, proposing rather a date "just a few years later" than 340–330. There is no evidence nor, I think, probability that the figurines represented a propagandizing campaign, "spinta ideologica" on the part of the state, rather than the private patriotism of individuals (*pace* Torelli 1988, 68f.). I note that the proposed date, in the 320s, is a generation earlier than is allowed for a Roman interest in Aeneas, by Bremmer and Horsfall (1987) 18. Cornell (1995) 66, 68, 414, with very different suppositions, does not persuade me.

26. See Zonaras 8.9 (II p. 200 Dindorf) and Cicero, *Verr.* II 4.33 (72). Cornell (1995) 65 sees the advantage ("political utility") as on the Roman side; but this misreads the realities.

27. Above, chap. 3 at nn. 11ff.

28. On the alleged debt of the Twelve Tables to Greek ideas, see Toher (2005); also Livy 5.21, 23, 25, 28 and Diodorus 14.93, where Camillus' vow in 395 produces a gold bowl as a gift to Apollo. On the two statues I adopt the view of Wallace (1990) 289. The wording of the story in Plutarch points to fabrication, cf. Humm (2005) 361f., who, however, like Hölscher (1978) 340, joins (556ff.) in the attempts to find deep meaning in the choice of the two personages. Coarelli (1983–85) 134 suggests a date "probably at the beginning of the third century", while Humm (2005) 556ff. prefers the later 300s.

29. Speaking about cults in Sicily, Cicero apologizes even to an upper-class if

not elite audience of his day, *Verr.* II 4.49 (109): the subject is no part of our everyday conversation, *aliena a . . . cotidiana dicendi consuetudine* (still more the case in the less globalized fourth or third century).

30. See in Torelli (1999) 24f. and (1988) 69, an altar to Pitumnus ancestor of Turnus, "a specifically Ardean deity" indicating the origin of colonists.

31. See Gros and Torelli (1988) 125, on Alba Fucens, Cosa, and Paestum; on Cosa's *mundus* on the *arx,* Brown (1980) 16f. On a dog's bones at the base of the city wall, see Rouveret and Theodorescu (2000) 193, dated to "early years" of the colony by Pedley (1990) 125.

32. See in Cazanove (2000) 74, ex-votos in Venusia, Paestum, Luceria, and elsewhere close to other Latin colonies, but sensible qualifications proposed by Glinister (2006); in Coarelli (2000) 199, 203f., a women's cult-college for Juno Lucina (third century?); Hercules cult of a Roman sort in Paestum and Alba Fucens but also noncolonial cities nearer Rome, in late fourth/ third century, Morel (1988) 57f.; Hercules and Minerva at Cosa, Scott (1988) 75; and on Pisaurum, Coarelli (2000) 197, 200ff., 204 (Salus, Feronia Mater Matuta, etc.), with the possibility that the founding date was not 283 but 184.

33. Cazanove (2000) 74.

34. See Torelli (1999) 52, 55f.; Pedley (1990) 113; and cultural continuity despite Roman hegemony or conquest (not by colonization) in the Pomptine and Campanian areas, in Attema and Leuven (2004) 159 and Humbert (1978) 403.

35. At Paestum, again: Greco and Theodorescu (1983) 84.

36. On a big atrial house, cf. Coarelli (1998) 64f.; on residential plots of a size reckoned in Roman units (*actus*), cf. Scott (1988) 75; on temples of Etrusco-Italic plan at Fregellae, Luceria, Interamna Lirenas, and other Latin colonies, cf. Torelli (1999) 126f.; and on Paestum's forum-side shops, Pedley (1990) 115, quoted.

37. See Gros and Torelli (1988) 125, thinking the pits served ritual, not voting; and Mouritsen (2004) 43–55 shows the great difficulties in seeing the pits as *saepta* markers; on the colonial *comitium* modeled on the Greek *ekklesiasterion,* see e.g., Coarelli (1998) 59, 129 Tav. 9, plans at Acragas and Samothrace, (2007) 53, and (2008) 57; also above, chap. 5 n. 35, Coarelli supposing a change from square to round at Rome only in the 260s, therefore not serving as a model to colonies, though both earlier and later he supposed the date was pre-Cosa (pre-273), cf. e.g., Coarelli (1983–85) 1.151 or (1998) 59 or (2005) 25; but Mouritsen (2004) 40 notes the circularity of the reasoning, that colonies must have copied Rome and therefore Rome's *comitium* must have been just like them; ibid. 43, he compares dimensions of several *comitia* with Rome's; at Paestum, see Greco (1988) 81, 83, Torelli (1999) 48, and Greco and Theodorescu (2000) 86f. and 96 fig. 1; at Alba Fucens the example can be dated by pottery to the founding, Mertens (1988) 94f. and fig. 9, and Torelli (1999) 34f.; at Fregellae, cf. Coarelli (1998) 59 and the reconstruction (my fig. 6.1) at Tav. 6, 11. Notice the replication of Rome's Curia (Hostilia) in Fregellae and later in Cosa and Paestum, in Lackner (2008) 259.

38. Greco and Theodorescu (1983) 83f.; Pedley (1990) 119.

39. Morel (1988) 55 on Latin used on makers' marks in Latin colonies com-

pared to Oscan in towns nearby; 57f., a colonial taste for pottery imported from Rome, a sort of piety in the general Roman colonial population; similarly in architectural terra-cotta decoration, Torelli (1999) 128; on the influence of Latin on other Italic languages, cf. Glinister (2006) 24; and Oscan words for magistracies yield to Latin after the third century, cf. Humbert (1978) 185, 292. Sabine was still in use among new Roman citizens, ibid. 80; further, Beloch (1926) 578 on Livy 40.43, where Capua's administration was all in the native tongue until the Capuans asked leave to use Latin; Etruscan was still in use far into the Empire, Giardina (1997) 44; and Attema and Leusen (2004) 159, quoted.

CHAPTER 7

1. Münzer appears first in vol. 8 (1913) of *Paulys Real-Encyclopädie der classischen Altertums,* ed. 2 (Stuttgart 1894), writing on the Hortensii, Horatii, Julii, Junii, etc., and he separately published a monograph on the Roman Republican nobility in 1920; Syme (1939) viii, pays tribute to "the supreme example and guidance of Münzer; but for his work on Republican family-history, this book [*The Roman Revolution*] could hardly have existed"; and Syme makes much use also of M. Gelzer who joined the encyclopedia in 1913.

2. Humbert (1978) 176 disposes of several attempts at analysis of "tendance politique"; further, Oakley (1997–2005) 2.26; Develin (2005) 302f. and (1985) 44–49, quoting Toynbee (1965) 1.331; and, on the misleading tendency of the literary sources, amplified by modern interpretation, to attribute almost heritable political character to *gentes,* see e.g., Martini (1998) 37ff. on the Valerii and Claudii, or Oakley (1997–2005) 1.98f. and 2.86 (the Manlii).

3. *LTUR* 1.222.

4. Humbert (1978) 52; Ogilvie and Drummond (1989) 291; Richard (1990) passim; Torelli (1990a) 76 and (1999) 16; and war bands, Holloway (2008) 123f.

5. Fig. 7.1 is a selective conflation of two fold-out maps, "Italia tributim discripta", in Taylor (1960), and Humbert (1978) maps III and V and Humbert (1984) 228, who draws on Beloch (1926) and Toynbee (1965). Much is simply a best guess. On bellicosity, see Harris (1979) 180, wars "almost uninterrupted"; according to Oakley (1993) 15f., Romans were "less than ten per cent of the time at peace" pre-264.

6. J. C. Meyer (1990) 549; Humphreys (1990) 549; Rosenstein (2004) 28f.; and below, chap. 8 n. 5. Speculation on the part played by agricultural slaves in freeing citizens to fight lacks figures that can be trusted, although the figures indeed are offered in Livy especially, and were gathered by Tenney Frank in 1933, and (with some differences in their totals) by Harris (1979) 59 and Oakley (1993) 24f., 34f. (a complete list of construction in Rome from 400 to 291). Hopkins (1978) 35, quoted in MacMullen (1980a) 8, estimates seventeen-year-olds at 3 percent of adult males, and if liable to service for ten years, a little under half of them would be needed for the annual two (later four) legions. Humm (2005) 278ff. supplies reasonable approximations as representative of the war effort over the years

509–264. Years of a double levy (after 326) or (after 320) year-round campaigning would change the level of demand, naturally.

7. On volunteers, Wolff (2010) 18ff. collects nine references from the 490s to the 290s, treating the sources without any reservations; on refusal of military service in a dozen different years (but always managed by tribunes), texts of 495–378 are gathered by Ridley (1990) 121f.; on demographic aspects, see below, chap. 8 at nn. 8f.

8. On the wolf, see Crawford (1985) 29; above, chap. 3 n. 16.

9. Gundel (1963) 292ff.; Malavolta (1997) 472.

10. See Kiernan (2007) 49–58, for Punic-war times. No doubt all earlier instances have been assembled and commented on somewhere, but I cite only Livy 3.8.10 (Volsci in 462); 9.25.9 (Ausones in 314); and 9.45.17 (Aequi in 304). A dozen peoples or cities of the sixth and fifth centuries, known to antiquarians, had disappeared by better-attested times and may hide stories of great savagery. For the bent of Livy's (and Dionysius') account toward the praise of earlier Romans, see e.g., Forsythe (1999) 65.

11. Livy 7.31; on the interpretation of the incident, Humbert (1978) 168, Cornell (1995) 347, or Humm (2005) 176; on Roman pride in honesty above tricks, MacMullen (1997) 116, evidence in Ennius and later.

12. Humbert (1978) 409ff. on Caere's ports, especially Pyrgi; on Antium, Livy 8.14.12 and Cassola (1962) 29ff.

13. At chap. 5 n. 11f.

14. Cf. chap. 8 at nn. 32, 36.

15. See e.g., Beard et al. (1998) 44; better, Muccigrosso (2006) 187–191, "the spatial pattern . . . shows that the over-riding concern of temple builders was political display".

16. On Victoria's temple, see Fears (1981) 774.

17. Frank (1933–40) 1.50, from Wissowa's list, beginning with Salus of the year 302 but vowed in 311, the conract let by the censor of 306, cf. Pais (1920) 62; 491–94, listing of twenty victory vows down to 264; 86 temples from that of Jupiter Capitolinus in ?507 down to the year 2 by Ampolo (1990a) 485, 487; and *LTUR* with information on locations s.vv. Bellona, Jupiter Invictus (3.143) and Victor (3.161), Jupiter Stator, Quirinus, and Summanus.

18. *LTUR* 4.363 and Hölscher (1978) 323f.; also p. 338 on the pair in the year 338, Livy 8.13.9; in 306, Livy 9.43.22 and Pliny, *Nat. hist.* 34.23, a *triumphator*'s, Q. Marcius Tremulus', equestrian image set up in the Forum in front of the temple of Castor, cf. Hölscher (1978) 339; also equestrian, Fabius Maximus Rullianus on the Capitoline, cf. Holliday (2002) 226; in 293, Spurius Carvilius' portrait along with a statue of Jupiter, Pliny 34.43; and on the *columna Maenia,* Muccigrosso (2006) 187.

19. On Pictor, see Degrassi (1987) 522; on Papirius Cursor's painted portrait on the Aventine, Hölscher (1978) 341; on Fulvius Flaccus, see Rawson (1990) 171 and the *New Pauly* (Leiden) 15.326 s.v. "Vertumnus", citing the *fasti triumphales* and other sources.

20. On the Volsinii statuettes, see Vessberg (1941) 21, Hölscher (1978) 320, and Holliday (2002) 30f.; for later pillage, Plutarch, *Fabius* 22.6, and on to Marcellus' from Syracuse.

21. On the shields, cf. Hölscher (1978) 319f.; on Samnite arms, Livy 10.46.8 and Rawson (1990) 165.

22. Plutarch, *Marcellus* 21, to which Wallace (1990) 288 refers.

23. Plutarch, *Pyrrhus* 25.6; Eutropius, *Breviarium* 2.14.3; Peruzzi (1990) 281–316, especially 301–04. and Tavv. XIIIf.; *Roma medio repubblicana* 33, 66, Tav. 9; and Scullard (1974) 113 and pl. VIIa.

24. Pais (1920) xxv misinterprets Livy 9.30.5f., which has nothing to do with triumphs, but correctly notes Livy 3.29.5 regarding the year 459, where Livy warns us, "it is said". Zonaras 7.21 (II p. 151 Dindorf) is very full, for the year 396, but I assume a retrojection.

25. See Livy 9.46.15 and *RE* s.v. "Transvectio equitum" (S. Weinstock, 1937) 2180; Oakley (1997–2005) 3.642, explaining that almost all comparative evidence regards Athens but likely the custom was to be seen everywhere, Livy being the earliest source, Dionysius the fullest who focuses on the year 496 (Lake Regillus by his chronology) and on the Dioscuri. For the revival by Augustus, see Suetonius, *Augustus* 38.3.

26. Quoted, Livy 3.29.4ff. and Florus 1.13.26f.; among early mentions, Livy 10.7.9 (in 300) with listing of various insignia, including the palm of victory; but, citing Livy 10.47.3 (by a slip, 10.27.3), Pais (1920) xxiv says the palm was only introduced after 293. On the singing, see Ogilvie (1965) 444; ibid. 273, 679, on other Hellenic elements in victory celebrations retrojected from later times (cf. also below, n. 28); they spread into Italy "especially from Tarentum", in Humm (2005) 507, also 502. The older interpretation of Roman triumph elements as mostly derived from Etruria is recently defended by Hölscher (2005) 474. For *triumphatores* outranking even consuls, cf. Valerius Maximus 2.8.6 for the period after my chosen one, and (without reference) Pais (1920) xxxvi.

27. I combine lists in Cornell (1989) 290 and Degrassi (1947) 69–73.

28. Rawson (1990) 171 points out one later triumphal element that was not in use pre-264.

29. A list of enumerated *praeda* boasts for 319–293 in Frank (1933–40) 1.43; further, Pais (1920) 45 and Rawson (1990) 166, accepting as historical Livy 6.29.9; also Livy 9.45.17 and Diodorus 20.101.5. For city images, Livy 37.59.3 of the year 189 and Zonaras 7.21 (II 150 Dindorf); for other paintings, virtually action-cartoons, in 201, see Appian, *Hist.* 8.66.

30. Tocqueville (1836) 1.84.

31. Harris (1979) in chaps. 1–2, with acknowledgment of the role of *gloria* and *laus*, offers the best treatment of the "expansionist", "imperialist", "bellicose" Roman nature, in a work rightly respected; or see Raaflaub (1996) 278 on *gloria* and *dignitas*.

32. MacMullen (2003) 32–35.

33. Discussion of the methodological problem in MacMullen (1980a) 8–14.

CHAPTER 8

1. On the First Secession, cf. Livy 2.32 and above, chap. 5 nn. 44f.; Ungern-Sternberg (2005) 80, one of many scholars to judge the so-called Second Decemvirate "pure fiction"; on the Second Secession, Livy 3.31–45 (excluding 3.44ff., "some of the finest pages in the whole of Livy", so, Cornell 1995, 273).

2. Notice Tocqueville (1836) 2.174–192, 219–36, pages where you would most expect to see at least some mention of parties in 1831–32.

3. Livy 3.58.6 and 8; a glorious suicide, above, chap. 5 n. 3, and heroes like the elder and younger P. Decius Mus.

4. From 5 to 15 percent participation in voting, cf. Humm (2005) 280 supposing a premanipular legion of 6,000, a total annual muster of two in the regal period, i.e., 12,000, rising to four manipular legions of 4,200, total 18,000 in an adult male citizen population of 115,000 in the year 304, i.e., 15 percent; the *equites* voted first. cf. e.g., Humm (2005) 164; and see Oakley (1997–2005) 2.20f. on the crucial importance of presiding at elections.

5. On the age category of most recruits (who were centuriate assembly voters), in their teens and twenties, see the good reasoning of Humphreys (1990) 549 and Rosenstein (2006) 231; on the restricted numbers of *gentes* in the *fasti*, cf. Forni (1994) 430ff. or Oakley (1997–2005) 2.23–25.

6. For the law of 358 against campaigning in smaller centers, markets, and crossroads (Livy 7.15.12f.), see Taylor (1960) 14 or Forni (1994) 431.

7. On the role of the tribes, see Mommsen (1844) 132f., citing Livy 4.46.1; Taylor (1960) 11, 74f. on rites and on the *tribus* as the universally indicated unit of census; also Humm (2006) 39, 47; and Humbert (1978) 312f. points to the Varronian derivation of *tributum* = taxes from *tribus*. The usual subunits were *pagi, fora,* and *conciliabula.* In the control of citizens' rights, Humbert (1978) 310 supposes (plausibly but without indication of the period treated) that lists were kept "centrally" at Rome; but Brunt (1971) 27 points out that Dionysius knew of "no public records for the period to 264", only *gens*-archives.

8. Cornell (1995) 208 instances a figure given by Fabius Pictor as "absurd" but goes on to defend the figures from 508 on to 392 ("one cannot simply dismiss them as fabrications, as Brunt for example does"), where actually Brunt (1971) 22 sees Pictor as "our best authority" but (27) simply agrees with Beloch (1886) 342, as quoted.

9. On Rome's population in ancient sources, see above, chap. 3 n. 32. As to mobilization, Livy 7.23.3f. in 350 and 9.43.4 in 307/6 reports a double levy, i.e., eight legions; 7.23.3f. and 7.25.8 in 350, a double levy raised to ten legions; and again, ten legions in 349, Livy 7.25.8 and 9.19.2, repeating that the levy was based *almost entirely in the city*—this, an idea which "is absurd and shows how little confidence we should have in his [Livy's] detailed information". So, Oakley (1997–2005) 2.127 and 234; and add Polybius 3.107.9 declaring that in 216 for the first time ever Rome raised eight legions (yet Polybius was certainly well acquainted with the sources such as Livy uses that he, Polybius, contradicts).

10. Beloch (1926) 217, 620f.; Brunt (1971) 12, "obliged in general to follow Beloch", cf. 30 table II; but (5) Beloch is quoted pronouncing population figures in the literary sources as "all fictitious". As to calculations by areas, full of problems, see recently Scheidel (2006) 210, admitting that we will never attain "a genuinely conclusive" estimate; and for various other scholars' doubt, cf. MacMullen (1980a) 8.

11. Scheidel (2006) 220, for the period of the mid-fourth century into the early third, sees the draft falling from 23 percent of males over seventeen, to 10 percent; similarly, Humm (2005) 371 (supposing a pool of 80,000 and a need of 18,000 in 300). Hopkins' different estimates (cit. at chap. 7, n. 6) are for the period post-200, so not relevant to my study. As to fairness in choice of, and by, legions, see Polybius 6.20.3 (though of course he does write at a second-century date); also resort to a lottery, Valerius Maximus 6.3.4 of the year 275.

12. Chap. 2 n. 32; chap. 3 n. 17.

13. Ogilvie (1965) 288 remarks on the practice of cavalry dismounting to fight; see also Polybius 3.65.9; 3.115.3; and 6.25.3f., where he describes this as common in olden times. On equipment, cf. Zimmerman (1986) 37–41; in Apulia (Daunia), see Volpe (1990) 37 and Cascarino (2007) 52; in Lanuvium, Colonna (2005) 507, 511.

14. Gelzer (1969) 5f., pointing out that even with a subsidy such service was costly; the number serving (1,800) is confirmed at least for the earlier second century by a fragment of Cato.

15. Free borrowing of fighting styles everywhere to be assumed, Cascarino (2007) 40. On *situlae*, Saulnier (1980) 81, 85, 87; on the Clusium art, Jannot (1984) 9f., 332f., and figs. 65 and 68 and Bringmann (2007) 12.

16. Above, chap. 4 nn. 33f., on the supposed early phalanx; Saulnier (1980) 10f., 69f., pre-500; post-500 depictions (Roman terra-cotta statuettes), 75–77; Daunia, Volpe (1990) 37 figs. 13f.; fourth-century paintings showing Samnite warriors with full corselet (back and front) or big round shield, Cascarino (2007) 52; a Capuan plaque, Humm (2005) 271 and pl. IV. On the "Corsini throne" the relief with warriors and arms is a copy, not ca. 400, cf. Torelli (1999) 156.

17. Quoted, Sumner (1970) 67, defending this starting point as against Livy, whose "whole farrago appears as an antiquarian reconstruction" (69); cf. Cornell (1995) 186 on a part of Livy's reconstruction of the army (Livy 1.43.5) as "patently absurd", and Mitchell (1990) 236f., grandly dismissive of Livy on the fourth-century army.

18. Polybius 1.33.9 regarding the year 255, where javelin men fight first, with many *semeia* = maniples behind in depth; 2.30.1, in 225 it is usual that javelin men fight first and then (§6) retire into the mass of the army, when the *speirai* = maniples "fall upon" the enemy using (§8) thrusting swords and big shields; 2.33.4, *triarii* stationed behind the maniples bear thrusting spears; and 2.33.7, "the formation unique to Roman warfare" can open space for the maniples (to fall back into); 3.19.5, a charge; 3.105.3 and 6, light-armed men in retreat confuse maniples; 3.113.3 and 3.115.12, an extra-deep maniple-formation (*semaia* = *manipulus*); on the three lines, 6.21.9 (add skirmishers, "the youngest", 6.22.1, 6.24.3); and 6.40.11, *hastati*,

triarii, and *principes* in a passage on marching formation. The word *manipulus* was familiar to Terence's audience, say, in the 170s (*Eunuch* 4.776). Quoted on "dynamic", Matthew (2009) 414, who goes on (415), "the terminology of the word *othismos* cannot be subject to one exclusive definition".

19. Livy 8.8.3, in the year 340, but "earlier" a Macedonian-type phalanx; also Dionysius, *Ant. Rom.* 4.16.2; Rawson (1971) 13; the phalanx could have been adopted from many peoples but it is asserted to be Etruscan, then Roman, by J. C. Meyer (1983) 139, Rawson (1990) 168, Cornell (1995) 184, or Bringmann (2007) 13.

20. In Mommsen (1844) 141, 147, see the two descriptions of the army based on Livy in tabular form, as are also many later descriptions, e.g., Keppie (1984) 16, 22; Humm (2005) 274 on the problem with the dating of army pay, about the date of which Livy contradicts himself (to the extent of a century and more, cf. Sumner [1970] 74); Cornell (1995) 188 and 354, also contradicting himself (maniples introduced in 406, but also in 311), as Rosenstein (2004) 203 points out; and Raaflaub (1996) 309.

21. Sumner (1970) 68; Humm (2005) 274–79 proposing a long development culminating in 311 in the manipular army.

22. See Humm (2005) 275 and Cascarino (2007) 76ff.

23. Maniples emerged in Italy before the Samnite wars but literary sources assign adoption by Romans to that long period, cf. Sumner (1970) 68f.; Cornell (1989a) 373; Cascarino (2007) 74f.; *pilum* and *scutum* were said to be adopted from the Samnites, as in fact seems very probable, cf. the sources collected in Humm (2005) 269f.

24. Above, chap. 5 n. 10 on the Foedus Cassianum; Livy 2.23.5f; and in Dionysius 6.19–21, speeches ending in 21.2, quoted.

25. Naturally these early colonies are ill-reported, hence their histories are in doubt, e.g., whether Antium should be included, as by Livy, Dionysius, and Salmon (1970) 110, but rightly excluded by Cassola (1962) 5f.; or whether to include Labici and others as does Salmon (1970) 42, 110; but they are excluded by Bringmann (2002) 28.

26. Taylor (1960) 79, instancing a Tusculan consul in 322, with many more to follow; Salmon (1970) 49; and Humbert (1978) 13, 29, 42, 138, 158, 288 n. 4 supposing magistracies of a certain type were imposed by Rome, and 419.

27. On Caere, see Taylor (1960) 79; Salmon (1970) 49f.; and Humbert (1978) 9, 31f., 141ff., 310, 421. On an earlier example of carving away of land from defeated enemies, to give to Romans in individual plots, at Veii, cf. Torelli (1999) 24.

28. As to numbers of colonists generally, a bad source (Dionysius) says 20,000 at Venusia, which Volpe (1990) 46 seems to accept, Torelli (1999) 94 to question, and Salmon (1970) 18 to reject, rightly as I judge. On rapprochement, see Humbert (1978) xii; ibid. 173 on collaborators, e.g., at Capua, also Gros and Torelli (1988) 127, and at Luceria, Volpe (1990) 35.

29. A wall at Minturnae was built by the in-settlers in 295 to separate their part of the city from the preexisting, cf. Johnson (1935) 1.2 and Salmon (1970) 179.

30. "The Aequi made it clear . . . in 304 (Livy 9.45.5–8) that they did not wish

to become *Romani* (that is, *cives*)", as Taylor (1960) 57 points out; cf. also earlier, Afzelius (1942) 31; later, Humbert (1978) passim on the frequent rejection of citizenship, e.g., 195f. by Fundi and Formiae; also 191f., "*civitas* was a verdict imposed on the vanquished"; 205f., 213 (Hernici), 406 (*civitas* is "submission"), and 419; and Oakley (1997–2005) 550 cites many instances of protest in the fourth century and later. Despite this easy consensus, Jehne and Pfeilschiften (2006) 14, in an essay loaded down with bibliographical references (but all post-1990), applaud another scholar as "pioneer" in his conclusion—to the above effect.

31. On land distribution after victory, Livy recounts much strife along the lines of Haves vs. Have-nots, e.g., 4.48.2 or 6.14.11; but notice Jehne (2000) 211f. on later practices retrojected to the later fifth century. On *clientes,* Watson (1975) 102 quotes Plautus (*Menaechmi* 572f.), that "everyone wants a large number of clients"; but this need speak only of the capital; and similarly, fifth- and fourth-century settlement patterns in the suburbs, Tomei (2009) 669f. Taylor (1960) 133 supposes much favoring of clients in settlements, but she supplies no evidence. It might only be in noblesse oblige. Cassola (1988) 16 recalls one incident of 291 when appointment to the *tresviri coloniae deducendae* was a big issue, and Humbert (1978) 198 n. 158 collects indications of individual *gentes* imposing their interests on postwar settlements of the later fourth century.

32. *Praefecturae* were in operation in independent cities and districts, Oakley (1997–2005) 2.553 (but necessarily only attested after the urban praetorship was instituted); on their operation, perhaps first in 318, Humbert (1978) 189, 201ff., 361–64, 380f.; and on some centrally imposed structures of local government, 288.

33. See Dionysius of Halicarnassus, *Ant. Rom.* 2.74.3.

34. The *centuriae* of later fame in centuriation, measuring twenty by twenty *actus,* are identified at Tarracina, cf. Gasparri (2000) 224 or Flackner (2008) 239, with doubts about the precise metric; ibid., showing the process might precede town plans, as at Ariminum.

35. On surveying for individual farming plots after conquest in 340, and again in 290 in Sabine country, see Gargola (1995) 39f.; around Signia in the second half of the fourth century, Attema and Leusen (2004) 159; at Terracina, cf. the preceding note; *per strigas* at Luceria, Schmiedt (1985) 263f. on the two phases/orientations of land division, with Volpe (1990) 46f. on plots of ten *iugera* and a few even larger; also 210, fig. 213, 212 and Radcliffe (2006) 96f., 174; at Paestum, again Gasparri (2000) 224, estimating more than 3,000 plots delimited at the end of fourth or the beginning of the third century.

36. See Volpe (1990) 46; *actus* measurements, Schmiedt (1985) 263, correcting the fifteen *actus* of Radcliffe (2006) 96; on Veian land, Manzo (2001) 93; on later very great owners, Brunt (1975) 619–22.

37. Torelli (1999) 6.

38. Sixth- and fifth-century *cuniculi* found throughout Latium, cf. Colonna (2005) 481, instancing some from the early fourth century to drain the Alban lake, cf. also Coarelli (1987) 167f. on major draining of Latin lakes, Alba (ca. 500) and Nemi (end of fourth century); on Nemi, Guldager Bilde (2006) 205f.; Colonna

(2005) 481 on projects in southern Etruria, these generally fifth century or later; Potter (1979) 84–87 on Etruria; special numbers of *cuniculi* around Veii, Velitrae, and Ardea, up to 4.5 km in length, ibid. and Hodge (1992) 45ff.

39. See Cicero, *Letters to Atticus* 4.15.5, in Taylor (1960) 63.

40. Potter (1979) 82f.

41. Riccobono (1941–43) 1.49, XII Tab. 7.6, regulating the width of roads; 7.7, paving, cf. Radke (1973) 1421; 1488 on the Via Latina; 1646 on the Via Curia, quite short; on a later date for the Latina, in 328, Coarelli (1988) 40; 36, on the Via Caecilia; on the Popilia of 316, Radke (1973) 1499f.

42. For the Via Salaria, cf. *LTUR* 5.37; on the Via Amerina in the early fourth century, Potter (1979) 104; the Appian, 1.84, but cf. Coarelli (1988) 37, the paving began only in 296; 36 on the Caecilia of late fourth or early third century, or of a later date (283), Wiseman (1970) 136, 149; the Tiburtina extended in 307 by the Via Valeria, Coarelli (1987) 85 and (1988) 40, 42, also Mari (2004) 23; and the Via Cassia in the early fourth and the Clodia in early third century, Potter (1979) 103f.

43. On milestones of the late third century (but recording the work of aediles much earlier), cf. Coarelli (1988) 37. Livy 10.47.3 in 292 reports a stretch of road built from the yield of fines; again, 9.43.5, unnamed roads *publica impensa factae;* and Diodorus 20.36.1f. notes the public monies in great amounts used by Appius Claudius on his highway.

44. Dionysius of Halicarnassus, *Ant. Rom.* 3.67.5, "I would propose as the three grandest works of Rome, from which the greatness of its rule best appears, the aqueducts, paved roads, and sewer works"; and quoted, Tocqueville (1836) 3.108, "ces longs rochers artificiels qu'on nomme des voies romaines".

45. On roads serving expansion, Coarelli (1988) 36; Alba Fucens accommodates the Via Valeria, Brown (1980) 12 or Gros and Torelli (1988) 136; the Via Appia is run through the middle of Terracina, Radke (1973) 1423, and through Venusia, Gros and Torelli (1988) 138; it runs through Minturnae before the colony is founded in that town, cf. Johnson (1935) 1f.; and the Via Aurelia was tied in to Cosa in 241, Coarelli (1988) 47.

46. On Greek and Etruscan models for a grid, Gargola 42; at Veii, for example, notice the early street grid, in Bartoloni (2006) 51 and fig. 6, 1; rituals are archaeologically attested at Veii, so it is argued, in Gargola (1995) 47, and 75, at Cosa; gridded towns planted by the Latin league, Gros and Torelli (1988) 133f.; rejection of the Roman army camp as the model for a town's grid, Torelli (1999) 29, and in fact the camp rather derives from the town plan, Gros and Torelli (1988) 130f.

47. Notice in Fregellae, founded in 328, unoccupied until 313, the housing blocks of 210 feet, Coarelli (1998) 31, 55 and Tav. 3; for the others, Gros and Torelli (1988) 138, 140.

48. Above, chap. 5 n. 35 and 6 n. 37; quoted, Coarelli (1998) 59. On the adaptation of plans to local topography in earlier settlements, down to Antium's, cf. Lackner (2008) 228f., 240 tab. 1 Blatt 1.

49. Pedley (1990) 115, quoted; for Cosa, Scott (1988) 75; "standardized", Salmon (1970) 35.

50. Coarelli (1998) 64f.

51. On wells, cf. Hodge (1992) 48; Muccigrosso (2006) 189. On the Appia substruction, see Ashby (1935) 10 and *LTUR* 1.83 on its eleven-thousand-foot aboveground parts; Dodge (2000) 171 on its sources; and 172 on the *aqua Anio vetus.* Diodorus 20.36.1 gave the *aqua Appia* eighty stadia in length (ca. nine miles).

52. Gagarin and Fantham (2010) 2.33, on sixth-century barrel vaulting in Rome, and arches for the *aqua Appia;* for the latter, also *LTUR* 1.83 and Dodge (2000) 171; barrel vaulting in the *porticus Aemilia,* Cornell (2000b) 51 and a date, below, chap. 9 n. 7; an arch in the city wall of Cosa, thus (?) not long after 273, Brown (1980) 19 and Salmon (1970) 34 and fig. 28; masonry bridges in a Roman road-bridge possibly of a third-century date in Etruria, Potter (1979) 101; an arched embrasure, possibly third century, in the city wall of Rome, Holloway (1994) 95f. and fig. 7.4; and an arch in a second-century bridge, Radke (1973) 1443.

53. On *opus caementicium* in use in central Italy by the end of the fourth century but by Romans only by the end of the third century, see Adam (1994) 79f. and Gagarin and Fantham (2010) 2.33; ibid., again in Rome by early second century, and also Holloway (1994) 95f.

CHAPTER 9

1. Perhaps enough of source criticism has been offered in chapters 1 and 5, above, though also at many other scattered points. I add only a word from the most effective modern critic of all, pointing to the inconsistency of another scholar who, "by admitting the existence of these [methodological] problems, felt he had done his duty and then went on confidently to establish . . . a reconstruction thus based in a rather straightforward manner on the information given by our ancient sources. I for my part consider this approach questionable because it pays only lip service to the most fundamental methodological question we moderns are confronted with". So, Raaflaub (1990) 87, slightly reworded; and often by this same scholar to the same effect, e.g., in the conference papers he edited in 2005. But he senses the consequence of challenging the traditional sources—the risks in "serious and determined skepticism. This conclusion will not be popular", he says in defense of that skepticism (2005, 71); also Horsfall (1994) 51, "it has become, in some quarters, difficult or dangerous to say, 'we do not know', or, worse, 'we cannot know', or so much as to hint that there is something disquieting about the evidence that remains".

2. Courtroom wisdom, see chap. 1 at n. 7; more fully in MacMullen (2003) 53 and 151 n. 2. Historians must resign themselves to some margin of error, much or little depending on the scope of their questions and data. Problems appear at their worst in such huge questions as, where and when did capitalism begin, or modernism, or patriarchy, and as fashions in method and paradigm come and go.

See e.g., Moelho and Wood (1998) 73f. (A. Lamoreaux), 249ff. (G. Spiegel), and passim.

3. The London *Daily Mail* of May 10, 2007, continuing, "Francis Grew, senior curator at the Museum of London, said, 'For the first time we have the beginnings of a link between the Roman city and the Saxon London of the 600s. Before, we always believed London collapsed into ruins quite quickly after AD 400'" (the reference, kindness of Salvatore Randazzo).

4. Quoted, Pliny, *Natural History* 35.84; and on the different capacities of different disciplines, see Ungern-Sternberg (2005) 82. He is one of those who sense the need to distinguish between classical philology and history, and thereby (apropos the Decemvirate and Livy) to protect the historical part of the record from the literary/artistic, so far as possible.

5. I quote from my essay (1980, 9) simply because it best says what I mean, and was also the point from which this present book took off.

6. Tocqueville (1836) 3.326, voicing an idea astir at the time, cf. e.g., A. Blanqui, *Cours d'économie industrielle*, recueilli par A. Blaine (1838–39) 79; and for many illustrations of the effect of modules and replication, see MacMullen (2000) chap. 5.

7. The "*porticus Aemilia*" has been often discussed, e.g., by F. Coarelli, *LTUR* 4.116f. and 439 with fig. 44. Tucci (2006) identifies it quite persuasively as originally a naval ship-shed only later used (197) for storage and commerce and (195) built probably after the year 167 (my thanks to L. Lancaster for the reference). Still, it remains to be seen where a home can be found for the "*porticus*" on the river's edge, if it must be displaced, and to explain also why the Romans would harbor their naval vessels not at Ostia, where they had a semimilitary installation, but twenty miles upstream to be rowed there after every exercise. Whatever the identification of the structure, the surviving parts allow study of the construction technique, *opus caementicium,* regarding which I borrow a bit from my book (2000) 124f. and my unpublished lecture ("Syme" 2000). See also Cornell (2000b) 51 who accepts the traditional date of the cement rebuilding, 174, and refers to cement work even earlier, in 191; and above, chap. 8 n. 53.

BIBLIOGRAPHY

Adam (1994) — Adam, J.-P., *Roman Building Materials and Techniques,* trans. A. Mathews (London).

Adam and Briquel (1982) — Adam, R., and D. Briquel, "Le miroir prénestin de l'Antiquario comunale de Rome et la légende des jumeaux divins en milieu latin à la fin du IVe siècle av. J.-C.", *Mélanges d'archéologie et d'histoire de l'École francaise de Rome, Antiquité* 94 (1982) 33–65.

Afzelius (1942) — Afzelius, A., "Die römische Eroberung Italiens (340–264 v. Chr.)", *Acta Jutlandica* 14 (1942) (Copenhagen: Aarsskrift for Aarhus Universitet 14).

Albertoni (2008) — Albertoni, M., "Il tempio dei Tarquini", *Il tempio di Giove e le origini del colle capitolino,* eds. M. Albertoni and I. Damiani (Milan) 14–17.

Aldrete (2007) — Aldrete, G. S., *Floods of the Tiber in Ancient Rome* (Baltimore).

Alföldi (1965) — Alföldi, A., *Early Rome and the Latins* (Ann Arbor, MI).

Ammerman (1996) — Ammerman, A. J., "The Comitium in Rome from the beginning", *American Journal of Archaeology* 100 (1996) 121–36.

Ampolo (1980) — "Periodo IVB (640/30–580 a. C.)", *La formazione della città nel Lazio. Seminario . . . 1977* (*Dialoghi di archeologia,* ser. 2, 2, Rome) 165–92.

Ampolo (1980a) — Ampolo, C., "Le condizione materiali della produzione. Agricoltura e paesaggio agrario", *La formazione della città nel Lazio. Seminario . . . 1977* (*Dialoghi di archeologia,* ser. 2, 2, Rome) 15–46.

Ampolo (1981) — Ampolo, C., "I gruppi etnici in Roma arcaica: posizione del problema e fonti", *Gli Etruschi e Roma. Atti dell'incontro di studio in onore di Massimo Pallottino . . . 1979* (Rome) 45–70.

Ampolo (1984) — Ampolo, C., "Il lusso funerario e la città arcaica", *Archeologia e storia antica* 6 (1984) 72–102.

Ampolo (1988) — Ampolo, C., "Roma arcaica tra Latini ed Etruschi: aspetti politici e istituzionali", *Etruria e Lazio arcaico. Atti dell'Incontro di Studio . . . 1986,* ed. M. Cristofani (Rome) 75–87.

Ampolo (1990) — Ampolo, C., "Discussion", *Staat und Staatlichkeit in der frühen römischen Republik. Akten eines Symposiums . . . 1988 . . . Berlin,* ed. W. Eder (Stuttgart) 210–11.

Ampolo (1990a) — Ampolo, C., "Aspetti dello sviluppo economico agl'inizi della repubblica romana", *Staat und Staatlichkeit in der frühen römischen Republik. Akten eines Symposiums . . . 1988 . . . Berlin,* ed. W. Eder (Stuttgart) 482–93.

Ampolo (1996) — Ampolo, C., "Roma ed i Sabini nel V a. C. secolo", *Identità e civiltà dei Sabini. Atto del XVIII convegno di studi etruschi ed italica . . . 1993* (Florence) 87–103.

Aronen (1989) — Aronen, J., "Il culto arcaico nel *Tarentum* a Roma e la *gens Valeria*", *Arctos* 23 (1989) 19–39.

Ashby (1935) — Ashby, T., *The Aqueducts of Ancient Rome,* ed. I. A. Richmond (Oxford).

Attema and Leusen (2004) — Attema, P., and M. van Leusen, "The early Roman colonization of South Lazio; a survey of three landscapes", *Centralization, Early Urbanization and Colonization in First Millennium BC Italy and Greece* (Leuven) 157–95.

Badian (1990) — Badian, E., "Diskussion", *Staat und Staatlichkeit in der frühen römischen Republik. Akten eines Symposiums . . . 1988 . . . Berlin,* ed. W. Eder (Stuttgart) 396–97.

Bakker (1994) — Bakker, J. T., *Living and Working with the Gods. Studies of Evidence for Private Religion and its Material Environment in the City of Ostia (100–500 AD)* (Amsterdam).

Baldassare et al. (2003) — Baldassare, I., et al., *La peinture romaine de l'époque hellénistique à l'Antiquité tardive* (Milan).

Bartoloni (2006) — Bartoloni, G., "Veio: l'abitato di Piazza d'Armi. Le terrecotte architettoniche", *Deliciae fictiles* III: *Archeological Terracottas in Ancient Italy: New Discoveries and Interpretations. Proceedings of the International Conference . . . 2002,* eds. I. Edlund-Berry et al. (Oxford) 50–76.

Bartoloni and Cataldi-Dini (1980) — Bartoloni, G., and M. Cataldi-Dini, "Periodo IVA (730/20–640/30 a. C.)", *La formazione della città nel Lazio. Seminario . . . 1977 (Dialoghi di archeologia,* ser. 2, 2, Rome) 126–64.

Bayet (1971) — Bayet, J., *Croyances et rites dans la Rome antique* (Paris).

Beard et al. (1998) — Beard, M., J. North, and S. Price, *Religions of Rome,* 2 vols. (Cambridge UK).

Bedini and Cordano (1980) — Bedini, A., and F. Cordano, "Periodo III (770–730/20 a. C.)", *La formazione della città nel Lazio. Seminario . . . 1977 (Dialoghi di archeologia,* ser. 2, 2, Rome) 97–124.

Beloch (1886) — Beloch, J., *Die Bevölkerung der griechisch-römischen Welt* (Leipzig; anastatic ed. Rome 1968).

Beloch (1926) — Beloch, J., *Römische Geschichte bis zum Beginn der punischen Kriege* (Berlin).

Bergonzi and Bietti Sestieri (1980) — Bergonzi, G., and A. M. Bietti Sestieri, "Periodi I e IIA", *La formazione della città nel Lazio. Seminario . . . 1977* (*Dialoghi di archeologia*, ser. 2, 2, Rome) 47–78.

Bianchi Bandinelli (1970) — Bianchi Bandinelli, R., *Rome the Center of Power. Roman Art to AD 200,* trans. P. Green (London).

Bickerman (1969) — Bickerman, E. J., "Some reflections on early Roman history", *Rivista di filologia e di istruzione classica* 97 (1969) 393–408.

Bietti Sestieri (1980) — Bietti Sestieri, A. M., "Periodo IIB (ca. 830–770 a. C.)", *La formazione della città nel Lazio. Seminario . . . 1977* (*Dialoghi di archeologia,* ser. 2, 2, Rome) 79–96.

Bietti Sestieri (1985) — Bietti Sestieri, A. M., "La tarda età del bronzo e gli inizi della cultura laziale", *Roma e il Lazio dall'età della pietra alla formazione della città. I dati archeologici,* eds. A. P. Anzideri et al. (Rome) 129–48.

Bietti Sestieri (1985a) — Bietti Sestieri, A. M., "Roma e il Lazio antico agli inizi dell'età del ferro", *Roma e il Lazio dall'età della pietra alla formazione della città. I dati archeologici,* eds. A. P. Anzideri et al. (Rome) 149–75.

Bietti Sestieri (1985b) — Bietti Sestieri, A. M., "Roma e il Lazio antico nell'8° sec. a.C.", *Roma e il Lazio dall'età della pietra alla formazione della città. I dati archeologici,* eds. A. P. Anzideri et al. (Rome) 176–94.

Bietti Sestieri and De Santis (1985) — Bietti Sestieri, A. M., and A. De Santis, "Roma e il Lazio antico fra la fine dell'8° e gli inizi del 6° sec. a.C.: il periodo orientalizzante", *Roma e il Lazio dall'età della pietra alla formazione della città. I dati archeologici,* eds. A. P. Anzideri et al. (Rome) 195–224.

Blanck (1991) — Blanck, H., "Un nuovo frammento del 'Catalogo' della biblioteca di Tauromenion", *La parola del passato* 52 (1997) 241–55.

Blomart (1997) — Blomart, A., "Die *evocatio* und der Transfer 'fremder' Götter von der Peripherie nach Rom", *Römische Reichsreligion und Provinzialreligion,* eds. H. Canjik and J. Rüpke (Tübingen) 99–111.

Bonfante Warren (1970) — Bonfante Warren, L., "Roman triumphs and Etruscan kings: the changing face of the triumph", *Journal of Roman Studies* 60 (1970) 48–66.

Bonfante and Whitehead (2007) — Bonfante, L., and J. Whitehead, "Letter to our readers", *Etruscan News* 8 summer (2007) 3.

Bremmer (1993) — Bremmer, J. N., "Three Roman aetiological myths", *Mythos in mythenloser Gesellschaft. Das Paradigma Roms* (Stuttgart) 158–74.

Bremmer and Horsfall (1987) — Bremmer, J. N., and N. M. Horsfall, *Roman Myth and Mythography* (London).

Bringmann (2007) — Bringmann, K., *A History of the Roman Republic,* trans. W. J. Smyth (Cambridge UK; German original, Munich 2002).

Briquel (2000) — Briquel, D., "La lente genèse d'une cité", *Histoire romaine,* 1. *Des origines à Auguste,* ed. F. Hinard (Paris) 47–83.

Broughton (1951–52) — Broughton, T. R. S., *The Magistrates of the Roman Republic,* 2 vols. (New York).

Brown (1980) — Brown, F. E., *Cosa. The Making of a Roman Town* (Ann Arbor, MI).

Bruns (1909) — Bruns, C. G., ed., *Fontes iuris Romani anteiustiniani,* 2 vols. in one (Tübingen).

Brunt (1971) — Brunt, P. A., *Italian Manpower, 225 B.C.–A.D. 14* (Oxford).

Brunt (1971a) — Brunt, P. A., *Social Conflicts in the Roman Republic* (London).

Brunt (1975) — Brunt, P. A., "Two great Roman landowners", *Latomus* 34 (1975) 619–35.

Burckhardt (1990) — Burckhardt, L., "The political elite of the Roman Republic: comments on recent discussion of the concepts *nobilitas* and *homo novus*", *Historia* 39 (1990) 77–99.

CAH — *Cambridge Ancient History* (Cambridge UK).

Calame (1990) — Calame, C., *Thésée et l'imaginaire athénien. Légende et culte en Grèce antique* (Lausanne).

Cambi (1999) — Cambi, F., "Demography and Romanization in central Italy", *Reconstructing Past Population Trends in Mediterranean Europe (3000 BC–AD 1800),* eds. J. Bintliff and K. Sbonias (Oakville CT) (*Archaeology of Mediterranean Landscapes,* eds. G. Barker and D. Mattingly vol. 1).

Campbell (1964) — Campbell, J. K., *Honour, Family and Patronage. A Study of Institutions and Moral Values in a Greek Mountain Community* (Oxford).

Capelli (2000) — "Il Lupercale più antico e più affollato: lo specchio di Bolsena", *Roma. Romolo, Remo e la fondazione della città,* eds. A. Carandini and R. Cappelli (Rome) 233–34.

Carafa (1998) — Carafa, P., *Il Comizio di Roma dalle origini all'età di Augusto* (Rome).

Carafa (2000) — Carafa, P., "I contesti archeologici dell'età romulea e della età regia", *Roma. Romolo, Remo e la fondazione della città,* eds. A. Carandini and R. Cappelli (Rome) 68–73.

Carafa (2006) — Carafa, P., "Esposizione e salvazione dei gemelli", *La leggenda di Roma* 1: *Dalla nascità dei gemelli alla fondazione della città,* ed. A. Carandini (Milan) 298–339.

Carandini (1997) — Carandini, A., *La nascità di Roma. Dèi, Lari, eroi all'alba di una civiltà* (Torino).

Carandini (2000) — Carandini, A., "Variazioni sul tema di Romolo. Riflessi dopo *La nascita di Roma* (1998–1999)", *Roma. Romolo, Remo e la fondazione della città,* eds. A. Carandini and R. Cappelli (Rome) 95–150.

Carandini (2006) — Carandini, A., *Remo e Romolo. Dai rioni dei Quiriti alla città dei Romani (775/750–700/675 a. C.)* (Turin).

Carandini (2006a) — Carandini, A., "Introduzione", *La leggenda di Roma* 1: *Dalla nascità dei gemelli alla fondazione della città,* ed. A. Carandini (Milan) xiii–lxxix.

Carandini (2007) — Carandini, A., *Roma: il primo giorno* (Milan).

Carandini and Bruno (2008) — Carandini, A., and D. Bruno, *La casa di Augusto. Dai 'Lupercalia' ad Natale* (Rome).

Carandini and Capelli (2000) — Carandini, A., and R. Capelli, eds., *Roma. Romolo, Remo e la fondazione della città* (Rome).

Carandini et al. (2008) — Carandini, A., et al., "La Leggenda di Roma. Riposte alle osservazioni di A. Fraschetti", *Archeologia classica* 59 (2008) 447–54.

Carettoni et al. (1960) — Carettoni, G., et al., *La pianta marmorea di Roma. Forma urbis Romae,* text and plates (Rome).

Carlucci (2006) — Carlucci, C., "Osservazioni sulle associazioni e sulla distribuzione delle antefisse di II fase appartenenti ai sistemi decorativi etrusco-laziale", *Deliciae fictiles* III: *Archeological Terracottas in Ancient Italy. New Discoveries and Interpretations. Proceedings of the International Conference . . . 2002,* eds. I. Edlund-Berry et al. (Oxford) 2–22.

Carruba (2006) — Carruba, A. M., *La Lupa Capitolina. Un bronzo medievale* (Rome).

Cascarino (2007) — Cascarino, G., *L'esercito romano. Armamento e organizzazione,* 1: *Dalle origini alla fine della Repubblica* (Rimini).

Cassola (1962) — Cassola, F., *I gruppi politici Romani nel III secolo a. C.* (Trieste).

Cassola (1988) — Cassola, F., "Aspetti sociali e politica della colonizzazione", *Dialoghi di archeologia,* ser. 3, 6, no. 2 (1988) 5–17.

Cazanove (2000) — Cazanove, O. de, "Some thoughts on the 'religious Romanization' of Italy before the Social War", *Religion in Archaic and Republican Rome and Italy. Evidence and Experience,* eds. E. Bispham and C. Smith (Edinburgh) 71–76.

Chassignet (1996–2004) — Chassignet, M., *L'annalistique romaine,* 3 vols. (Paris).

Cifani (2005) — Cifani, G., "Roma. Una stipe votiva al IV miglio tra le vie Latine e Labicana", *Mélanges d'archéologie et d'histoire de l'École française de Rome, Antiquité* 117 (2005) 199–221.

Cifani (2008) — Cifani, G., *Architettura romana arcaica. Edilizia e società tra Monarchia e Repubblica* (Rome).

Cifani (2009) — Cifani, G., "Indicazioni sulla proprietà agraria nella Roma arcaica in base all'evidenza archeologica", *Suburbium* II. *Il suburbio di Roma dalla fine dell'età monarchica alla nascita del sistema delle ville (V–II secolo a. C.),* ed. V. Jolivet (Rome) 311–24.

CIL — *Corpus inscriptionum latinarum* (Berlin 1863–).

Classen (1963) — Classen, C. J., "Zur Herkunft der Sage von Romulus und Remus", *Historia* 12 (1963) 447–57.

Coarelli (1974) — Coarelli, F., *Roma* (Milan).

Coarelli (1981) — Coarelli, F., *Roma,* ed. 2 (*Guide archeologiche Laterza* 6) (Rome).

Coarelli (1983) — Coarelli, F., "Le pitture della tomba François a Vulci: una proposta di lettura", *Dialoghi di archeologia,* ser. 3, 1, no. 2 (1983) 43–69.

Coarelli (1983–85) — Coarelli, F., *Il foro romano,* 2 vols. (Rome).

Coarelli (1986) — Coarelli, F., *Il foro romano. Periodo arcaico,* ed. 2 (Rome).

Coarelli (1987) — Coarelli, F., *I santuari del Lazio in età repubblicana* (Rome).

Coarelli (1988) — Coarelli, F., "Colonizzazione romana e viabilità", *Dialoghi di archeologia,* ser. 3, 6, no. 2 (1988) 35–48.

Coarelli (1998) — Coarelli, F., "La storia e lo scavo", *Fregellae* 1: *Le fonti, la storia, il territorio,* eds. F. Coarelli and P. G. Monti (Rome) 29–69.

Coarelli (2000) — Coarelli, F., "Il Lucus Pisaurensis e la romanizzazione dell'Ager Gallicus", *The Roman Middle Republic. Politics, Religion, and Historiography c. 400–133 B.C. (Papers from a Conference . . . 1998)*, ed. C. Bruun (Rome) 195–205.

Coarelli (2005) — Coarelli, F., "Pits and fora: a reply to Henrik Mouritsen", *Papers of the British School at Rome* 73 (2005) 23–30.

Coarelli (2007) — Coarelli, F., *Rome and Environs. An Archaeological Guide*, trans. J. C. Clauss and D. P. Harmon (Berkeley).

Coarelli (2008) — Coarelli, F., *Roma,* new edition (Rome).

Codagnone (1989) — Codagnone et al., "La viabilità", *Minturnae,* ed. F. Coarelli (Rome) 143–47.

Colonna (1973–74) — Colonna, G., "Nomi etruschi di vasi", *Archeologia classica* 25–26 (1973–74) 132–50.

Colonna (1977) — Colonna, G., "Nome gentilizio e società", *Studi etruschi* 45 (1977) 176–92.

Colonna (1981) — Colonna, G., "Quali Etruschi a Roma", *Gli Etruschi e Roma. Atti dell'incontro di studi in onore di Massimo Pallottino . . . 1979* (Rome) 159–72.

Colonna (1981a) — Colonna, G., "Tarquinio Prisco e il tempio di Giove Capitolino", *La parola del passato* 36 (1981) 41–59.

Colonna (1988) — Colonna, G., "L'Etruria e Lazio nel età dei Tarquini", *Etruria e Lazio arcaico. Atti dell'Incontro di Studio . . . 1986,* ed. M. Cristofani (Rome) 55–66.

Colonna (2005) — Colonna, G., *Italia ante Romanum imperium. Scritti di antichità etrusche, italiche e romane (1958–1998)* I, 2: *Tra storia e archeologia* (Pisa).

Cornell (1978) — Cornell, T. J., " 'Rome's debt to Greece' ", *Classical Review* 28 (1978) 11–12.

Cornell (1989) — Cornell, T. J., "Rome and Latium to 390 B. C.", *CAH,* ed. 2 (1989), 7, 2, 243–308.

Cornell (1989a) — Cornell, T. J., "The conquest of Italy", *CAH,* ed. 2 (1989), 7, 2, 351–419.

Cornell (1995) — Cornell, T. J., *The Beginnings of Rome. Italy and Rome from the Bronze Age to the Punic Wars (c. 1000–264 BC)* (London).

Cornell (2000) — Cornell, T. J., "Il Lupercale piu antico e piu affollato: lo specchio di Bolsena", *Roma. Romolo, Remo e la fondazione della città,* eds. A. Carandini and R. Cappelli (Rome) 45–50.

Cornell (2000a) — Cornell, T. J., "The Lex Ovinia and the emancipation of the senate", *The Roman Middle Republic. Politics, Religion, and Historiography c. 400–133 B. C. (Papers from a Conference . . . 1998),* ed. C. Bruun (Rome).

Cornell (2000b) — Cornell, T. J., "The city of Rome in the Middle Republic (c. 400–100 BC)", *Ancient Rome: The Archaeology of the Eternal City,* eds. J. Coulston and H. Dodge (Oxford) 42–60.

Cornell (2004) — Cornell, T. J., "The nature and reliability of the historical tradition", *Samnium. Settlement and Cultural Change. Proceedings of the Third Togo Salmon Conference on Roman Studies* (Providence) 115–31.

Cornell (2005) — Cornell, T. J., "The value of the literary tradition in archaic

Rome", *Social Struggles in Archaic Rome. New Perspectives on the Conflict of the Orders,* ed. K. A. Raaflaub, ed. 2 (Malden MA) 47–74.

Crawford (1974) — Crawford, M. H., *Roman Republican Coinage,* 2 vols. paged continuously (Cambridge UK).

Crawford (1985) — Crawford, M. H., *Coinage and Money Under the Roman Republic. Italy and the Mediterranean Economy* (Berkeley).

Cristofani (1985) — Cristofani, M., *I bronzi degli etruschi* (Novara).

Cristofani (1985a) — Cristofani, M., ed., *Civiltà degli Etruschi* (Milan).

Cristofani (1987) — Cristofani, M., *Saggi di storia Etrusca arcaica* (Rome).

Cristofani (1996) — Cristofani, M., *Etruschi e altre genti nell'Italia preromana. Mobilità in età arcaica* (Rome).

Croisille (2005) — Croisille, J.-M., *La peinture romaine* (Paris).

D'Alessio (2006) — D'Alessio, M. T., "La nascita dei gemelli", in *La leggenda di Roma* 1: *Dalla nascita dei gemelli alla fondazione della città,* ed. A. Carandini (Milan) 247–97.

Danner (1993) — Danner, P., "Die Dekoration auf First und Giebelschrägen in der archaischen Baukunst Mittelitaliens", *Deliciae fictiles. Proceedings of the First International Conference on Central Italic Architectural Terracottas at the Swedish Institute in Rome . . . 1990,* eds. E. Rystedt et al. (Stockholm) 93–107.

Danti (2008) — Danti, A., "Il tempio nell'età repubblicana", *Il tempio di Giove e le origini del colle capitolino* (Rome) 26–29.

Dardenay (2010) — Dardenay, A., *Les mythes fondateurs de Rome. Images et politique dans l'Occident romain* (Paris).

DE — *Dizionario epigrafico di antichità romane* (Rome 1910–).

Degrassi (1937) — Degrassi, A., ed., *Inscriptiones Italiae* 13, 3: *Elogia* (Rome).

Degrassi (1947) — Degrassi, A., ed., *Inscriptiones Italiae* 13, 1: *Fasti consulares et triumphales* (Rome).

A. Degrassi (1963) — Degrassi, A., *Fasti anni Numani et Iuliani* (*Inscriptiones Italiae Academiae Italicae consociatae ediderunt* 13: *Fasti et elogia* 2) (Rome).

D. Degrassi (1987) — Degrassi, D., "Interventi edilizi sull'isola tiberina nel I secolo a. C.", *Athenaeum* 65 (1987) 521–27.

Delcourt (2005) — Delcourt, A., *Lecture des Antiquités romaines de Denys d'Halicarnasse. Un historien entre deux mondes* (Brussels).

De Martino (1979) — De Martino, F., *Diritto e società nell'antica Roma,* eds. A. Dell'Agli and T. Spanuolo Vigorita, 2 vols. (Rome).

De Santis (1985) — De Santis, A., "Roma e il Lazio antico fra la fine dell'8° and gli inizi del 6° sec. a. C'", *Roma e il Lazio dall'età della pietra all formazione della città. I data archeologici* (Rome) 195–224.

Develin (1985) — Develin, R., *The Practice of Politics at Rome 366–167 B. C.* (Brussels).

Develin (2005) — Develin, R., "The integration of plebeians into the political order after 366 B. C.", *Social Struggles in Archaic Rome. New Perspectives on the Conflict of the Orders,* ed. K. A. Raaflaub, ed. 2 (Malden MA) 293–311.

Dillery (2009) — Dillery, J., "Roman historians and the Greeks: audiences and models", *The Cambridge Companion to the Roman Historians,* ed. A. Feldherr (Cambridge UK) 77–107.

D'Ippolito (1998) — D'Ippolito, F. M., "Le origini del Senato e la prima età repubblicana", *Il senato nella storia: Il senato nell'età romana* 1 (Rome) 29–84.

Dodge (2000) — Dodge, H., "Greater than the Pyramids: the water supply of ancient Rome", *Ancient Rome: The Archaeology of the Eternal City,* eds. J. Coulston and H. Dodge (Oxford) 166–209.

Donati and Stefanetti (2006) — Donati, N., and P. Stefanetti, *Dies natalis. I calendari romani e gli anniversari dei culti* (Rome).

Ducati (1927) — Ducati, P., *Storia dell'arte etrusca,* 2 vols., text and plates (Florence).

Dulière (1979) — Dulière, C., *Lupa Romana. Recherches d'iconographie et essai d'interprétation,* 2 vols. (Brussels).

Dumézil (1987) — Dumézil, G., *La religion romaine archaïque,* ed. 2 (Paris).

Eder (1990) — Eder, W., "Der Burger und seine Staat—Der Staat und seine Bürger. Eine Einführung zum Thema Staat und Staatlichkeit in der frühen römischen Republik", *Staat und Staatlichkeit in der frühen römischen Republik. Akten eines Symposiums . . . 1988 . . . Berlin,* ed. W. Eder (Stuttgart) 12–32.

Elster (2009) — Elster, J., *Alexis de Tocqueville, the First Social Scientist* (Cambridge UK).

Farney (2007) — Farney, G. D., *Ethnic Identity and Aristocratic Competition in Republican Rome* (Cambridge UK).

Farrell (2005) — Farrell, J., "The origins and essence of Roman epic", *Vergangenheit in mündlicher Überlieferung,* eds. J. von Ungern-Sternberg and H. Reinau (Stuttgart) 417–28.

Fears (1981) — Fears, J. R., "The theology of Victory at Rome: approaches and problems", *Aufstieg und Niedergang der römischen Welt,* ed. H. Temporini (Berlin) II, 17, 2, 736–826.

Flobert (1985) — Flobert, P., ed., *Varron: La langue latine, livre VI* (Paris).

Formigli (1985) — Formigli, E., "La tecnica", in Cristofani (1985) 35–53.

Forni (1994) — Forni, G., *Scritti vari di storia, epigrafia e antichità romana,* eds. M. Gabriella and A. Bertinelli, 2 vols. (Rome).

Forsén (1991) — Forsén, B., *Lex Licinia Sextia de modo agrorum—Fiction or Reality?* (Helsinki).

Forsythe (1999) — Forsythe, G., *Livy and Early Rome. A Study in Historical Method and Judgement* (Stuttgart).

Forsythe (2005) — Forsythe, G., *A Critical History of Early Rome. From Prehistory to the First Punic War* (Berkeley).

Fraccaro (1957) — Fraccaro, P., "The history of Rome in the regal period", *Journal of Roman Studies* 47 (1957) 59–65.

Frank (1933–40) — Frank, T., ed., *An Economic Survey of Ancient Rome,* 6 vols. (Baltimore).

Franke (1989) — Franke, P. R., "Pyrrhus", *CAH,* ed. 2 (1989), 7, 2, 456–85.

Fraschetti (2007) — Fraschetti, A., "Alcune osservazioni a proposito di un recente volume su La leggenda di Roma", *Archeologia classica* 58 (2007) 317–35.

Frier (1999) — Frier, B. W., *Libri annales pontificum maximorum: The Origins of the Annalistic Tradition,* ed. 2 (Ann Arbor, MI).

Fröhlich (1991) — Fröhlich, T., *Lararien- und Fassadenbilder in den Vesuvstädten. Untersuchungen zur "volkstümlichen" pompejanischen Malerei* (Mainz).

Gabba (1991) — Gabba, E., *Dionysius and The History of Archaic Rome* (Berkeley).

Gagarin and Fantham (2010) — Gagarin, M., and E. Fantham, eds., *The Oxford Encyclopedia of Ancient Greece and Rome,* 7 vols. (Oxford).

Gale, Giardino, and Parisi Presicce (2005) — Gale, N., C. Giardino, and C. Parisi Presicce, "La provenienza del metallo adoperato nella fabrica della Lupa Capitolina", *Studi etruschi* 71 (2005) 129–41.

Gargola (1995) — Gargola, D. J., *Lands, Laws, & Gods. Magistrates & Ceremonies in the Regulation of Public Lands in Republican Rome* (Ithaca NY).

Gasparri (2000) — Gasparri, D., "La colonia latina di Paestum: indagini sulla centuriazione", *Paestum. Scavi, studi, ricerche. Bilancio di un decennio (1988–1998),* eds. E. Greco and F. Longo (Paestum, Salerno) 219–26.

Gelzer (1969) — Gelzer, M., *The Roman Nobility,* trans. R. Seager (Oxford [Ger. 1912]).

Gerhard (1840–97) — Gerhard, E., *Etruskische Spiegel,* 5 vols. (Berlin).

Gianferrari (1995) — Gianferrari, A., "Robigalia: un appuntamento per la salvezza del raccolto", *Agricoltura e commerci nell'Italia antica* (Rome) 127–40.

Giardina (1997) — Giardina, A., *L'Italia Romana. Storie di un'identità incompiuta* (Rome).

Glinister (2000) — Glinister, F., "Sacred rubbish", *Religion in Archaic and Republican Rome and Italy. Evidence and Experience,* eds. E. Bispham and C. Smith (Edinburgh) 54–70.

Glinister (2006) — Glinister, F., "Reconsidering religious Romanization", *Religion in Republican Italy,* eds. C. E. Schultz and P. B. Harvey (Cambridge UK).

Gomme (1967) — Gomme, A. W., *The Population of Athens in the Fifth and Fourth Centuries B.C.* (Chicago).

Grandazzi (1991) — Grandazzi, A., *La fondation de Rome. Réflexion sur l'histoire* (Paris).

Grandazzi (2008) — Grandazzi, A., *Alba Longa, histoire d'une légende. Recherches sur l'archéologie, la religion, les traditions de l'ancien Latium,* 2 vols. paged continuously (Rome).

Greco (1988) — Greco, E., "Archeologia della colonia latina di Paestum", *Dialoghi di archeologia,* ser. 3, 6, no. 2 (1988) 79–86.

Greco and Theodorescu (1983) — Greco, E., and D. Theodorescu, *Poseidonia—Paestum* II. *L'agora* (Paris).

Greco and Theodorescu (2000) — Greco, E., and D. Theodorescu, "L'agora, 1: premessa", *Paestum. Scavi, studi, ricerche. Bilancio di un decennio (1988–1998),* eds. E. Greco and F. Longo (Paestum, Salerno) 85–90.

Gros (1996–2001) — Gros, P., *L'architecture romaine du début du IIIe siècle av. J.-C. à la fin du Haut-Empire*, 2 vols. (Paris).

Gros and Torelli (1988) — Gros, P., and M. Torelli, *Storia dell'urbanistica. Il mondo romano* (Bari/Rome).

Gruen (1992) — Gruen, E., *Culture and National Identity in Republican Rome* (Ithaca NY).

Guaítoli (1981) — Guaítoli, M., "Gabii", *La parola del passato* 36 (1981) 152–73.

Guldager Bilde (2006) — Guldager Bilde, P., "Gli scavi nordici della Villa di S. Maria sul Lago di Nemi (1998–2002)", *Lazio e Sabina 3: Atti del Convegno. Terzo Incontro di Studi sul Lazio e la Sabina, Roma . . . 2004*, ed. G. Ghini (Rome) 203–6.

Guldager Bilde and Poulsen (2008) — Guldager Bilde, P., and B. Poulsen, *The Temple of Castor and Pollux* (Rome).

Gundel (1963) — Gundel, H. G., "Der Begriff Maiestas im politischen Denken der römischen Republik", *Historia* 12 (1963) 283–320.

Gustafsson (2000) — Gustafsson, G., *Evocatio deorum. Historical and Mythical Interpretations of Ritualised Conquests in the Expansion of Ancient Rome* (Uppsala).

Hansen (1985) — Hansen, M. H., *Demography and Democracy. The Number of Athenian Citizens in the Fourth Century B.C.* (Vojens, Denmark).

Hansen (1991) — Hansen, M. H., *Athenian Democracy in the Age of Demosthenes. Structure, Principles, and Ideology* (Oxford).

Harris (1979) — Harris, W. V., *War and Imperialism in Republican Rome 327–70 B.C.* (Oxford).

Harris (1990) — Harris, W. V., "Roman warfare in the economic and social context of the fourth century B.C.", *Staat und Staatlichkeit in der frühen römischen Republik. Akten eines Symposiums . . . 1988 . . . Berlin*, ed. W. Eder (Stuttgart) 494–510.

Henige (1974) — Henige, D. P., *The Chronology of Oral Tradition. Quest for a Chimaera* (Oxford).

Herzog (1988) — Herzog, R., "Zwei Beispiele afrikanischer mündlicher Überlieferung", *Vergangenheit in mündlicher Überlieferung*, eds. J. von Ungern-Sternberg and H. Reinau (Stuttgart) 72–76.

Hill (1961) — Hill, J. E. C., "Notes and comments", *Past & Present* 20 (1961) 3–5.

Hodge (1992) — Hodge, A. T., *Roman Aqueducts & Water Supply* (London).

Hofstede (2001) — Hofstede, G., *Culture's Consequences: Comparing Values, Behaviors, Institutions, and Organizations Across Nations*, ed. 2 (Thousand Oaks CA).

Hölkeskamp (2000) — Hölkeskamp, K.-J., "*Fides—deditio in fidem—dextra data et accepta:* Recht, Religion und Ritual in Rom", *The Roman Middle Republic. Politics, Religion, and Historiography c. 400–133 B.C. (Papers from a Conference . . . 1998)*, ed. C. Bruun (Rome) 224–49.

Holliday (2002) — Holliday, P. J., *The Origins of Roman Historical Commemoration in the Visual Arts* (Cambridge UK).

Holloway (1994) — Holloway, R. R., *The Archaeology of Early Rome and Latium* (London/New York).

Holloway (2008) — Holloway, R. R., "Who were the *tribuni militum consulari potestate?*" *Antiquité classique* 77 (2008) 107–25.

Holloway (2009) — Holloway, R. R., "Praetor maximus and consul", *Palaia philia. Studi di topografia antica in onore di Giovanni Uggeri,* eds. C. Marangio and G. Laudizi (Milan) 71–75.

Hölscher (1978) — Hölscher, T., "Die Anfänge römischer Repräsentationskunst", *Mitteilungen des deutschen archäologischen Instituts, römische Abteilung* 85 (1978) 314–57.

Hölscher (2005) — Hölscher, T., "The public monumentalism of the Roman Republic", *Journal of Roman Archaeology* 18 (2005) 472–78.

Hopkins (1978) — Hopkins, K., *Conquerors and Slaves. Sociological Studies in Roman History,* 1 (Cambridge UK).

Hoving (1996) — Hoving, T., *False Impressions. The Hunt for Big-Time Art Fakes* (New York).

Humbert (1978) — Humbert, M., *Municipium et civitas sine suffragio. L'organisation de la conquête jusqu'à la Guerre Sociale* (Rome).

Humbert (1984) — Humbert, M., *Institutions politiques et sociales de l'Antiquité* (Paris).

Humm (2005) — Humm, M., *Appius Claudius Caecus. La République accomplie* (Rome).

Humm (2006) — Humm, M., "Tribus et citoyenneté: extension de la citoyenneté romaine et expansion territoriale", *Herrschaft ohne Integration? Rom und Italien in republikanischer Zeit,* eds. M. Jehne and R. Pfeilschifter (Frankfurt am Main) 39–64.

Humphreys (1990) — Humphreys, S. C., "Diskussion", *Staat und Staatlichkeit in der frühen römischen Republik. Akten eines Symposiums . . . 1988 . . . Berlin,* ed. W. Eder (Stuttgart) 549–51.

ILLRP — *Inscriptiones latinae liberae rei publicae* 1, ed. A. Degrassi (Florence 1965).

Isman (2007) — Isman, F., "The She-wolf is mediaeval, no longer Etruscan?" *Etruscan News* 8 (summer 2007) 14.

Izzet (2000) — Izzet, V., "Tuscan order: the development of Etruscan sanctuary", *Religion in Archaic and Republican Rome and Italy. Evidence and Experience,* eds. E. Bispham and C. Smith (Edinburgh) 34–53.

Jannot (1984) — Jannot, J.-R., *Les reliefs archaïques de Chiusi* (Rome).

Jehne (2000) — Jehne, M., "Jovialität und Freiheit. Zur Institutionalität der Beziehungen zwischen Ober- und Unterschichten in der römischen Republik", *Mos maiorum. Untersuchungen zu den Formen der Identitätsstiftung und Stabilisierung in der römischen Republik,* eds. B. Linke and M. Stemmler (Stuttgart) 207–35.

Jehne and Pfeilschiften (2006) — Jehne, M., and R. Pfeilschiften, "Einleitung: zum Charakter der römischen Herrschaft in Italien", *Herrschaft ohne Integration? Rom und Italien in republikanischer Zeit,* eds. M. Jehne and R. Pfeilschiften (Frankfurt am Main) 7–22.

Johnson (1935) — Johnson, J., *Excavations at Minturnae* I: *Monuments of the Republican Forum* (Philadelphia).

Johnson et al. (1961) — Johnson, A. C., et al., *Ancient Roman Statutes, a Translation* (Austin TX).

Jolowicz (1952) — Jolowicz, H. F., *Historical Introduction to the Study of Roman Law* (Cambridge UK).

Jolowicz and Nicholas (1972) — Jolowicz, H. F., and B. Nicholas, *Historical Introduction to the Study of Roman Law*, ed. 3 (Cambridge UK).

Keppie (1984) — Keppie, L., *The Making of the Roman Army. From Republic to Empire* (London).

Kiernan (2007) — Kiernan, B., *Blood and Soil. A World History of Genocide and Extermination from Sparta to Darfur* (New Haven).

Lackner (2008) — Lackner, E.-M., *Republikanische Fora* (Munich).

Last (1928) — Last, H. M., "Chronological notes, 1: The date of the first treaty between Rome and Carthage", *CAH* 7 (1928) 859–62.

Lendon (2009) — Lendon, J. E., "Historians without history: Against Roman historiography", *The Cambridge Companion to the Roman Historians,* ed. A. Feldherr (Cambridge UK) 41–61.

Lenski (2008) — Lenski, N., "Evoking the pagan past: *Instinctu divinitatis* and Constantine's capture of Rome", *Journal of Late Antiquity* I (2008) 204–57.

Linderski (1990) — Linderski, J., "The auspices and the Struggle of the Orders", *Staat und Staatlichkeit in der frühen römischen Republik. Akten eines Symposiums . . . 1988 . . . Berlin,* ed. W. Eder (Stuttgart) 34–48.

Linderski (2005) — Linderski, J., "Religious aspects of the conflict of the orders: the case of *confarreatio*", *Social Struggles in Archaic Rome. New Perspectives on the Conflict of the Orders,* ed. K. A. Raaflaub, ed. 2 (Malden MA) 223–38.

Linderski (2007) — Linderski, J., *Roman Questions 2: Select Papers* (Stuttgart).

Lombardi (2002) — Lombardi, G., "A petrographic study of the casting core of the Lupa Capitolina bronze sculpture (Rome, Italy) and identification of its provenance", *Archaeometry* 44 (2002) 601–12.

LTUR (1993–2000) — *Lexicon topographicum urbis Romae,* ed. E. M. Steinby, 6 vols. (Rome).

Luce (1977) — Luce, T. J., *Livy. The Composition of His History* (Princeton).

Lulof (1997) — Lulof, P. S., "Myths from Greece. The representation of power on the roofs of Satricum", *Mededelingen van het Nederlands Instituut te Rome* 56 (1997) 85–114.

Lulof (2006) — Lulof, P., "Roofs from the South: Campanian architectural terracottas in Satricum", *Deliciae fictiles* III: *Archeological Terracottas in Ancient Italy. New Discoveries and Interpretations. Proceedings of the International Conference . . . 2002,* eds. I. Edlund-Berry et al. (Oxford) 235–42.

MacMullen (1974) — MacMullen, R., *Roman Social Relations 50 B.C. to A.D. 284* (New Haven).

MacMullen (1980) — MacMullen, R., "How many Romans voted?" *Athenaeum* 68 (1980) 454–57.

MacMullen (1980a) — MacMullen, R., "Roman elite motivation: three questions", *Past & Present* 88 (1980) 3–16.

MacMullen (1981) — MacMullen, R., *Paganism in the Roman Empire* (New Haven).

MacMullen (1991) — MacMullen, R., "Hellenizing the Romans (2nd century BC)", *Historia* (1991) 419–38.

MacMullen (1997) — MacMullen, R., "Tracking value changes", *Aspects of the Fourth Century A.D. Proceedings of the Symposium* Power and Possession: State, Society, and Church in the Fourth Century A.D. . . . *Leiden 1993* (Leiden) 115–34.

MacMullen (2000) — MacMullen, R., *Romanization in the Time of Augustus* (New Haven).

MacMullen (2003) — MacMullen, R., *Feelings in History, Ancient and Modern* (Claremont CA).

MacMullen (2009) — MacMullen, R., *The Second Church. Popular Christianity A.D. 200–400* (Atlanta/Leiden).

MacMullen (2010) — MacMullen, R., "Christian ancestor worship in Rome", *Journal of Biblical Literature* 129 (2010) 591–607.

Magdelain (1971) — Magdelain, A., "Remarques sur la société romaine archaïque", *Revue des études latines* (1971) 103–27.

Maggiani (1983) — Maggiani, A., "Le pitture del 'Sarcofago del Sacerdote' nel Museo Nazionale di Tarquinia", *Dialoghi di archeologia,* ser. 3, 1, no. 2 (1983) 79–84.

Maier (2008) — Maier, F. G., *Nordost-Tor und persische Belagerungsrampe in Alt-Paphos* III. *Grabungsbefund und Baugeschichte* (*Ausgrabungen in Alt-Paphos auf Cypern* 6: Mainz am Rhein).

Malavolta (1997) — Malavolta, M., "Maiestas", *DE* 5, fasc. 15–16, 469–81.

Manganaro (1974) — Manganaro, G., "Una biblioteca storica nel ginnasio di Tauromenion e il P. Oxy. 1241", *La parola del passato* 29 (1974) 389–409.

Manichetti (1994) — Manichetti, M., "Praenestinus Aeneas. Il culto di Iuppiter Imperator e il trionfo su Mesenzio . . ." *Ostraka* 3 (1994) 7–30.

Mansuelli (1968) — Mansuelli, G. A., "Individuazione e rappresentazione storica nell'arte etrusca", *Studi etruschi,* ser. 3, 36 (1968) 3–19.

Manzo (2001) — Manzo, A., *La lex Licinia Sextia de modo agrorum: Lotte e legge agrarie tra il V e il IV secolo a. C.* (Napoli).

Mari (2004) — Mari, Z., "Acquisizioni lungo la *via Valeria* e gli acquedotti della valle dell'Aniene", *Lazio e Sabina* 2: *Atti del Convegno. Secondo Incontro . . . 2003,* ed. G. Ghini (Rome) 23–38.

Marincola (2009) — Marincola, J., "Ancient audiences and expectations", *The Cambridge Companion to the Roman Historians,* ed. A. Feldherr (Cambridge UK) 11–23.

Martini (1998) — Martini, M. C., *Due studi sulla riscrittura annalistica dell'età monarchica a Roma* (Brussels).

Mastrocinque (1996) — Mastrocinque, A., "Sabini o Latini? A proposito di due episodi di storia romana antiqua", *Identità e civiltà dei Sabini. Atto del XVIII convegno di studi etruschi ed italica . . . 1993* (Florence) 41–47.

Matthew (2009) — Matthew, C. A., "When push comes to shove: what was the *othismos* of hoplite combat?" *Historia* 58 (2009) 395–415.

Mattusch (2007) — Mattusch, C., "More light on the Lupa controversy", *Etruscan News* 8 (summer 2007) 14.

Mertens (1988) — Mertens, J., "Alba Fucens", *Dialoghi di archeologia,* ser. 3, 6, no. 2 (1988) 87–104.

E. A. Meyer (2004) — Meyer, E. A., *Legitimacy and Law in the Roman World. Tabulae in Roman Belief and Practice* (Cambridge UK).

J. C. Meyer (1983) — Meyer, J. C., *Pre-Republican Rome. An Analysis of the Cultural and Chronological Relations 1000–500 BC* (Odense).

J. C. Meyer (1990) — Meyer, J. C., "Diskussion", *Staat und Staatlichkeit in der frühen römischen Republik. Akten eines Symposiums . . . 1988 . . . Berlin,* ed. W. Eder (Stuttgart) 54.

Michels (1967) — Michels, A. K., *The Calendar of the Roman Republic* (Princeton).

Mills and Mansfield (1982) — Mills, T. Fitz-M., and J. M. Mansfield, *The Genuine Article. The Making and Unmasking of Fakes and Forgeries* (New York).

Mitchell (1990) — Mitchell, R. E., *Patricians and Plebeians. The Origins of the Roman State* (Ithaca NY).

Moelho and Wood (1998) — Moelho, A., and G. S. Wood, eds. 1998. *Imagined Histories. American Historians Interpret the Past* (Princeton).

Momigliano (1963) — Momigliano, A., "An interim report on the origins of Rome", *Journal of Roman Studies* 53 (1963) 95–121 (reprinted, *Terzo contributo alla storia degli studi classici e del mondo antico,* Rome 1966, 543–98).

Momigliano (1989) — Momigliano, A., "The origins of Rome", *CAH,* ed. 2 (1989), 7, 2, 85–112.

Mommsen (1844) — Mommsen, T., *Die römischen Tribus in administrativer Beziehung* (Altona).

Mommsen (1969) — Mommsen, T., *Römisches Staatsrecht* (*Handbuch der römischen Altertümer,* eds. J. Marquardt and T. Mommsen, ed. 3, vols. 1–3, Graz).

Morel (1988) — Morel, J.-P., "Artisanat et colonisation dans l'Italie romaine aux IVe et au IIIe siècles av. J.-C.", *Dialoghi di archeologia,* ser. 3, 6, no. 2 (1988) 49–63.

Morel (1989) — Morel, J.-P., "The transformation of Italy, 300–133 B. C. The evidence of archaeology", *CAH,* ed. 2 (1989), 7, 2, 477–516.

Moscati (1997) — Moscati, S., *Così nacque l'Italia. Profili di antichi popoli riscoperti* (Turin).

Mouritsen (2001) — Mouritsen, H., *Plebs and Politics in the Late Roman Republic* (Cambridge UK).

Mouritsen (2004) — Mouritsen, H., "Pits and politics: interpreting colonial fora in Republican Italy", *Papers of the British School at Rome* 72 (2004) 37–68.

Muccigrosso (2006) — Muccigrosso, J., "Religion and politics: did the Romans scruple about the placement of their temples?" *Religion in Republican Italy,* eds. C. E. Schultz and P. B. Harvey (Cambridge UK) 181–206.

Munzi (1994) — Munzi, M., "Sulla topografia dei Lupercalie", *Studi classici e orientali* 44 (1993) 347–64.

Mura Sommella (1993) — Mura Sommella, A., "Ancora sulla decorazione plastica del tempio arcaico del Foario Boario: statue e acroterie", *Deliciae fictiles. Proceedings of the First International Conference on Central Italic Architectural Terracottas at the Swedish Institute in Rome . . . 1990,* eds. E. Rystedt et al. (Stockholm) 225–32.

Naso (2001) — Naso, A., "The Etruscans in Lazio", *The Etruscans Outside Etruria,* ed. G. Camporeale (Los Angeles) 220–35.

Neppi Modona (1977) — Neppi Modona, A., C*ortona etrusca e romana nella storia e nell'arte* (Florence).

Neue Pauly — Der Neue Pauly Enzyklopädie der Antike, eds. H. Cancik and H. Schneider, 10 vols. (Stuttgart 1996–2003).

Nicolet (1980) — Nicolet, C., *The World of the Citizen in Republican Rome,* trans. P. S. Falla (London).

North (1989) — North, J. A., "Religion in Republican Rome", *CAH,* ed. 2 (1989), 7, 2, 573–624.

North (1990) — North, J., "Diviners and divination at Rome", *Pagan Priests. Religion and Power in the Ancient World,* eds. M. Beard and J. North (Ithaca NY) 51–71.

North (1995) — North, J. A., "Religion and rusticity", *Urban Society in Roman Italy,* eds. T. J. Cornell and K. Lomas (London) 135–50.

Oakley (1993) — Oakley, S. P., "The Roman conquest of Italy", *War and Society in the Roman World,* eds. J. Rich and G. Shipley (London) 9–37.

Oakley (1997–2005) — Oakley, S. P., *A Commentary on Livy Books VI–X,* 5 vols (Oxford).

Oakley (2002) — Oakley, S. P., "Appendix. The evidence", in *Livy. The Early History of Rome. Books I–V,* trans. A. de Selincourt, reprint (London) 451–58.

OCD — Oxford Classical Dictionary, ed. 3, eds. S. Hornblower and A. Spawforth (Oxford 2003).

Ogilvie (1965) — Ogilvie, R. M., *A Commentary on Livy, Books 1–5* (Oxford).

Ogilvie (1971) — Ogilvie, R. M., "Introduction", in *Livy. The Early History of Rome. Books I–V of The History of Rome from its Foundations,* trans. A. de Selincourt, ed. 2 (London) 1–25.

Ogilvie and Drummond (1989) — Ogilvie, R. M., and A. Drummond, "The sources for early Roman history", *CAH,* ed. 2 (1989), 7, 2, 1–29.

Orr (1978) — "Roman domestic religion", *Aufstieg und Niedergang der römischen Welt,* ed. H. Temporini (Berlin) II, 16, 2, 1557–91.

Pais (1920) — Pais, E., ed., *Fasti triumphales populi Romani* (Rome).

Pallottino (1987) — Pallottino, M., "Il fregio dei Vibenna e le sue implicazioni storiche", *La tomba François di Vulci. Mostra organizzata . . . 1987,* ed. F. Buranelli (Rome) 225–33.

Palmer (1970) — Palmer, R. E. A., *The Archaic Community of the Romans* (Cambridge UK).

Parisi Presicce (2000) — Parisi Presicce, C., ed., *La Lupa capitolina* (Rome).

Pascal (1981) — Pascal, C. B., "October horse", *Harvard Studies in Classical Philology* 85 (1981) 261–91.

Patterson (2010) — Patterson, J. R., "The city of Rome revisited: from mid-Republic to mid-Empire", *Journal of Roman Studies* 100 (2010) 210–32.

Patterson et al. (2004) — Patterson, H., et al., "Three south Etrurian 'crises': first results of the Tiber Valley Project", *Papers of the British School at Rome* 72 (2004) 1–36.

Pedley (1990) — Pedley, J. G., *Paestum. Greeks and Romans in Southern Italy* (London).

Pensabene (1998) — Pensabene, P., "Vent'anni di studi e scavi dell'Università di Roma 'La Sapienza' nell'area Sud Ovest del Palatino (1977–1997)", *Il Palatino: Area sacra sud-ovest e Domus Tiberiana,* ed. C. Giavarini (Rome) 1–155.

Pensabene (2000) — Pensabene, P., "Le reliquie dell'età romulea e i culti del Palatino", *Roma. Romolo, Remo e la fondazione della città,* eds. A. Carandini and R. Cappelli (Rome) 74–82.

Pensabene (2006) — Pensabene, P., "'I luoghi del sacro: elementi di topografia storica", *Scienze dell'antichità* 13 (2006) 329–55.

Peruzzi (1990) — Peruzzi, E., *I romani di Pesaro e i sabini di Roma* (Florence).

Pesando et al. (2005) — Pesando, F., et al., *L'Italia antica. Culture e forme del popolamento nel I millennio a. C.* (Rome).

Peter (1967) — Peter, H., *Historicorum Romanorum reliquiae,* ed. 2, 2 vols. (Stuttgart).

Pierson (1938) — Pierson, G. W., *Tocqueville and Beaumont in America* (Oxford).

Poma (1984) — Poma, G., *Tra legislatori e tiranni. Problemi storici e storiografici sull'età delle XII Tavole* (Bologna).

Potter (1979) — Potter, T. W., *The Changing Landscape of South Etruria* (New York).

Poucet (1985) — Poucet, J., *Les origines de Rome. Tradition et histoire* (Brussels).

Prosdocimi (1996) — Prosdocimi, A. L., "Etnici e strutture sociali nella Sabina", *Identità e civiltà dei Sabini. Atto del XVIII convegno di studi etruschi ed italica . . . 1993* (Florence) 227–45.

Raaflaub (1990) — Raaflaub, K. A., [remarks, in:] "Diskussion", *Staat und Staatlichkeit in der frühen römischen Republik. Akten eines Symposiums . . . 1988 . . . Berlin,* ed. W. Eder (Stuttgart) 87.

Raaflaub (1996) — Raaflaub, K. A., "Born to be wolves? Origins of Roman imperialism", *Transitions to Empire. Essays in Greco-Roman History, 360–146 B.C., in Honor of E. Badian,* eds. R. W. Wallace and E. M. Harris (Norman OK) 273–314.

Raaflaub (2005) — Raaflaub, K., "Epic and history", *A Companion to Ancient Epic,* ed. J. M. Foley (Oxford) 55–70.

Raaflaub (2005a) — Raaflaub, K. A., "The conflict of the orders in archaic Rome:

a comprehensive and comparative approach", *Social Struggles in Archaic Rome. New Perspectives on the Conflict of the Orders,* ed. K. A. Raaflaub, ed. 2 (Malden MA) 1–46.

Raaflaub (2005b) — Raaflaub, K. A., "From protection and defense to offense and participation: stages in the conflict of the orders", *Social Struggles in Archaic Rome. New Perspectives on the Conflict of the Orders,* ed. K. A. Raaflaub, ed. 2 (Malden MA) 185–222.

Radcliffe (2006) — Radcliffe, F. F., ed., *Paesaggi sepolti in Daunia. John Bradford e la ricerca archeologica dal cielo 1945–1957* (Foggia).

Radke (1973) — Radke, G., "Viae publicae Romanae", *RE* Suppl. 13, 1417–1686.

Rasmussen (2005) — Rasmussen, T., "Urbanization in Etruria", *Proceedings of the British Academy* 126 (2005) 71–90.

Rathmann (2005) — Rathmann, M., ed., *Diodoros griechische Weltgeschichte Buch XVIII–XX. Kommentar und Anhang* (Stuttgart).

Rawson (1971) — Rawson, E., "The literary sources for the pre-Marian army", *Papers of the British School at Rome* 39 (1971) 13–31.

Rawson (1972) — Rawson, E., "Cicero the historian and Cicero the antiquarian", *Journal of Roman Studies* 62 (1972) 33–45.

Rawson (1990) — Rawson, E., "The antiquarian tradition: spoils and representations of foreign armour", *Staat und Staatlichkeit in der frühen römischen Republik. Akten eines Symposiums . . . 1988 . . . Berlin,* ed. W. Eder (Stuttgart) 73–83.

RE — *Realencyclopädie der classischen Altertumswissenschaft* (Stuttgart 1960–).

Riccobono (1941–43) — Riccobono, S., *Fontes iuris romani antejustiniani in usum scholarum.* ed. S. Riccobono et al., ed. 2, 3 vols. (Florence).

Richard (1978) — Richard, J.-C., *Les origines de la plèbe romaine. Essai sur la formation du dualisme patricio-plébéien* (Rome).

Richard (1990) — Richard, J.-C., "Historiographie et histoire: l'expédition des Fabii à la Crémère", *Staat und Staatlichkeit in der frühen römischen Republik. Akten eines Symposiums . . . 1988 . . . Berlin,* ed. W. Eder (Stuttgart) 174–99.

Richard (2001) — Richard, J.-C., "Annalistique et fastes: l'histoire d'une invention?" *Revue des études latines* 79 (2001) 19–25.

Richard (2005) — Richard, J.-C., "Patricians and plebeians: the origin of a social dichotomy", *Social Struggles in Archaic Rome. New Perspectives on the Conflict of the Orders,* ed. K. A. Raaflaub, ed. 2 (Malden MA) 107–27.

Ridley (1990) — Ridley, R. T., "Patavinitas among the patricians? Livy and the Conflict of the Orders", *Staat und Staatlichkeit in der frühen römischen Republik. Akten eines Symposiums . . . 1988 . . . Berlin,* ed. W. Eder (Stuttgart) 103–38.

Roma medio repubblicana. Aspetti culturali di Roma e del Lazio nei secoli IV e III a. C. (Rome 1973).

Romana Fortunati (1993) — Romana Fortunati, F., "Il tempio delle stimmate di Velletri", *Deliciae fictiles. Proceedings of the First International Conference on Central Italic Architectural Terracottas at the Swedish Institute in Rome . . . 1990,* eds. E. Rystedt et al. (Stockholm) 255–65.

Roncalli (1987) — Roncalli, F., "La decorazione pittorica", *La tomba François di Vulci. Mostra organizzata . . . 1987*, ed. F. Burunelli (Rome) 79–115.

Rosenstein (2004) — Rosensteiin, N. S., *Rome at War. Farms, Families, and Death in the Middle Republic* (Chapel Hill).

Rosenstein (2006) — Rosenstein, N., "Recruitment and its consequences for Rome and the Italian allies", *Herrschaft ohne Integration? Rom und Italien in republikanischer Zeit*, eds. M. Jehne and R. Pfeilschifter (Frankfurt am Main) 227–41.

Rouveret and Theodorescu (2000) — Rouveret, A., and D. Theodorescu, "Recherches à Porta Marina: rapport préliminaire", *Paestum. Scavi, studi, ricerche. Bilancio di un decennio (1988–1998)*, eds. E. Greco and F. Longo (Paestum, Salerno) 85–90.

Rüpke (1990) — Rüpke, J., *Domi militiae. Die religiöse Konstruktion des Krieges in Rom* (Stuttgart).

Rüpke (2007) — Rüpke, J., *Religion of the Romans*, trans. R. Gordon (Cambridge UK).

Sabatucci (1988) — Sabatucci, D., *La religione di Roma antica dal calendario festivo all'ordine cosmica* (Milan).

Sacchi Lodispoto (1983) — Sacchi Lodispoto, G., "Contributi degli istituti stranieri in Roma agli scavi nel Lazio", *Il Lazio nell'antichità romana*, ed. R. Lefevre (Rome) 75–101.

Sandberg (2000) — Sandberg, K., "Tribunician and non-tribunician legislation in mid-Republican Rome", *The Roman Middle Republic. Politics, Religion, and Historiography c. 400–133 B.C. (Papers from a Conference . . . 1998)*, ed. C. Bruun (Rome) 121–40.

Saulnier (1980) — Saulnier, C., *L'armée et la guerre dans le monde étrusco-romain (VIIIᵉ–IVᵉ s.)* (Paris).

Schäfer (1980) — Schäfer, T., "Zur Ikonographie der Salier", *Jahrbuch des deutschen archäologischen Instituts* 95 (1980) 342–73.

Scheidel (2006) — Scheidel, W., "The demography of Roman state formation in Italy", *Herrschaft ohne Integration? Rom und Italien in republikanischer Zeit*, eds. M. Jehne and R. Pfeilschifter (Frankfurt am Main) 207–26.

Schmiedt (1985) — Schmiedt, G., "Le centuriazioni di Luceria e di Aecae", *L'Universo* 65 (1985) 260–304.

Schultz (2006) — Schultz, C. E., "Juno Sospita and Roman insecurity in the Social War", *Religion in Republican Italy*, eds. C. E. Schultz and P. B. Harvey (Cambridge UK) 207–27.

Scott (1988) — Scott, R. T., "The Latin colony of Cosa", *Dialoghi di archeologia*, ser. 3, 6, no. 2 (1988) 73–77.

Scullard (1974) — Scullard, H. H., *The Elephant in the Greek and Roman World* (London).

Sellers (1991) — Sellers, C., *The Market Revolution. Jacksonian America 1816–46* (New York/Oxford).

Shackleton-Bailey (1966) — Shackleton-Bailey, D. R., ed., *Cicero's Letters to Atticus* (Cambridge UK).

Sherwin-White (1973) — Sherwin-White, A. N., *The Roman Citizenship*, ed. 2 (Oxford).

Sinclair (1988) — Sinclair, R. K., *Democracy and Participation in Athens* (Cambridge UK).

Simone (1972) — Simone, C. de, "Per la storia degli imprestiti greci in etrusco", *Aufstieg und Niedergang der römischen Welt*, ed. H. Temporini (Berlin) I, 2, 490–521.

Simone (1981) — Simone, C. de, "Gli Etruschi a Roma: evidenza linguistica e problemi metodologici", *Gli Etruschi e Roma. Atti dell'incontro di studio in onore di Massimo Pallottino . . . 1979* (Rome) 93–103.

Smith (1996) — Smith, C. J., *Early Rome and Latium. Economy and Society c. 1000 to 500 BC* (Oxford).

Smith (2000) — Smith, C., "Worshipping Mater Matuta: ritual and context", *Religion in Archaic and Republican Rome and Italy. Evidence and Experience*, eds. E. Bispham and C. Smith (Edinburgh) 135–55.

Smith (2000a) — Smith, C., "Early and archaic Rome", *Ancient Rome. The Archaeology of the Eternal City*, eds. J. Coulston and H. Dodge (Oxford) 16–41.

Smith (2005) — Smith, C., "The beginnings of urbanization in Rome", *Proceedings of the British Academy* 126 (205) 91–111.

Smith (2006) — Smith, C. J., *The Roman Clan. The gens from Ancient Ideology to Modern Anthropology* (Cambridge UK).

Spivey and Stoddart (1990) — Spivey, N., and S. Stoddart, *Etruscan Italy* (London).

Starr (2009) — Starr, R. J., "*Annos undeviginti natus:* Augustus and Romulus in *Res gestae* 1.1", *Historia* 58 (2009) 366–69.

Steinby (1993–2000) — Steinby, E. M., ed., *LTUR*, 6 vols. (Rome).

Stillwell et al. (1976) — Stillwell, R., et al., eds., *Princeton Encyclopedia of Classical Sites* (Princeton).

Sumner (1970) — Sumner, G. V., "The legion and the centuriate organization", *Journal of Roman Studies* 60 (1970) 67–78.

Syme (1939) — Syme, R., *The Roman Revolution* (Oxford).

Tagliamonte (1996) — Tagliamonte, G., *I Sanniti. Caudini, Irpini, Pentri, Carricini, Frentani* (Milan).

Taylor (1960) — Taylor, L. R., *The Voting Districts of the Roman Republic. The Thirty-five Urban and Rural Tribes* (Rome).

Taylor (1966) — Taylor, L. R., *Roman Voting Assemblies from the Hannibalic War to the Dictatorship of Caesar* (Ann Arbor MI).

Thommen (1995) — Thommen, L., "Les lieux de la plèbe et de ses tribuns dans la Rome républicaine", *Klio* 77 (1995) 358–70.

Thuillier (1975) — Thuillier, J. -P., "Denys d'Halicarnasse et les jeux romains (*Antiquités romaines*, VII, 72–73)", *Mélanges d'archéologie et d'histoire de l'École française de Rome, Antiquité* 87 (1975) 563–81.

Tocqueville (1836) — Tocqueville, A. de, *Democracy in America*, trans. Henry Reeve, ed. 2, 4 vols. (London).

Toher (2005) — Toher, M., "The tenth table and the conflict of the orders", *Social Struggles in Archaic Rome. New Perspectives on the Conflict of the Orders*, ed. K. A. Raaflaub, ed. 2 (Malden MA) 268–92.

Tomei (2009) — Tomei, M. A., "Attività di scavo e di tutela della Soprintendenza speciale per i beni archeologici", *Suburbium* II. *Il suburbio di Roma dalla fine dell'età monarchica alla nascita del sistema delle ville (V–II secolo a. C.)*, ed. V. Jolivet (Rome) 664–72.

Torelli (1984) — Torelli, M., *Lavinio e Roma. Riti iniziatici e matrimonio tra archeologia e storia* (Rome).

Torelli (1988) — Torelli, M., "Aspetti ideologici della colonizzazione romana piu antica", *Dialoghi di archeologia*, ser. 3, 6, no. 2 (1988) 65–72.

Torelli (1989) — Torelli, M., "Archaic Rome between Latium and Etruria", *CAH*, ed. 2 (1989), 7, 2, 30–51.

Torelli (1990) — Torelli, M., "Riti di passagio maschili di Roma arcaica", *Mélanges d'archéologie et d'histoire de l'École française de Rome, Antiquité* 102 (1990) 93–106.

Torelli (1990a) — Torelli, M., "Kommentar", *Staat und Staatlichkeit in der frühen römischen Republik. Akten eines Symposiums . . . 1988 . . . Berlin*, ed. W. Eder (Stuttgart) 73–83.

Torelli (1997) — Torelli, M., "Il culto romano di Mater Matuta", *Mededelingen van het Nederlands Instituut te Rome* 56 (1997) 165–76.

Torelli (1999) — Torelli, M., *Tota Italia. Essays in the Cultural Formation of Roman Italy* (Oxford).

Torelli (2006) — Torelli, M., "Ara Maxima Herculis. Storia di un monumento", *Mélanges d'archéologie et d'histoire de l'École française de Rome, Antiquité* 118 (2006) 573–620.

Toynbee (1965) — Toynbee, A. J., *Hannibal's Legacy. The Hannibalic War's Effects on Roman Life*, 2 vols. (London).

Tucci (2006) — Tucci, P. L., "L'iscrizione e le precedenti identificazioni", *Archeologia classica* 57 (2006) 176–99.

Ungern-Sternberg (1988) — Ungern-Sternberg, J. von, "Überlegungen zur frühen römischen Überlieferung im Licht der Oral-Tradition-Forschung", *Vergangenheit in mündlicher Überlieferung*, ed. J. von Ungern-Sternberg and H. Reinau (Stuttgart) 237–65.

Ungern-Sternberg (2005) — Ungern-Sternberg, J. von, "The formation of the 'Annalistic tradition': the example of the decemvirate", *Social Struggles in Archaic Rome. New Perspectives on the Conflict of the Orders*, ed. K. A. Raaflaub, ed. 2 (Malden MA) 75–97.

Ungern-Sternberg (2005a) — Ungern-Sternberg, J. von, "The end of the Conflict of the Orders", *Social Struggles in Archaic Rome. New Perspectives on the Conflict of the Orders*, ed. K. A. Raaflaub, ed. 2 (Malden MA) 312–32.

Vansina (1985) — Vansina, J., *Oral Tradition as History* (London).

Vagnetti (1971) — Vagnetti, L., *Il deposito votivo di Campetti a Veio (Materiale degli scavi 1937–1938)* (Florence).

Versnel (1970) — Versnel, H. S., *Triumphus. An Inquiry into the Origin, Development and Meaning of the Roman Triumph* (Leiden).

Vessberg (1941) — Vessberg, O., *Studien zur Kunstgeschichte der römischen Republik* (Lund).

Volpe (1990) — Volpe, G., *La Daunia nell'età della romanizzazione. Paesaggio agrario, produzione, scambi* (Bari).

Waarsenburg (1995) — Waarsenburg, D. J., *The Northwest Necropolis of Satricum. An Iron Age Cemetery in Latium Vetus* (Amsterdam).

Wagner (1984) — Wagner, C. G., "El comercio punico en el Mediteráneo a la luz de una nueva interpretación de los tratados concluidos entre Cartago y Rome", *Historia Antigua* 6 (1984) 211–24.

Walbank (1957–79) — Walbank, F. W., *A Historical Commentary on Polybius*, 3 vols. (Oxford).

Wallace (1990) — Wallace, R. W., "Hellenization and Roman society in the late fourth century B.C. A methodological critique", *Staat und Staatlichkeit in der frühen römischen Republik. Akten eines Symposiums . . . 1988 . . . Berlin*, ed. W. Eder (Stuttgart) 278–92.

Waltzing (1895–1900) — Waltzing, J.-P., *Étude historique sur les corporations professionelles chez les Romains, depuis les origines jusqu'à la chute de l'Empire d'Occident*, 4 vols. (Louvain).

Waszink (1947) — Waszink, J. H., *Quinti Septimi Florentis Tertulliani, de anima* (Amsterdam).

Watson (1975) — Watson, A., *Rome of the XII Tables. Persons and Property* (Princeton).

Weems (1850) — Weems, M. L., *The Life of George Washington* (Philadelphia).

Welch (2006) — Welch, K. E., "Introduction", *Representations of War in Ancient Rome*, eds. S. Dillon and K. E. Welch (Cambridge UK) 1–26.

Willems (1878–85) — Willems, P., *Le sénat de la République romaine. Sa composition et ses attributions*, 2 vols. (Louvain).

Winter (2005) — Winter, N. A., "Gods walking on the roof: the evolution of terracotta statuary in Archaic Etruscan architecture in light of the kings of Rome", *Journal of Roman Archaeology* 18 (2005) 241–51.

Wiseman (1970) — Wiseman, T. P., "Roman Republican road-building", *Papers of the British School at Rome* 38 (1970) 122–52.

Wiseman (1979) — Wiseman, T. P., *Clio's Cosmetics. Three Studies in Greco-Roman Literature* (Leicester UK).

Wiseman (1993) — Wiseman, T. P., "The she-wolf mirror: an interpretation", *Papers of the British School at Rome* 61 (1993) 1–6.

Wiseman (1995) — Wiseman, T. P., "The god of the Lupercal", *Journal of Roman Studies* 85 (1995) 1–22.

Wiseman (1995a) — Wiseman, T. P., *Remus. A Roman Myth* (Cambridge UK).

Wiseman (2008) — Wiseman, T. P., *Unwritten Rome* (Exeter UK).

Wissowa (1912) — Wissowa, G., *Religion und Kultus der Römer*, ed. 2 (Munich).

Wolff (2010) — Wolff, C., "Les volontaires dans l'armée romaine jusqu'à Marius", *Latomus* 69 (2010) 18–28.

Zeggio (2000) — Zeggio, S., "Il deposito votivo di Santa Maria della Vittoria", *Roma. Romolo, Remo e la fondazione della città*, eds. A. Carandini and R. Cappelli (Rome) 332.

Zevi (1981) — Zevi, F., "Note sulla leggenda di Enea in Italia", *Gli Etruschi e Roma. Atti dell'incontro di studio in onore di Massimo Pallottino . . . 1979* (Rome) 145–58.

Zevi (1988) — Zevi, F., "I santuari di Roma agli inizi della repubblica", *Etruria e Lazio arcaico. Atti dell'Incontro di Studio . . . 1986*, ed. M. Cristofani (Rome) 121–32.

Zevi (1996) — Zevi, F, "Les débuts d'Ostie", *Ostia. Port et porte de la Rome antique*, eds. J.-P. Descoeudres et al. (Geneva) 3–7.

Zimmermann (1986) — Zimmermann, J.-L., "La fin de Falerii Veteres: un témoignage archéologique", *J. Paul Getty Museum Journal* 14 (1986) 37–42.

INDEX

Printed and bound by CPI Group (UK) Ltd, Croydon, CR0 4YY

09/06/2025